Government Procedures and Operations

e-Governance in India

Problems, Prototypes and Prospects

Government Procedures and Operations

Additional books in this series can be found on Nova's website
under the Series tab.

Additional e-books in this series can be found on Nova's website
under the eBooks tab.

GOVERNMENT PROCEDURES AND OPERATIONS

E-GOVERNANCE IN INDIA

PROBLEMS, PROTOTYPES AND PROSPECTS

PUNEET KUMAR
RAJESH SHARMA
AND
URMANI KAUSHAL
EDITORS

nova publishers
New York

Library of Congress Cataloging-in-Publication Data

Names: Kumar, Puneet (Assistant professor), editor. | Sharma, Rajesh (Assistant professor), editor. | Kaushal, Urmani, editor
Title: E-governance in India : problems, prototypes and prospects / editors: Puneet Kumar, Rajesh Sharma, and Urmani Kaushal (Dept. of Computer Application, Mody University of Science and Technology, Laxmangarh, Sikar, Rajasthan, India, and others).
Description: Hauppauge, New York : Nova Science Publisher's, Inc., 2016. |
Series: Government procedures and operations | Includes index.
Identifiers: LCCN 2016007425 (print) | LCCN 2016008706 (ebook) | ISBN 9781634848305 (hardcover) | ISBN 9781634848442 (Ebook) | ISBN 9781634848442 ()
Subjects: LCSH: Internet in public administration--India.
Classification: LCC JQ229.A8 E25 2016 (print) | LCC JQ229.A8 (ebook) | DDC 352.3/802854678--dc23
LC record available at http://lccn.loc.gov/2016007425

Published by Nova Science Publishers, Inc. † New York

Dedication

This edited compendium is dedicated to our esteemed Ph.D. supervisors.

Prof. (Dr.) Dharminder Kumar

(Guru Jambheshwar University, Hisar, Haryana, India)

Dr. Avanish Kumar

(Bundelkhand University, Jhansi, Uttar Pradesh, India)

Dr. Manish Didwania

(Mody University of Science and Technology, Laxmangarh, Sikar, Rajasthan, India)

CONTENTS

FOREWORD

Dr. Mahi Pal
IES
Director (Retd)
Ministry of Rural Development
Government of India

The changes that have taken place in various sectors of infrastructure particularly in Information & Communication Technology (ICT) have put the world on high connectivity pedestal. Access to internet and mobile phones has brought out visible changes in mitigating the hardship faced by both rural and urban population of the country. From road to digital world connectivity has truly transformed the ambience of Indian society and economy. E-government and E-governance are the integral strategy of the Government to increase productivity, improve the quality and efficiency of its various programmes, promote transparency & accountability and enhance access to information. The digital India initiative initiated by the Government of India last year has empowered citizen with e-access to government services and livelihood related services. The initiative to connect 2.5 lakh villages of India through National Broadband Network will have a cascading effect on rural connectivity, creativity and prosperity. The digital India has three core components namely creation of digital infrastructure, delivering services digitally and digital literacy. Among others, it requires a lot of effort on the part of Government and other stakeholders towards building technological human capital among our people with regard to various components of digitization mentioned above.

In view of above, the present book "E-Governance in India: Problems, Prototypes and Prospects" edited by Dr. Puneet Kumar, Dr. Rajesh Sharma and Dr. Urmani Kaushal is timely value addition in the field of ICT as it through sidelights on different facets of digitalization ranging from its conceptualization to application. A bunch of 14 papers written by different scholars are broadly related to five areas of e-governance namely conceptualization, processes , impact of e-application on poverty alleviation and other social sectors like women and vulnerable sections, international experiences and challenges. The e-application and its impact have been evaluated with the help of case studies carried out in some part of the country.

The book has eloquently surfaced that e-inclusion and inclusive e-governance in terms of fulfilling people's expectations could only be materialized if resources, efforts of citizenry , government and industry are unified as single force. Awareness building about the importance of the usages of ICT should be given serious attention because the e-participation of people in the country is very less as compared to other countries. The networking among different stakeholders of ICT is also sine que non for effective delivery of e-services to all particularly to technologically backward people . Two clear messages emerge from the book are i) ICT has generated new opportunities for economic growth and ii) achieving sustained and rapid growth sustained technological innovations are required.

The contents of the book have well emphasized on focusing and strengthening the supply side and demand side of the ICT in deepening the application of ICT in the governance, planning and development of the country. The book is very useful to policy makers, researchers, trainers , teachers , students and all those who are engaged in ICT activities.

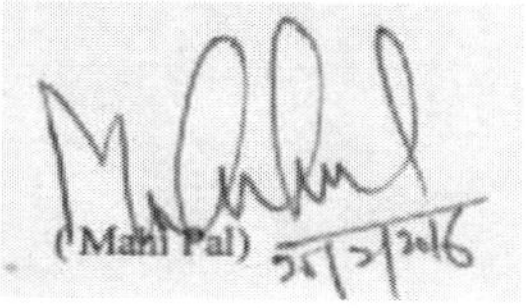

PREFACE

In the current era, e-Governance has emerged as a most prominent tool for strengthening democracy. Therefore, in year 2006, the Government of India has launched National e-Governance Plan (NeGP) which encompasses 31 Mission Mode Projects to automate high priority mundane tasks associated with rural and urban areas of country. However, the government is spending an enormous amount of funds in deployment of e-governance, but, success ratio of e-governance projects in India is not overwhelming. The study of e-Governance mechanism for improvement in its implementation through various research articles motivated the editors to select this domain as a focus area for proposed research compendium.

The fourteen chapters are fascinating this book compendium as precious gems, reflecting light on diversified aspects of the intents converged towards e-governance in India viz evolution and spread, implementation challenges, impact on societal issues, development of novel frameworks, involved legal issues and prognosis.

The success stories of various countries suggest that the effective utilization of e-governance services enable its stakeholders to tackle various problems related to socio-economic aspects. In order to strengthen the deployment of e-governance and its services, political environment, technological involvement in national education policy, adequate promotion of in-house research and development, minimization of vendor locking, apt people's participation and involvement of new technologies like cloud computing, virtualization techniques are the prerequisites. Since, government is spending gigantic amount in deployment of e-governance, therefore, the involvement of novel technologies will reduce infrastructure requirements and cost incurred. Moreover, aforesaid factors will certainly help in generating positive multiplier effect on other areas such as employment generation, GDP growth, rapid mobilization of resources and favorable socio-economic environment.

The international experience also affirms that, the countries who have minimized aforesaid issues and challenges, have attained high EGDI, which leads towards increase in their GDP.

It's high time for Government of India to ponder upon the issues highlighted in the book through various researches in order to disseminate more, effective, transparent, and rapid deployment of e-governance. Hopefully, the issues raised and suggestions inferenced during the course of this book will bring massive and favorable changes certainly if, employed for welfare of the nation. The attempt can also be proved useful for the researchers working in several related areas of e-Governance.

ACKNOWLEDGMENT

"People see the things and say why? And I dream the matter and say why not?" G.B. Shaw's above statement truly speaks about our inquisitive tendencies. Due to God's benign grace we got the thirst for knowledge and our family members, research contributors, helped us to quench it.

After bowing our head to God, Almighty, and thanking of His grace, we express our deep sense of reverence, gratitude and indebtedness to the eminent persona of field Prof. Dharminder Kumar, Dean, Dept. of Computer Science and Engineering, Guru Jambheshwar University of Science and Technology, Dr. Avanish Kumar, Associate Professor, Bundelkhand University and Dr. Manish Didwania, Associate Professor, COBMEC, Mody University of Science and Technology, who bestowed their valuable guidance to carry out this work, without them, none of this, would be possible.

We are extremely thankful to Prof. J. V. Desai, Dean, College of Engineering and Technology, Prof. Jagdish Rai Luthra, Dean, College of Arts, Science and Humanities, Prof. Suresh Kumar Advani, Dean, College of Business, Management, Economics and Commerce, Mody University of Science and Technology, for his seamless support and unreserved cooperation and providing necessary facilities to us for this work.

We are especially thankful to Prof. A. K. Sharma, College of Engineering and Technology, Mody University of Science and Technology, for his valuable suggestions, persistent motivation, endless encouragement, ever helping attitude throughout the work.

Further, we want to extend our gratitude to all members of Department of Computer Application, College of Engineering and Technology and Department of Economics, College of Business, Management, Economics and Commerce, Mody University of Science and Technology, for their academic dialogues and research aptitude provided to us.

We must also pay regards and thanks to other faculty members and non-teaching staff of the University for their Helping Attitude during the research work.

I find myself incompetent in selecting proper words with which we can express our feelings and gratefulness to our parents for their kind perpetual encouragement and constant blessings during this work. The privilege can only be remembered with utmost splendor and ravishing feelings.

Thanks is a word which has lost its significance by wear and tear due to improper and over usages, still paucity of an apt substitute serves me to use the same word for my friends especially Dr. Puran Singh Yadav, Dr. Rajendra Singh Chundawat, Mr. Prateek Bhanti, Dr.

N. S. Chundawat, Mr. Hitesh Jangir and Dr. S. K. Rai for their seamless support at every moment and creating an atmosphere for high academic pursuits.

Above all, we are extending our thanks and feeling of gratitude from core of our heart to all the friends, and cooperative hands whose names could not be mentioned here.

(Editors)

In: e-Governance in India: Problems, Prototypes and Prospects ISBN: 978-1-63484-830-5
Editors: P. Kumar, R. Sharma and U. Kaushal

Chapter 1

e-GOVERNANCE IN INDIA: AN ANALYTICAL PERSPECTIVE

Ajai Pal Sharma[*]
Department of Management Studies, School of Law,
Governance, Public Policy and Management,
Central University of Haryana, Jant-Pali Villages, Mahendergarh, India

ABSTRACT

In a developing country like India, the success of the government plans lies with the people's participation, transparency, rapid dissemination of information and apt and just public administration. Moreover, transparency with people's participation in governance enables leaders and bureaucrats to perform efficiently which is very essential for any healthy and inclusive democracy. Therefore, technological involvement is essential and required in these spheres. The infusion of e-governance has helped in bridging the gap between public and government. And it has opened new avenues for growth and development for developing countries by generating positive socio-economic environment. The present chapter is an attempt to highlight the involvement of e-governance in various sectors in India. Further, it shows the major steps initiated by the government of India for strengthening e-governance services; and in the end, in order to strengthen the delivery mechanism of e-services, some suggestions have been given.

1. INTRODUCTION

Democracy is a system of governance which enables citizens of great nations to moan and groan about themselves. This can be possible only when there is inclusive democracy. And democracy can't be inclusive unless every individual has access to economic, political and social justice and have their aspirations to be included in public policies. To achieve this

[*] Dr. Ajai Pal Sharma is an Assistant Professor, Department of Management Studies, School of Law, Governance, Public Policy and Management, Central University of Haryana, Jant-Pali Villages, Mahendergarh. E-mail: ajaipalsharma@cuh.ac.in.

objective the concept of good governance has emerged as the bigger issue today than any other issues.

We may be living in many boundaries but governance knows no boundaries whether it is geographic, social, cultural, economic, or political. Good governance as a concept is applicable to all the institutions including government, legislative, and judiciary, media, private sector enterprises, corporate sector and even the NGOs. For any result to be achieved, it requires a concrete call from political and administrative will of the highest order apart from all innovations.

"We can't meet 21st century challenges with 20th century bureaucracy." (Sadashivam & Tabassum, 2011) At the time of independence in 1947, our country had many problems and challenges like illiteracy, poverty, social tensions, lack of facilities and more importantly, the challenge of 'Nation Building.' To meet all these challenges a planned economic model was adopted to achieve the status of democratic social welfare state and bureaucracy was given the major role in that process. Unfortunately this target has not been achieved till date, probably because of ineffective role played by our leaders and bureaucracy in past. Today, bureaucracy needs to be dynamic so that it can withstand the changing situation at regional and global level, particularly when we are living in a technological era.

In this direction ICT has played a major role to benefit the citizens and also to improve efficiency in administration. The working of public services, processes of administration and knowledge on policy making are the important areas of governance which were kept under secrecy in the traditional model of governance, whereas the emergence of e-governance has made it more transparent and open by facilitating citizens' participation through many means. e-Governance has the potential to improve the speed, convenience, quality and transparency of public administrative services. It has enhanced the ability of individual citizens to express and exercise their democratic rights. Transparency in governance through e-mode has made the leaders and bureaucrats more accountable and responsible which is very essential for any healthy and inclusive democracy.

2. Essence of e-Governance

"e-Governance is not about hardware, software, connectivity, change management, or citizens' participation to increase stakeholders but the assimilation of all these to bring speed and transparency in governance for inclusive democracy." The word 'e' means, easy, economic and effective governance which enables the citizens to feel the government without seeing it. Rapid changes in Information and Communication Technologies during the past few decades have paved the way for electronic governance. (Gupta, 2004)

Generally the intervention of ICT in public domain managed by government is referred as e-government whereas participation of citizens in the governing process is referred as e-governance. (ICT and Rural Development, 2012) However e-governance has greater scope and connotation than e-government, even though ordinarily the terms are used interchangeably. e-Governance permits new ways of participation of citizens and communities for debating which facilitate provision of accurate information about social problems and their possible solutions, if any. The present union government under the dynamic leadership of Prime Minister has started such governance using e-way which is better known as My Gov. This has been started to involve more and more citizens to share their views and opinions about the good governance. There has been noticeable involvement of the citizens in this process and helping the government to make the governance more participative and transparent.

e-Governance does not mean only using technological tools but it strives to bring a change in mind-set and work culture to integrate government processes and functions to serve the citizens in better way. Generally it is considered that interaction between a citizen and a government agency takes place in government offices but with the emergence and introduction of ICTs, it is now possible to locate services closer to the citizens' location. In this process, it is crucial that the capacity of government is open to citizens as well as the application of a new social context between all stakeholders.

However, we should not forget that the existing e-governance models are technology-based which have been aped from west and thus do not completely assure good governance and development in context of developing countries like India when the nation is suffering with the problems of illiteracy, poverty, inequality, etc.

3. E-GOVERNANCE IN INDIA

Accomplishment of e-governance in any country to a greater extent depends on the level of Information Technology literacy among its constituents and the level of participation of citizens in democratic process. Recognizing the increasing importance of electronics, the Government of India established the Department of Electronics in 1970 and subsequently established the National Informatics Centre in 1977 as a first major step towards e-governance in India and in 2006 the Government of India formally launched its National e-Governance Plan. The present union government of India has started a website 'My Gov' to invite suggestions and opinions about various issues concerning to public and that initiative is working fast towards making the governance more participative, transparent and effective.

Given the current developments in India, the position of e-governance is not so good or in rudimentary stage as compared to developed countries. As far as the IT literacy in India is concerned, there is 'digital divide' which has posed another kind of social segregation between those who are information rich and those who are information poor. This divide is because of uneven distribution and quick development of ICTs in India and is seen as a threat to the concept of developing egalitarian society, as it enables the rich to become richer and the knowledgeable to become more knowledgeable. This gap has been seen more in rural areas which are often regarded as information poor and lagging behind urban areas in terms of essential infrastructure and services. (Hazra, 2012) But with the continuing efforts of the governments this gap is decreasing and now rural people are also found more informed than earlier.

Digital connectivity is one of the roads ahead that can help the nation in connecting the governments to common people irrespective of areas whether it is urban or rural. Pitching India as the world's destination for the next big idea, recently Prime Minister Narender Modi at the launch of the Digital India week said "I dream of Digital India where 1.2 billion connected Indians drive the nation, which will take technology to the villages and block levels over the course of the next week." This clearly indicates that the focus of the present government is not only to develop the rural India through digital connectivity but to connect the whole India using ICTs.

As per the report (2012) released by United Nations Department of Economics and Social Affairs on E-Governance Development at world level, the condition of India does not seem to be good. India ranks 124th out of 190 Nations in using e-governance practices with index of 0.383 in comparison to world average index of 0.497. Infrastructure index is 0.110 in comparison to world index of 0.326 and e-participation index is 0.184 in comparison to 0.268. The basic factors taken for this survey are information dissemination, access, service delivery capability and citizen participation. (E-Governance Development Data, 2012)

4. Brighter Side of e-Governance

Although, India has been a late starter in using Information and Communication Technologies yet its impact on governance has been great and has influenced the process of governance to a great extent.

4.1 Creative Role: Use of ICT in governance has initiated new public services by facilitating improved delivery of services and has created more job opportunities for many others.

4.2 Reduction in Cost and Delays in Services Delivery: e-Governance allows the information to move quicker, easier and at cheaper cost on behalf of the government.

4.3 Expansion in Citizens' Access to Public Sector Information: The electronic communication serves as a bridge connecting individual citizens to decision makers. The best example is the Right to Information Act enacted in 2005 for the convenience of the citizens so that they can seek information from the government agencies in their areas of intention. This has made the governance process more transparent and people feel accountable for their acts.

4.4 Ability to Provide Immediate Communication: Through e-mail, citizens can register their views and concerns on current issues and can provide immediate communication between citizens and officials. All the offices starting from local to PMO office are under this ambit and the e-mail addresses are being given on the respective websites. The movement of Civil Society led by Anna Hazare is the best example of use of ICT. Anna team mobilized and sensitized the citizens by sending e-mails and SMSs to popularize their movement and it was noticed that it was effective and worked to their expectations.

4.5 Provides Database: In addition to all the above advantages it provides comprehensive database which helps policy makers to design, formulate and evaluate policies. (Vayunandan, 2003)

4.6 E-Learning: The broadband has increased the reach and delivery of learning opportunity to provide higher quality education to a wider population. It aids delivery of interactive learning possible, anytime, anywhere by combining voice, video and data and can be used to support collaborative e-learning. A group of persons can interact remotely with interactive learning material. The learning group can add further elements in the process of learning and can track the history of discussion. They can search across all added discussion and can refer the part for future discussion. This has made the governance in education sector easy and more accessible to all.

4.7 E-Health Care: With the help of advance broadband services it is now utilized as a tool to save lives and extend health care services, especially in areas where mobility or access is impinged. Robust growth in mobile phone and broadband penetration helps patients to gain access to doctors over long distances. Broadband enables integrated "healthcare in the cloud," supports the use of digital tools, enables high-speed exchanges of bulk data and gives physicians access anywhere, anytime, on any device. All data concerning to patient report can be gathered at a central database and distributed across different hospitals for detailed and thorough medical history. With these innovations consumers are benefited highly by keeping track of their reports, manage and improve their health on their own.

4.8 E-Banking: Access to basic financial services continues to be an unrealized dream for millions; even more so for those in rural and remote areas. Banking industry is slowly morphing into a paperless system with the help of ICT facilities. Even with rapid growth in the number of mobile phone subscribers, banks in collaboration with telecom companies are seeking to develop an alternate channel to deliver banking services. Mobile banking objective is to consolidate the services of the group into a single, self-service and fully integrated branch kiosk.

4.9 Mobile Governance: Technology is a best medium for sharing the information with citizens and for recording their suggestions and feedback. Electronic governance or e-governance is the key in bringing the rural people in the mainstream of the digital technologies. E-governance increases the participation of rural people for better prospects and opportunities for economic development, social transformation, agricultural management and marketing management, etc. through electronic medium. e-Governance helps to exploit the power of communication network to transform accessibility, quality and the cost-effectiveness of public services. Under e-governance initiative Indian ministries and government departments are developing their e-portal to digitize their operations to make them simpler and increasingly accessible for Indian citizens.

Mobile Governance, or m-governance, is an upcoming area too with more potential impact than e-governance programmes. Lot of m-governance initiatives active in rural areas like, in Karnataka Land owners register with "Bhoomi" application get an SMS whenever there is a transaction on the land. In Chhattisgarh registered phone numbers at Fair Price shop (FPS) can access the information regarding availability and supply of food grains and about times and truck numbers that deliver supplies to the FPS. Central and state governments have already shown remarkable progress in developing the e-governance and mobile governance initiatives. Filling e-return is a good example of tax payers filling their return online. Firstly the government made e-filing mandatory for those earning over Rs. 5 Lakhs and secondly the process is more user friendly with step by step guidelines which make it easy for all citizens to use this medium, overcoming the barriers of consumer awareness and education.

Recent m-commerce initiative has been activated through Vodafone regarding pension disbursement in Haryana. Vodafone has partnered with the Government of Haryana to facilitate mobile-based disbursement of monthly social security pension. Mobile money transfer and payment service is currently carried out as a pilot initiative, covering 868 beneficiaries at five villages in Karnal and Mahendergarh districts in Haryana. Vodafone M-Pesa allows beneficiaries with any active mobile number to directly receive pension, offering a safe and secure mechanism to transfer funds. The users get SMS, mentioning the amount of the pension, the withdrawal code and the withdrawal procedure. They can then withdraw the amount by simply authorizing the transaction with the withdrawal code at a nearby Vodafone M-Pesa retail outlet.

5. Darker Side of e-Governance

It is feared that governments are not utilizing the technology to its fullest extent as they lack the attitude to exploit the full capacity of ICT for improving democratic system. It is also expected that information technology (IT) may not always replace face to face interactions and meetings particularly when it comes to discussion phase. Even though IT might have widened the scope of governance but it is also true that it cannot handle very large meetings and even millions of e-mails can't be responded without resulting into delays. Therefore, heavy reliance on ICT to carry on the plans and processes of democracy may even reduce the ability of the government to debate, analyze and implement its plans for its citizens.

There is problem of inequality in gaining access to public sector services between various sections of citizens, especially between urban and rural communities, educated and illiterate, and rich and poor which needs to be addressed immediately, if the goal of e-governance has to be achieved. The dominance of English language on the internet is also a serious issue which prevents the access to public information to non-English speaking population.

In line with global trend, India might have undertaken massive initiatives to introduce e-governance at the national, state and local levels but there are fears that this whole enterprise of ICT may create a new class of 'untouchables' living in 'information poverty' compromising equal access to government services and eroded accountability and individual privacy. It is true that all the government offices including ministries are well in the reach of the common people through websites and e-mails and provides a wider opportunity for public servants to interact directly with the public in the process of receiving feedback from citizens and responding to their queries and complaints through electronic means. But we should not forget that making the system so open has also given access to anti-social elements which may prove dangerous not only to individual privacy but to National security.

Another big factor is that most of the political leaders whether computer literate or not have to depend on the ICT-skilled public servants for day to day functioning and replying to public concerns. In this process the public servants might assume a political role and increase their bureaucratic power thus leading to politicization of the bureaucracy.

6. Recent Initiatives of Union Government

A Case of Unique Identification Authority of India (UIDAI), Railway Reservation System, E-Voting in India, Online Dispute Resolution, Public Utility Services: Electricity bills, Agricultural inputs, Registration of vehicles, etc.

Some Cases from States

6.1. E-Connectivity of Prisons - A Case of Dhanbad

Dhanbad administration in Bihar has e-connected it's all block headquarters to the prison to facilitate videoconferencing between relatives and friends of under trials and prisoners lodged in Dhanbad jail so that they will no longer have to wait for hours in long queue to meet them. This move is expected to reduce the stress among the prisoner regarding well-being of their family members as most often they do not get an opportunity to interact with them due to heavy rush at the jail gate during meeting hours. This effect is being co-ordinated by block Pragya Kendras, a key element in the Centre's National e-governance plan under which unemployed youth are used to give their services. The family member of a jail inmate would have to contact the nearest Pragya Kendra to be allotted a time slot for meeting. (Telegraph, 2010).

6.2. E-Connectivity of Prisons in Haryana

Going in the same line with Bihar and adhering the directions received from the High Court of Punjab and Haryana, Haryana Police has e-connected all jails and courts using ICTs. (Tribune, 2010) Videoconferencing facilities have been installed in all jails and courts to reduce down the movements of prisoners for hearings. This will cut down the expenses borne by the state in transportation and security of inmates, who are brought to various courts across the state. State police will also be eased out from the immense load of taking the prisoners to jail and back. There are instances when inmates have escaped out of police custody, this system will be helpful in checking such instances.

6.3. E-Challan – Case of Chennai and Bangalore

Chennai and Bangalore are practicing e-challan system using Blackberry devices to record all offences digitally in a central server. In this system once a vehicle is flagged down for an offence, the registration details of the vehicle are entered into the device and a communication is established through GPRS with central server that houses the records of all vehicles in the city. If there is any discrepancy in the details than vehicle could be considered as stolen and investigation can be started. Since every policeman is given separate password, greater transparency and accountability is achieved.

6.4. Mother Child Health Tracking System - A Case of Haryana

Under the aegis of National Health Rural Mission the government of Haryana has started a program "Mother Child Health Tracking System." The prime objective of this mission is to keep a track on sex ratio in the state and to decrease the mortality rate of mother and child both. To avail the facilities every mother need to register themselves at Central Health Centres (CHC) or Primary Health Centre (PHC). All the registered mothers are being provided information through Short Service Messages (SMSs) not only about their vaccination but about the type of diets they are supposed to take during and after the pregnancy. As reported 12058 pregnant women and 9058 newly born babies exclusively from district Mahendergarh have been registered by 6th April 2012. (Jagran, 2012).

Under this scheme all the pregnant women who come for delivery to CHCs or PHCs are being registered on the spot through the software which is connected to Headquarters at

Panchkula. The officer sitting in their offices can contact the individuals to find out the status of services being provided by the CHCs or PHCs. It is well known that district Mahendergarh is at the bottom in sex ratio in Haryana and this mission is expected to control this rate in the near future. This initiative taken by the Haryana Government is another latest example of the e-governance to meet the expectations of the citizens and to include everyone in the main stream so that growth can be inclusive.

6.5. Computerization of Public Distribution System

Ministry of Consumer Affairs and Public Distribution have given top priority to PDS reforms and have urged the state governments to computerize the public distribution system. In this direction most of the state governments have completed the process of digitalization of ration card database for all the beneficiaries and Smart cards have been issued. Monitoring of transportation of essential commodities can be done using GPS, whenever PDS commodities are being dispatched to Fair Price Shops (FPSs) from the warehouses. Also an e-mail will be sent to all the registered beneficiaries for that FPS so that they can go and collect their quota from that shop. This process has been already started in Gujarat, Himachal Pradesh, Karnataka, Maharashtra, Meghalaya, Pondicherry, Rajasthan, Sikkim and Tamil Nadu. There are various instances of malpractices in the PDS at large level, this system is expected to bring transparency and accountability. Citizens will be able to voice their complaints through call centres if any malfunctioning is observed in the system.

7. Realty Check

Despite well introduced initiatives taken by the Centre and State Governments, the system would not bring desired results unless it is given the shape of nationwide campaign to provide adequate finances, enough electricity in the rural areas, and awareness to the illiterate citizens about the various programmes run by the centre and state governments for the welfare of the citizens. In order to improve the efficiency, effectiveness and responsiveness of the governments, the e-governance planners are required to expand the number and variety of services, improve access to the technology especially in context of computers. Thus, the people who do not have access to computers or being prevented from accessing information online to be addressed immediately.

The 8th edition of the global information technology report prepared by the 'World Economic Forum' in partnership with 'INSEAD' a leading business school, ranked India 54th among 134 countries after evaluating the capability of nation to leverages ICTs for their economic progress. Despite India's ranking 3rd worldwide for the availability of Scientists and Engineers and 27th for the quality of is research institutions, there are less than 3 personal computers and only 7 internet users for every 100 people. (The Hindu, 2009) The tele-communication revolution might have arrived, but internet penetration is still minuscule. In India, the possession of mobile phone might have increased to 63.2% in 2011 in comparison to 9.1% in 2001 but the internet connectivity has increased only to 10.2 percent as on 31st Dec 2011 from 0.7 percent in 2001 which is not adequate to take full advantage of e-governance. (Today, 2012) However recent data has shown some improvements in accessibility of internet penetration in India but this is not sufficient enough in such a large country, hence lot more need to be done if we have to be a successful e-governed nation.

CONCLUSION

Over the last 20 years, large number of initiatives have been taken in e-governance. Some of them have been very successful while some not so successful but one thing is common i.e., even in successful initiatives by the time we complete a project there are new demands. Similarly, by the time we run through those demands we have another set of fresh demands. At times it is felt that we always leave everyone wanting for more. Sufficient has not been enough. E-governance is a moving target and the expectation of people and organizations continuously change.

Therefore in order to try and build a system for e-governance we need to integrate expectation of citizens, especially because when we talk of e-inclusion and inclusive e-governance, it's important we try and synergize resources and efforts of the citizenry, government and industry into single unified force. Only then we will be in a position to fully harness benefits of ICT tools that we have today.

REFERENCES

E-Governance Development Data. (2012, 11th May). Retrieved August 2012, from United Nations Department of Economics and Social Affairs.

Gupta, A. (2004). Globalization, Technological Innovations and Public Administration: Challenges and Constraints. In N. J. Bave, *Publice Administration in the 21st Century* (p. 234). New Delhi: Indian Istitute of Public Administration.

Hazra, A. (2012). ICT and Sustainable Rural Growth. *Kurkshetra: A Journal of Rural Development, 60*(3), 9.

Hindu, T. (2012, May). *Cities News*. Retrieved August 2015, from The Hindu: www.thehindu.com.

ICT and Rural Development. (2012). *Kurukshetra: A Jorunal of Rural Development, 60*(2), 32.

Jagran, D. (2012, April 12). Rewari-Mahendergarh News. *Dainik Jagran*.

Sadashivam, T. and Tabassum, S. (2011, Oct-Dec.). Revisiting Indian Administration. *The Indian Journal of Political Science, 72*(4), 971.

Telegraph, T. (2010, August 17). *The Telegraph*.

The Hindu. (2009, August 29). *The Hindu*.

Today, B. (2012, April). *Business Today*, pp. 24-25.

Tribune, T. (2010, September 20). *The Tribune*.

Vayunandan, E. (2003). *Good Governance Initiatives in India*. New Delhi: Prentice Hall India Pvt. Ltd.

In: e-Governance in India: Problems, Prototypes and Prospects ISBN: 978-1-63484-830-5
Editors: P. Kumar, R. Sharma and U. Kaushal

Chapter 2

RURAL DEVELOPMENT AND INFORMATION TECHNOLOGY: THE WAY AHEAD

***Puran Singh Yadav*[1,*] *and Anshu Parashar*[2,†]**
[1]Director and [2]Assistant Professor of
Haryana Institute of Rural Development Nilokheri,
Karnal, Haryana, India

ABSTRACT

The soul of India lives in villages. Therefore, rural development has become a national necessity and has considerable importance. Rural development has always been accorded priority during the five year plans of Government since independence. The programmes of rural development aim to improve the quality of life of the rural people. To make the implementation of programmes to access the last men, the use of ICTs can complement the conventional methodology for proper planning and monitoring. This paper discusses the concept of rural development and various flagship programmes of rural development including the challenges of rural development. Secondly, it elaborates the use of ICT in rural development and thirdly different challenges to enhance the use of ICT in rural areas. Lastly the paper has concluded that ICT applications can play a vital role for effective implementation and monitoring of the rural development programmes despite so many challenges of its application and also to provide common services to the door step of the stakeholders' i.e., weaker sections by real time monitoring.

Keywords: rural development, rural development programme, ICT applications

* Dr. Puran Singh Yadav, Director, Haryana Institute of Rural Development, Nilokheri, Karnal, Haryana. E-mail: psyadav59@rediffmail.com.
† Er. Anshu Parashar, Assistant Professor, Haryana Institute of Rural Development, Nilokheri, Karnal, Haryana.

INTRODUCTION

"India lives in villages," said Mahatma Gandhi. It is true even today with more than 68% (Census-2011) of India's population still living in the villages (Affairs, 2015) and find their livelihoods support there. In Indian context agriculture development is synonymous with rural development. No wonder that the rural development has always been a primary concern of the successive Governments since independence. It has always been accorded top priority in the Five Year Plans of the Government of India. It goes without saying that rural areas are chronically suffering from unemployment, underemployment, disguised unemployment and infrastructure gaps leading to low levels of income, education, nutrition and poor health standards and unhygienic living conditions. The first in the series of Rural Development Programmes was launching of the Community Development Programme (CDP) way back in 1952 as an attempt to tackle the problems of Rural Development (Mondal, 2015) (Nayar, 1960). Its objectives were to improve all aspects of village life and to mobilize local initiative and resources through self-help and cooperation for the betterment of rural conditions. It could achieve only partial success for lack of effective delivery mechanism. It is generally believed that performance of the Rural Development Programmes is better when the locals are involved in the planning and its implementation (Mondal, 2015). The successive Five Year Plans have laid emphasis on strengthening of delivery mechanism through Panchayati Raj for this purpose (India, 2015). The Planning Commission of India has been consistently laying stress on planning for village development by grassroots institutions since the First Five Year Plan (1952-57) (India, 2015). Notably, the period from the 60s-70s was crucial for Rural Development. It witnessed the introduction of a large number of programmes targeted to the upliftment of the poor as mentioned below. Subsequently, the concept of Basic Minimum Needs was also added to the policy paradigm. Financial sector reforms had also been initiated with nationalization of banks (1969) and establishing of Regional Rural Banks (1975).

Broadly, the rural areas have been infested with problems such as

- Low levels of sustainable employment and income with shrinking employment opportunities in agriculture and allied sectors;
- Lack of resources i.e., deprivation;
- Social backwardness and barriers;
- Low levels of literacy and lack of know how hence lack of confidence and leadership qualities;
- Rain-fed agriculture leading to low levels of productivity coupled with poor marketing facilities as well as over exploitation of natural resources;
- In adequate infrastructure like electricity, transport, educational institutions, communication, health, storage facilities etc and lack of basic necessities of life like water, sanitation and shelter;
- Non-committal delivery mechanism and
- Lack of social security and cooperation among the people etc.

Present paper r contains seven sections. After having introduced the topic in section-I, Rural Development and Rural Development Programmes have been discussed in section-II.

In section-III challenges in Rural Development have been explained. Role of ICT in Rural Development is given in section-IV and role of ICT applications in RDPs is discussed in section-Ve. The challenges to application of ICT in Rural Development explained in section-VI. The conclusions have been drawn in section-VII.

RURAL DEVELOPMENT AND RURAL DEVELOPMENT PROGRAMMES

Rural Development has been defined as an improvement in socio-economic conditions, standards of living and quality of life of the people, especially of the low-income groups living in rural areas with perceptible changes in their incomes, employment opportunities and reduction in poverty levels. It involves helping the poorest among those who seek a livelihood in the rural areas. These groups include the small/marginal farmers, tenants, and the landless. In the present chapter Rural Development refers to the socio-economic development of the poor i.e., the families living below the poverty line (BPL), living marginally above the poverty line and the marginalized sections of the society such as scheduled castes, women, physically handicapped and old aged and those having very small holdings like small and marginal farmers.

Rural Development Programmes are those activities or schemes, which, if implemented, help to generate employment and to improve incomes of the poor to bring an overall upward change in their living standards of the people. The following categories of Rural Development Programmes (India, Schemes-Department of Rural Development, 2015) (India, Ministry of Panchayati Raj, 2015) have been/are under implementation presently:

1) **Rural Self-Employment Programmes:** Integrated Rural Development Programme (IRDP-1979), Training of Rural Youth for Self-Employment (TRYSEM)-1979, Development of Women and Children in Rural Areas(DWCRA-1982), Scheme of Improved Toolkit to Rural Artisans(SITRA-1992), Ganga Kalyan Yojana (GKY-1997) subsumed into Swaranjayanti Gram Swarozgar Yojana (SGSY) in 1999, remodeled as National Rural Livelihood Mission (NRLM) in 2011 and Deen Dayal Upadhyay - Gramin Kaushal Yojana DDU-GKY in 2015.
2) **Rural Wage-Employment Programmes:** National Rural Employment Programme (NREP-1980), Rural Landless Employment Guarantee Programme (RLEGP-1983)converted into Jawahar Rozgar Yajana (1988) Millions Well Scheme (MWS), Employment Assurance Scheme (EAS-1993) subsumed into Jawahar Gram Samiridhi Yojana (JGSY) in 1999 and remodeled as Sampooran Gramnm Rozgar Yojana in 2001 which was later made National Food for Work Programmes in 2004 and ultimately into Mahatma Gandhi National Rural Employment Guarantee Act (MGNREGA) in 2006.
3) **Rural Housing:** Indira Awas Yajana (IAY) since 1983, earlier it was a part of RLEGP and since 1996 an independent Scheme.
4) **Area Development Programmes:** Draught Prone Area Programme (DPAP-1974), Desert Development Programme (DDP-1977), Integrated Wastelands Development Projects (IWDP-1989), Watershed Development Projects 1995, named as Hariyali in

2001 and Integrated Watershed Development Programme (IWMP-2011) and made part of Pradhanmantri Krishi Sinchai Yojana 2015.

5) **Digitization of Land Records**
6) **Social Assistance Programmes:** Indira Gandhi National Old Age Pension Scheme (IGNOAPS), Indira Gandhi National Widow Pension Scheme (IGNWPS) Indira Gandhi National Disability Pension Scheme (IGNDPS), and National Family Benefit Scheme (NFBS) 2.7) Infrastructure Programmes: Pradhan Mantri Gram Sadak Yojana (PMGSY).
7) **Rural Sanitation Programmes:** Central Rural Sanitation Programme (1986), Total Sanitation Campaign (TSC-1999), named as Nirmal Bharat Abhiyan (NBA-2012) and remodeled as Swachh Bharat Mission –Gramin (SBM-G) in the year 2014 in 2012 SBM-G.
8) **Rural Drinking Water Supply Programmes:** Accelerated Rural Water Supply Programmes (ARWSP-1973) now as National Rural Drinking Water Programme (NRDWP).
9) **Other related Programes of Ministry of Panchayati Raj**

In this manner, the Ministry of Rural Development, Ministry of Panchayati Raj and Ministry of Drinking Water and Sanitation have been implementing hosts of programmes for rural development and poverty alleviation and have to access the remotest of the areas across the length and breadth of the country. Besides, the other Ministries have been implementing a numerous programmes relating to health, education, welfare of women and children, welfare of minorities and weaker sections, which has not only a wider coverage but also access to teeming millions.

CHALLENGES IN RURAL DEVELOPMENT

Rural Development is a national necessity for India and at the same time accessing such a big number about 85 cr people spread over huge area is really a gigantic and challenging task. The task involves eradication of poverty and providing basic necessities of life to the people in order to bring about and improvement in the quality of life of the people by raising the living standards of the rural people in general and poor and marginalized in particular through

- Creating employment opportunities by developing skill, knowledge, attitude and other abilities and also by infrastructure development for income generation.
- Developing infrastructure facilities.
- Providing minimum basic necessities/facilities to rural mass in terms of drinking water, education, transport, electricity and communication.
- Developing institutions of local self-governance like Panchayats for wider community participation and sustainable development through good governance.
- Providing financial assist to develop the artisans in the rural areas, farmers and agrarian unskilled labor, small and big rural entrepreneurs to improve their economy.

- Developing rural industries through the development of handicrafts, small scaled industries, village industries, rural crafts, cottage industries and other related economic operations in the rural sector.
- Developing agriculture, animal husbandry and other agricultural related areas.
- Restoring uncultivated land, provide irrigation facilities and motivate farmers to adopt improved seed, fertilizers, package of practices of crop cultivation and soil conservation methods and restoring ecological balance.
- To develop leadership quality of rural area.
- To improve rural marketing facility.
- To improve rural people's participation in the development of state and nation as whole.

To meet the challenges of rural backwardness and poverty, the Government of India has launched a large number of programmes as mentioned above from time to time (Nair, 2014). Various studies have indicated that despite huge spending on these programmes since independence, the results have not been very encouraging and about 28% of rural people still living below the poverty line though the percentage has come down from 55% in 1973, the absolute number remains almost the same. Poverty remains a chronic condition for almost 30 per cent of India's rural population. This state of affairs has been mainly attributed to lack of proper monitoring of programme implementation.

It has been now well settled and recognized that Information and Communication Technology (ICT) can play a great role in real time monitoring of implementation of these programmes and to see that the benefits reach the actual beneficiary well in time. Through the application of ICT real-time implementation of the Rural Development Programmes can be monitored sitting at one place like where the work site is located, what is the progress, whether the workers are being paid wages in time, where a self-help group is formed, whether the members are benefitted or not, where a house is being constructed, where a toilet constructed and being used, whether a person is getting the benefits of social security programmes in time or not. The financial progress/spending can also be monitored on real time basis and accounts maintenance by the Gram Panchayats can be monitored through different softwares. Sitting at a place, we can find out whether the village has been provided with the safe drinking water or not. In fact through the application of ICT direct benefit transfer (DBT) can happen to the satisfaction of actual beneficiaries. The beneficiaries can get information via SMS through mobile phone. The application of ICT in RDPs is discussed in the next section.

ICT AND RURAL DEVELOPMENT

In the developed world, the Information and Communication Technologies (ICT) revolution has affected every sphere of life and has been of immense benefit to the rural people. ICT refers to systems for producing, storing, sending and retrieving digital form of data. These data can contain text, sounds and images, both still and moving. Though Information Technology and Communication Technology were developed independently, both are greatly fused together to produce a new environment commonly referred to as

Information and Communication Technology (ICT). Moreover, the emergence of new wireless and satellite-based solutions is positioning the country to take advantage of the benefits to be derived from ICTs. Over last decade, the beginning of remote sensing, Geographic Information System (GIS), Global Positioning System (GPS) and survey technologies have potentially increased the capacity to collect huge volume of Geospatial or Geographical data. The Global Positioning System (GPS) is a satellite based navigation system used a lot for quite some time for sensing and navigation (Rout, Ojha, Pradhan, and Samal, 2012) (ISRO, 2015). The GIS is a distinct and powerful tool which strengthens the integration of spatial and attribute data and the layering of information in a number of different themes, which may be superimposed upon each other, revealing complex spatial relationships between variables (ISRO, 2015).

ICT, and particularly the Internet, are transforming all human activities dependent on information, including those in rural areas and especially in India. ICT has immense potential as an information technology based extension services in rural area. Remote Sensing, GPS and GIS technology has become an integral tool in a number of applications including land use, wastelands, urban planning, water exploration, environmental conservation and management, ecosystem studies, etc. (ISRO, 2015). These technologies have helped in improving the accuracy of data for disaster management, land use, wastelands, rural and urban planning, water exploration, environmental conservation, ecosystem studies, etc. (Rout, Ojha, Pradhan, and Samal, 2012) (ISRO, 2015).

Role and Applications of ICT in Development Programmes

The use of ICTs could therefore, complement the conventional Rural Development methods for betterment of rural people. The use of computers has increased tremendously while the numbers of Internet Service Providers (ISPs) have also increased. Main attractions of ICTs in rural areas are Mobile telephony and Internet both has now reached most parts of rural areas. Now days rural peoples are very much familiar with the use of SMS (Short Message Service) and audio/video clips through internet enabled smart phones. ICT holds tremendous potential for Rural Development in India and some of its potential applications are listed under:

Implementation and Monitoring of Rural Development Programmes of Ministry of Rural Development (MoRD), Ministry of Panchayati Raj (MoPR) and MDWS.

ICT is playing vital role in implementing and monitoring the various central and state programmes for the Rural Development. Management of real time information for all Rural Development Programmes/schemes/projects through ICT helps the central/state government agencies/officials to effectively plan, implement and monitor the actual outcome in the rural areas. Various ICTs applications are deployed as Management Information System (MIS) of various government schemes, for self-help schemes/projects, to mobilize/aware people for the schemes/projects and to keep track beneficiaries as well as fund flow at all levels.

MIS are used for implementing and monitoring various Rural Development and Panchayati Raj Programmes like MGNREGAsoft for wage employment (India, Mahatma Gandhi NREGAsoft Releases, 2015), MIS-SBM for Swachh Bharat Mission (Sanitation, 2015), MIS-IWMP for watershed management (Development, 2015), Aawasoft for Indira Aawas Yojna (Development, Indira Awaas Yojana, 2015), PES for Panchayati Raj

Institutions including PRIASoft (Model Accounting System for PRIs) (India, Panchayat Enterprise Suite, 2015) etc. These ICT based applications bring transparency, accountability and provide single window interface for all the stake holders. It helps to track transfer of funds and its utilization to various implementing agency. All stakeholders can monitor the programme implementation in real time as and when transactions happen. It assists in tracking inventory of works/assets and also used for redressal mechanism for grievances of all the stakeholders.

If we take NREGAsoft for wage-employment as an example, it is effectively deployed as a work flow based transaction level local language enabled e-Governance system (Richard and Vijayan, 2012). It is available in Online as well as offline mode to capture all the activities under MGNREGA. Each stakeholder can access relevant information through this portal. e-payment can be made through eFMS (PFMS) module implemented in Online. The portal provides single point access to all stake holders of MGNREGA. It includes separate pages for approximately 2.5 lakh Gram Panchayats, 6600 Blocks, 644 districts and 34 States and UTs. It generates all registers/documents and make them available on public domain, specially; registration, job cards, employment demanded and allocated, days worked, mustrolls, unemployment allowance, payments and compensations due, sanctioned shelf of works, work progress, measurement, inventory of works/assets, financial proposals, funds available/spent, amount paid as wages, materials and administrative expenses, track transfer of fund to various implementing agencies, online processing of labour budgets, strategy for timely payments of wages, reports/alerts for corrective action, social audit findings, register grievances of workers and track complaints and action taken (Richard and Vijayan, 2012) (India, Mahatma Gandhi NREGAsoft Releases, 2015).

Besides the above the ICT plays great role in the following areas:

ICT for Citizen Centric Services

ICT is playing important role for establishing CSCs (Common Service Centres) in rural areas through PPP Model (Technology, 2015). Haryana was the first state to roll-out 100% rural CSCs in the country. These CSCs started providing G2B, G2G, G2C Services. Now, the CSCs project is being remodelled under the brand name "e-Seva" and using the IVISS (Integrated Village Information and Services System) software as the citizen service delivery front-end application. The farmers sitting at a place can see the market rates for their produce.

Agricultural Goods Sales and Purchase Information System

From where to purchase fertilizers to ''how to use them,' information on pesticides, herbicides, storage etc. 'where to sell their goods,' "current price" such type of information can be easily available to the farmer (Cooperation, 2015).

Enhanced Decentralization

The decentralization of government means that rural areas must be capable of playing the new roles prescribed by the government. Some of these include the promotion of rural tourism which is done better and more cheaply with the use of web pages than traditional advertising media, participation in governance at the local level through the district websites and initiation of development projects with funds generated at the local level. Through the availability of FM and Community Radio stations and the advent of mobile applications in the rural areas, rural people are able to bring their views and problems to the attention of their related officers for response. SMEs in rural areas are now taking advantage of the Community and FM radio stations to advertise their products and services to many communities within and beyond their areas of operation. This enlarges the frontiers of their market and ensures the sustainability of their businesses.

Climate and Water Resources

Using ICT techniques, climatology and agronomics, is also dealing for analyzing the weather conditions to help the world's farmers adapt to climate change. Large amount of data are produced at different spatiotemporal scales by many sensors observing earth and model simulations. For climate studies, climate data with coverage of the entire earth and a long time period are often required to extract useful climate change information and patterns. In the field of water resources ICTs are being applied for scientific planning, management and monitoring (ISRO, 2015).

Health Care Facilities for Rural Areas though Telemedicine

Information and Communication Technologies (ICTs) contributes to improving the coverage of national health services in rural areas. ICT offers a variety of specialized applications and tools for health care services for rural and remote areas. It includes the collection of doctor databases, visual design of medical reports, geographical disease pattern, hospital MIS and disease data analysis for rural community health assessment. The application of ICTs to rural health-care delivery, called telemedicine, enables access to professional doctors irrespective of the geographical location of the patient or the doctor. ICTs have helped rural health workers to communicate easily with the district and regional health centers for fast and prompt supply of drugs and medical equipment to save lives in the rural areas.

Disaster Management in Rural Areas

ICT techniques are very useful and effective tools during disaster management in rural areas especially for remote locations in the situations of various disasters like earthquakes, landslides, floods and fires. Whether natural (flood etc.) or man-made (release of chemical or toxic substances, etc.) disasters require that emergency personnel be able to move affected populations to safer locations in as short a time as possible. ICT applications using remote sensing and satellite are performing very crucial task for managing public safety in rural areas (ISRO, 2015).

Distance Learning Services for Rural People

The introduction of online distance education by most universities provides learning opportunities to rural people, who, because of geographical distance to the centres of education or for limited financial resources, would be otherwise excluded from improving on their educational qualifications. The use of radio, television, video conferencing, webcasts etc. in education is now very common. Computers have been acquired for the study centres so that both tutors and students can make use of them to facilitate effective teaching and learning (Anand, Saxena, and Saxena, 2012).

SOME SPECIALIZED ICT AND E-GOVERNANCE SERVICES

a) **Property Registration** using ICT based e.g., HARIS (Haryana Registration Information System) application. HARIS provide services like collector rates of property, stamp duty calculations, deeds writing – standard deed templates, buyers/sellers photographs capturing, registration of property deeds, issuance of copy of registered deed, issuance of mutation notice, information on registered deeds etc. (Centre, 2015).

b) **Land Records Management** (Development, Department of Land Resources, 2015) using HALRIS (Haryana Land Records Information System). It is sngle window interface for deed writing, registration, mutation, jamabandi and ROR. It has Integrated Cadastral Maps with land records for on-line updating of mussavies as well as jamabandies, to provide copy of sajra aksh alongwith RoR. It provide on-line updated nakal of ROR to public helps in reduction of litigations and frauds, as now it is not possible to sell a same piece of land to multiple parties/peoples.

c) **Unique Identification (UID)/Aadhaar System** (India, Unique Identification Authority of India, 2015) for establishment of state resident's identity data. Integration of UID enrolled residents and issued UID numbers has been done with the smart card based PDS project and Direct Benefit Transfer (DBT) for subsidies for the beneficiaries. Now the disbursement of scholarships, pensions and subsidies through banking systems have been introduced. Unique ID cards are also issued to senior citizens, facilitating them to avail the benefits of schemes launched for them. The Aadhaar based linkage with bank accounts and implementation of DBT Scheme effectively enhancing transparency and reducing the level of corruption.

d) **Haryana Pension Processing and Information System (HaPPIS)** is an e-Governance application for social justice and empowerment (Reach, 2015). It is used for providing social security and economical assistance to the old aged, widows and handicapped of the state, in the form of monthly pension, who are unable to sustain themselves from their own resources and are in need of financial assistance. HaPPIS is a web enabled; centralized system has been developed and implemented across the state. This system has helped in reduction in time of pension disbursement to the beneficiaries, dramatically on one hand and detection of fraudulent cases on other hand.

e) **The e-DISHA Kendra's** are providing the services, which are strictly in government domain. Services include issue of various certificates, driving license, vehicle registration, birth and death certificates, and related to arms licenses etc. It is an IT driven electronic interface, aimed for delivery of a bucket of G2C services under a single roof (Haryana, 2015). Its time bound service delivery has resulted (a) in improving the efficiency of delivery of the services, (b) in elimination of corruption and middlemen from the process and c) in saving citizens from trouble of running around various dept.

f) **Video Conferencing Services** in all districts and multi point VC at State HQ. Extensive VC services are being provided regularly covering intra state, interstate and with central government departments.

g) **Websites and Portals Services** like design and development, hosting and management of departmental websites, web portals and interactive contents of major state government websites. Registration, activation and renewal of .gov.in and .nic.in domains for all state and central government websites and web Portals located in Haryana,
h) **SMS Gateway and On-line Payment Gateway** with the identified e-Governance projects. government official e-mail services over https://mail.gov.in and https://mail.nic.in domains.
i) **Digital Signatures Certificates** (DSCs e-Tokens) Registering and issuing services are being provided to government officers
j) **GIS Applications** to various departments for collecting data of village boundaries with important layers have been digitized and geo-referenced. Digitization and geo-referencing of cadastral maps for entire state.

CHALLENGES OF ICT IN RURAL DEVELOPMENT

Rural areas are still underserved in terms of ICT infrastructure and capacity building. As a result, ICTs have not been able to play their expected roles in the development of rural areas. However, there are some serious challenges against the full realization of ICTs role in rural development. The role of ICT in rural development is faced by many challenges. Issues such as unavailability of electricity, lack of ICTs equipment, high level of illiteracy, user acceptance and local content have to be addressed before the full potential of ICTs role in rural development can be achieved.

Unavailability of Electricity and High Cost ICTs Equipment

Many rural areas have limited access to electricity. The poor electricity power supply also restrains ICT centres in districts/blocks where they are mostly connected to the national grid for regular supply of power. Another challenge in ICTs for rural development is unavailability and affordability of computers and other equipment, as well as their maintenance. At present, the major means of access to ICTs in the rural areas is through the few common service centers and computer centers at panchayat that have been established in these areas.

Low Literacy Levels and Lack of ICT Personnel

Literacy rates are very low in rural area. The situation gets worse when it comes to computer literacy. There are fewer computer-literate personnel in the rural areas compared to the urban centres. On the other hand, if farmers are to make good use of ICTs, the extension officers who advise and train farmers need to acquire more knowledge and skills in ICTs. As this is presently not the situation, it has created a negative effect in the use of ICTs in the rural areas.

Lack of Telecommunications and Internet Services

The provision of ICTs in rural areas also requires access to telecommunication and internet services. However, as in the case of electricity, most of the internet and telecommunication companies are reluctant to move to the rural areas due to lack of electricity and fear of incurring losses. The problem of access to the internet in the rural areas is a major pre-requisite to the provision of effective ICT services to these places.

Local Language Problem

Poor local language content and unavailability of instructional manuals in local languages is also a major challenge in the role of ICT rural development. Maximum percent of the content on the internet is in English. Thus, if one is not literate in English, there is very little or no benefit to be derived from the internet.

Acceptance in Rural People

Another challenge is user acceptance of ICTs in the rural areas. It is often taken for granted that any technology transfer to the rural areas would be accepted. But it is always ignored that the rural people have their own established cultural and traditional ways of doing things. Any outside imposition of ideas or systems might therefore not be easily accepted.

CONCLUSION

Therefore, in order to utilize the ICTs effectively for Rural Development, a strong policy framework is needed. Fortunately, India has an ICT policy and Digital India Programme (DIP). According to these, the government encourages, promote and support the implementation of nation-wide ICT systems for rural areas. This includes a) use of ICT for providing common government services the modernization of agriculture to encourage Rural Development in order to achieve long-term growth in the agricultural sector and the economy as a whole. Sensitization of the importance of ICTs in the development of the rural areas should be given serious attention in the planning of ICT programmes in the rural areas. It is imperative for the government and other development agencies to ensure that the content of ICT policies and programmes are relevant to the needs of rural people. Last but not the least, the application of ICT in Rural Development will go a long way in improving the quality of not only of the implementation of the programmes but also help in improving the daily life of lot of people by real time direct benefit transfer. It will also infuse transparency in the system and eliminate the leakages by fast tracking the utilization of funds meant for the poor and weaker section of rural communities.

REFERENCES

Affairs, M. O. (2015, October 12). *Rural-Urban Distribution*. Retrieved from Census of India Website: http://www.censusindia.gov.in/Census_Data_2001/India_at_Glance/rural.aspx.

Anand, R., Saxena, S. and Saxena, S. (2012). E-Learning and Its Impact on Rural Areas. *IJMECS*, 46-52.

Centre, N. I. (2015, May 14). *Haryana Registration Information System*. Retrieved from http://www.nic.in/hi/projects/haryana-registration-information-system-haris.

Cooperation, D. O. (2015, October 22). *Delhi Kisan Mandi*. Retrieved from http://delhikisanmandi.in/.

Development, M. O. (2015, October 11). *Department of Land Resources*. Retrieved from http://iwmpmis.nic.in/.

Development, M. O. (2015, October 22). *Indira Awaas Yojana*. Retrieved from http://iay.nic.in/netiay/home.aspx.

Haryana, G. O. (2015, November 4). *e-Disha*. Retrieved from https://edisha.gov.in/.

India, G. O. (2015, November 5). *Mahatma Gandhi NREGAsoft Releases*. Retrieved from Ministry of Rural Development Website: http://nrega.nic.in/releases.htm.

India, G. O. (2015, October 11). *Ministry of Panchayati Raj*. Retrieved from http://www.panchayat.gov.in.

India, G. O. (2015, September 22). *Panchayat Enterprise Suite*. Retrieved from Ministry of Panchayati Raj website: http://panchayatonline.gov.in/viewPESHome.do.

India, G. O. (2015, October 11). *Planning Commission*. Retrieved from http://planning commissionarchive.nic.in/.

India, G. O. (2015, October 11). *Schemes-Department of Rural Development*. Retrieved from Ministry of Rural Development website: http://rural.nic.in/sites/programmes-schemes.asp.

India, G. O. (2015, September 19). *Unique Identification Authority of India*. Retrieved from https://uidai.gov.in.

ISRO. (2015, October 22). *National Remote Sensing Centre*. Retrieved from http://www.nrsc.gov.in/.

Mondal, P. (2015, September 15). *The Community Development Programme of India*. Retrieved from Online Library: http://www.yourarticlelibrary.com/india-2/the-community-development-programme-of-india-2405-words/4866/.

Nair, I. (2014). Challenges of Rural Development and Opportunities for Providing Sustainable Livelihood. *International Journal of Research in Applied, Natural and Social Science*, 111-118.

Nayar, B. R. (1960). Community Development Programme-Its Political Impact. *Economic and Political Weekly, 12*(38).

Reach, E. (2015, November 14). *Haryana*. Retrieved from A NASSCOM Initiative: http://egovreach.in/social/Haryana.

Richard, C. and Vijayan, P. K. (2012). Sustainable rural development with the application of Spatial Information. *International Journal of Geomatics and Geosciences*, 1048-1061.

Rout, J., Ojha, A., Pradhan, S. and Samal, R. (2012, June 5). *GIS for rural development and spatial planning system*. Retrieved from Geospatial World: http://geospatialworld.net/Paper/Application/ArticleView.aspx?aid=25039.

Sanitation, M. O. (2015, October 12). *Swach Bharat Mission*. Retrieved from http://sbm.gov.in/tsc/NBA/NBAHome.aspx#bottom.

Technology, D. O. (2015, September 13). *Common Services Centres Scheme*. Retrieved from http://www.csc.gov.in/index.php?option=com_content&view=article&id=236&Itemid=213.

In: e-Governance in India: Problems, Prototypes and Prospects ISBN: 978-1-63484-830-5
Editors: P. Kumar, R. Sharma and U. Kaushal

Chapter 3

CHALLENGES TO IMPLEMENT E-GOVERNANCE IN RURAL INDIA

D. Suresh Kumar[1]* and Jelsy Joseph[2]

[1]College of Business Management, Economics and Commerce,
Mody University of Science and Technology, Lakshmangarh, Rajasthan, India
[2]Professor and Head, Department of Commerce, COBMEC,
Mody University of Science and Technology, Lakshmangarh, Rajasthan, India

ABSTRACT

India is a nation of villages. The real India is represented by censes 2011 data which shows that there are 638,387 villages in India and they produce more than 72 per cent of the total population (e-Governance in Rural Agricultural Development, 2012). Information and Communication Technologies (ICTs) play a key role in economic growth of Rural India. So development of these rural areas is one of the important considerations of the policy makers. Therefore, they have been immersed in upgrading the living standard of the rural people by providing sufficient and quality social services. In order to eradicate the rural poverty various e-governance programmes have been launched by the Government of India. These programmes focus on poverty alleviation, better livelihood opportunities, provision of basic facilities and infrastructure through innovative programmes of wage and self-employment etc., which promote the overall quality of life of rural people. However, due to the lack of ICT education and awareness, rural people are not comfortable in accessing e-governance services. This paper addresses the challenges of implementing e-governance in rural areas. The government needs to overcome technical, organizational and economical challenges to successfully implement the e-governance programmes.

Keywords: ICT, e-panchayats, government, poverty alleviation

* Assistant Professor, College of Business Management, Economics and Commerce, Mody University of Science and Technology, Lakshmangarh, Sikar, Rajasthan, E-mail: dsureshkumarku@gmail.com.

1. Introduction

E-government refers to "the use of digital technologies to transform government operations in order to improve effectiveness, efficiency and service delivery."*(Forman, 2005)* Generally, the more services that are available online and the more widespread their use, the greater the impact that e-government will have. "In addition to the internet, mobile phones offer an even more convenient channel through which to distribute government information. By utilizing text messaging, governments are able to send out region-wide and specific emergency warnings, provide up-to-the-minute information upon request, and in essence make governments accessible to the people no matter where they may be, at any time." (McGuigan, 2015) E-governance has often defined as the application of Information and Communication Technology (ICT) for delivering government services, exchange of information communication transactions, integration of various stand-alone systems and services from the Government to its customers, businesses, other governments, and also management of the entire back office processes and interactions within the government system. The Government of India has launched National e-Governance Plan (NeGP) for disseminating e-governance services(Kapoor, 2015) The National e-Governance Plan (NeGP) has been formulated by the Department of Electronics and Information Technology (DEITY) and Department of Administrative Reforms and Public Grievances (DARPG). The NeGP targets to quality delivery of government schemes to peoples and trades with the idea of "A common man can access the all government services in his locality, through common service delivery outlets and ensure efficiency, transparency and reliability of such services at affordable costs." (Kapoor, 2015)

2. History of e-Governance in India

In 1970, the Government of India set up the Department of Electronics, which was later followed up with the setting up of National Informatics Center (NIC) in 1976. This was the first time that the country's ruling elite focused on technology and communications for the first time as an area of importance. In a decade, the government was able to create a national satellite-based computer network called NICNET. Using this technological infrastructure, a drive to digitize and computerize all the district level offices in the country was started. States were offered free software and hardware and by 1990, the NICNET connectivity had been extended from the State Capitals to the District headquarters. (Kapoor, 2015)

3. National Informatics Centre (NIC)

It was established in 1976, National Information Center (NIC) is providing network backbone and e-governance support to government bodies. NIC has been playing a vital role in directing e-government/e-governance applications in government ministries/departments at the Centre, States, Districts and Blocks, assisting upgrading in government services, wider transparency, promoting devolved planning and management, causing in better efficiency and responsibility to the people of India. In order to derive competitive advantage by implementing ICT applications in social and public administration the government has organized the programme of "Informatics-led-development."(National Informatic Center, 2013) The following key activities are being undertaken under this:

- Setting up of ICT Infrastructure
- Implementation of National and State Level e-governance Projects
- Products and Services
- Consultancy to the government departments
- Research and Development
- Capacity Building

4. Models for E-Governance

E-governance is all about flow of information between the government and citizens, government and businesses and government and government. E-governance also covers all these relationships as follows:

Primarily there are four e-governance models:

1) Government to Citizens (G2C)
2) Government to Government (G2G)
3) Government to Employees (G2E)
4) Government to Business (G2B)

The Table No. 4.1 explains the different models in context of India.

Table 4.1. E-governance models and their usage

E-Goverance Model	Uses	Services Offered in India
Government to Citizens (G2c)	Involves initiatives designed to facilitate people's interaction with government as consumers of public services and as citizens.	E-Citizenship E-Registration E-Transportation E-Health E-Education E-Help E-Taxation
Government to Government (G2G)	Involves sharing data and conducting electronic exchanges between governmental actors. This involves both intra-and inter-agency exchanges at the national level and local levels.	E-administration E-police E-courts
Government to Employees (G2E)	Includes online tools, sources and articles that help employees maintain communication with the government	E- Data submission E- Complaints and dissatisfaction E - Rules and Regulation E- Payment and working record E- Forms
Government to Business (G2B)	Involves business-specific transactions (e.g., payments with regard to sale and purchase of goods and services) as well as provision on line of business-focused services.	E-Taxation E-Licensing E-Tendering

Source: http://www.patheos.com.

5. OBJECTIVES OF E-GOVERNANCE

The object of e-governance is to provide a SMARRT Government. The Acronym SMARRT refers to Simple, Moral, Accountable, Responsive, Responsible and Transparent Government.

Simple	Moral	Accountable	Responsive	Responsible	Transparent
The use of ICT brings simplicity in governance through electronic documentation, online submission, online service delivery, etc.	It brings Morality to governance as immoralities like bribing, red-tapism, etc. are eliminated.	Government is account-able as all the data and information of Government is available online for consideration of every citizen, the NGOs and the media.	Due to reduced paperwork and increased communication speeds and decreased communication time, the Government agencies become responsive.	Technology can help the Government Responsible. Increased access to information makes more informed citizens. And these empowered citizens make a responsible Government.	With increased morality, online availability of information and reduced red-tapism the process of governance becomes transparent

Source: http://indiaegovernance.blogspot.in.

6. NEED OF E-GOVERNANCE IN RURAL INDIA

Development of rural economy is the real challenge for developing countries where large sections of people reside in villages and smaller towns. And this is the area where development interventions either fail to penetrate or bounce back without creating a significant impact. The foremost reason is the ineffective public investment being made in rural areas which is not allowing rural areas to develop as rapidly as their urban counterparts. The disparity in rural-urban infrastructure, in terms of roads, power, transport, water, and telecommunications is a severe bottleneck. Private investment in rural areas fails to provide basic facility to rural population. As large section of rural population continue to be employed in agriculture because of lack of alternate job opportunities in rural areas, especially for younger population and absence of technological revolution. (The Digital Governance Initiative, 2015) In order to improve the standard of living in rural areas Government of India has started many programmes aiming at providing opportunities, information and easy access of the rural development schemes to all citizens in rural India. The government efforts in various areas (National, State, District, Block and Panchayat level) have been initiated by Ministry of Rural Development for strengthening the ICT infrastructure. Due to the diversity, government faced various types of challenges in delivering government services. The intervention of ICT has eased out these challenges for government.

7. E-GOVERNANCE SCHEMES IN RURAL INDIA

Online Land Records: The Computerization of Land Records (CLR) is one of the earliest initiatives of e-governance in India at the grass-roots level. The focus of the entire operation has always been to employ state of the art Information Technology (IT) to galvanize and transform the existing land record system of the country. This service is a value addition and modernization in land administration. (e-Governance in Rural Agricultural Development, 2012)

Rural Agricultural Development: There have been several initiatives by the State and Central Governments to meet the various challenges facing the agriculture sector in the country. The online services cater up to the Panchayat level. The major e-governance initiatives in agriculture sector are: Rashritya Krishi Vikas Yojana, information to farmers on government programmes and schemes, Agricultural Marketing Information Network, Agriculture Credit, Agriculture Marketing, Drought Management, Macro Management Unit, Networking of Directorates and Field Units, Seeds, Kisan Call Center, Agricultural Census, Registration of Pesticides, Integrated Nutrient Management, Rainfed Farming System, Cooperation, Horticulture Development.

E-Panchayats: This represents the first-level of government interaction for over 60 percent of the Indian population, and provides a large number of basic services for millions of citizens living in rural locations across the nation. It is against this backdrop that the Panchayat Mission Mode Project has been included in NeGP. The MMP aims to address and overcome the typical challenges faced in the villages, like delay in delivery of services to citizens and lack of trustworthy communication structure, low revenue mobilization for implementing schemes at the Gram Panchayat level, and problems in the onitoring mechanisms for schemes. (e-Panchayats, 2012)

Mahatma Gandhi National Rural Employment Guarantee Act (MGNREGA): It aims at by guaranteeing hundred days wage employment of unskilled manual work to enhancing the livelihood security of people in rural areas. The central and state governments have been adding various e-governance advantages in this scheme. The important online modules in MGNREGA contain: Queries, Suggestions, and Complaints, Feedback in Panchayats level, Grievance Redressal System, Workers Information and Description, District/Block Administrator, State specific information and Social Audit.

Indira Awaas Yojna: In order to provide housing facilities to the rural poor, Indira Awaas Yojana (IAY) was launched in May 1985 as a sub-scheme of the Jawahar Rozgar Yojana. It is being implemented as an independent scheme since 1 January, 1996. It aims to providing grant-in-aid to construction of housing units and upgradation of kutcha houses for rural people, who live in below poverty-line belonging to SCs/STs, free bonded labourers and non-SC/ST categories. The new e-governance systems have been included, AWAAS Soft, Lodge Public Grievances, Check Redressal of Grievance, Complaint Register.

CAPART: It was made by the amalgamation of two agencies, the 'Council for Advancement of Rural Technology' (CART) and People's Action for Development in India (PADI). It is functioning under the guidance of the Ministry of Rural Development, Government of India. CAPART is a self-governing body listed under the Societies Registration Act 1860; this agency is assisting over 12000 voluntary organizations all over the country in implementing development initiatives. This agency is the main promoter of rural development in India.

National Social Assistance Programme (NSAP): It was introduced on 15th August, 1995. E-governance in NSAP includes: Indira Gandhi National Old Age Pension Scheme (IGNOAPS) Indira Gandhi National Widow Pension Scheme Indira Gandhi National Disability Pension Scheme (IGNDPS).

Pradhan Mantri Gram Sadak Yojana (PMGSY): The Pradhan Mantri Gram Sadak Yojana (PMGSY) was launched by the Government of India to provide connectivity to unconnected rural habitations as part of a poverty reduction strategy. A citizen can track the day to day progress report in the scheme. The e-governance initiatives include: Habitation Coverage, Sanctioned Projects, Pending Proposals, Completion of Packages, Physical and Financial Projects Summary, Physical Progress of Works, Financial Progress of Works, Financial Progress as per Accounts, State Profile, National Projects Summary, and Per Kilometer Cost.

Swarnjayanti Gram Swarozgar Yojana (SGSY): It is to bring the assisted poor families above the Poverty Line by ensuring constant level of income over a period of time. This objective is to be achieved by organizing the rural poor into Self Help Groups (SHGs) through the process of social mobilization, The SHG approach helps the poor to build their self-confidence through community action. This process ultimately leads to improve their collective bargaining power and socioeconomic empowerment of the rural poor. (e-Governance in Developmental Schemes, 2012)

8. Challenges for e-Governance Implementation

E-governance's management and coordination with other departments is very difficult for center and state governments. There is a lack of technical, organizational and economical management. It is not possible to give reliable and timely information every time. It is very challenging to control, supervise and ensure conformity of government instructions. If any problem occurs in portal, it is very difficult to maintain the trust of citizens. The resistance to change, training programmes, collaboration, leadership, technological skills and capabilities, cost and finance of the project, network creation are some of very common problems in implementation of e-governance. (Bhavneet Dhindsa, 2013)

8.1. Technical Challenges

8.1.1. Interoperability

It is more pragmatic than other approaches, such as bidding to make all systems compatible at the code level, focusing solely on adding new layers of middleware that try to make all systems look and act the same, or seeking to make different systems interchangeable. With a common understanding of basic protocols, with little or no specific knowledge different software can interact smoothly. At times interoperability is also disordered with open source software. Open source is a methodology for licensing and developing software that may or may not be interoperable. (Gates, 2005)

8.1.2. Secrecy and Safety

A critical problem in implementing e-governance is the secrecy and safety of an individual's personal data that he/she provides to get government services. With the implementation of e-government projects, some important actions must be taken to protect the personal information of the end-users. Lack of safety standards can be one of the limitations of development of e-government projects in rural areas.

8.1.3. Multi Service Interactions

The Web is an important medium for receiving, providing information and an accessible web can also help citizens more effectively interact with the society and government. Thus multiple service interaction is important that the Web be accessible in order to deliver equal access and equal opportunity to citizens with disabilities and older citizens. Given that people with disabilities represent between ten and twenty percent of the population of most countries, ensuring accessibility of government Web sites is an important aspect of openness and transparency of government data. This need has been made more explicit by the 2008 passage of the United Nations Convention on the Rights of Persons with Disabilities [UN-ACC] which among other fundamental human rights includes the right of access to information. The web is an opportunity for people with disabilities to access the information, there are accessibility barriers to print, audio and visual media can be much more easily overcome through web technologies.

An accessible Web expands opportunities for communication, interaction, and employment for rural people with disabilities throughout governments. (Convention on the Rights of Persons with Disabilities, 2008)

8.2. Organisational Challenges

8.2.1. Populace

Populace of India is undoubtedly the main challenge in implementing e-governance schemes. Indian government is making efforts for providing unique identity to its citizens, for example, as populace deals with the challenges of establishing person identities. Gauging the populace and keeping the data base updated and then providing the e-governance services to the entire populace are major challenges.

8.2.2. Lack of Combined Services

Communication gap between different department of central and state governments may be the major cause. The e-governance services which are offered by the central and state governments are not combined. Thus, the information that exists in one department has no or little meaning to some other departments of the government.

8.2.3. Lack of Awareness in People

Most of the people in rural India are not aware about the benefits of e-governance services. The government also does not pay more attention to make the people aware about e-governance activities. Unawareness is a major challenge in the implementation of e-governance in rural area.

8.2.4. Variety of Languages

In India people speaking different languages. The language diversity is a very big challenge for implementing e-governance projects as e-governance applications are written in English language. Rural people are facing problem in accessing e-governance services because they do not know any other language than their regional language. So it is a challenge for the government to write e-governance applications more than one language.

8.2.5. Literacy Rate and ICT Literacy

In rural India the literacy rate is very low, minimum educational standard is not necessary to be considered as literate and to access web sites. Rural people are not technically literate to use the technology. Government launched many e-governance services to develop rural India but because of lack of technical knowledge they are incapable of using such facilities. Without increase the IT literacy rate, the efforts of the government do not get much success.

8.3. Economic Challenges

8.3.1. Cost

Cost is one of the most important problems in implementation of e-governance in India. Majority of the people are living below poverty line in rural India. In order to provide e-governance services, government invested huge amount of money on implementation, operational and maintenance tasks. Success of e-governance in rural areas is always doubtful. In remote areas generally the cost for developing infrastructure like connectivity and electricity are very high.

8.3.2. Maintenance of Electronic Devices

As the cost of information technology changes very fast and it is very difficult for developing country like India to modernize existing system immediately. Maintenance is the important factor for rapidly changing technical environment. Different devices and their different characteristics may vary and the system in use must be capable to handle all the emerging needs.

8.3.3. Low Per Capita Income

The GDP per capita is obtained by dividing the country's gross domestic product, adjusted by inflation, by the total population. According to International Monetary Fund World Economic Outlook (April-2015), GDP (nominal) per capita of India in 2014 at current prices is $1,627 compared to $1,508 in 2013. India is the ninth largest economy of the world. However, due to its huge population of more than 1.26 billion, India is at 145th position in term of GDP (nominal) per capita. Per capita income of India is 6.69 times lower than world's average around of $10,880. This Figure is 68.66 times lower than richest country of world and 6.5 times greater than poorest country of the world. India is at 34th position in the list of Asian countries. (GDP per capita of India, 2015) Therefore, people cannot afford on-online services provided by the government which is a challenge for implementation of e-governance.

8.3.4. Limited Financial Resources

In line with the Government's commitment to medium term fiscal consolidation, and to ensure macroeconomic stability in the short run, the budget inherited a targeted fiscal deficit of 4.1 percent of GDP, down from 4.5 percent in the previous year. How ambitious a target was this? Evaluating the budget from the revenue side suggests that the target was ambitious. An overestimation of revenue can result from an overestimation of nominal GDP growth as well as an overestimation of optimism. (Finance, 2014-2015) India has limited financial source so as to implement and maintain the e-government projects properly.

9. SUGGESTIONS

- The effectiveness of Panchayat and Block level functions will depend upon state and central government and they have to take various innovative steps to promote e-governance. Government of India has drawn up a roadmap for IT implementation and delivery of services to the citizens online. The applications that have been implemented are targeted towards providing Government to Citizen (G2C), Government to Business (G2B), Government to Employees (G2E) and Government to Government (G2G) services with emphasis on use of local language.
- ICTs should be integrated within the education curriculum within government, government-aided and private schools, public and private institutes in rural areas. This will enable developing countries a source of IT-trained population.
- Enabling IT policies requires countries to develop broadband network in rural areas. All schools, colleges, institutions, and post offices in rural areas should be connected via broadband network. Right kind of education and training can become a lifeline for our youngsters who want to find employment opportunity for earning.
- Often NGOs working for rural development, NGOs need to transform too, they should adapt themselves to changing technologies and educate themselves on vast potential of IT in rural areas when applied innovatively for increasing employment opportunities and income.
- Sound communication channels should be made effective to make rural people understand the features and process. Through television advertisement government could very easily communicate to rural people.
- In order to find out rural infrastructure requirements, the Gram Sabha meetings may be conducted through media participation.
- In rural areas people have not awareness about ICT and e-governance. They do not know how to check their registration, employment details, unemployment allowance, working days and payments lodge complaint and to trace the subsequent response. It has a provision of payment of wages through bank/post office thereby ensuring the correct payment to a worker.
- In order to create participative, transparent and responsive government, the government of India has launched "Digital India" programme. The initiative includes plan to connect rural areas with high-speed internet networks. The effort which is made by the government will give bright future to rural India. Therefore, government

has to provide digital literacy so that people may take full advantage of these activities.

Conclusion

E-governance is the key to good governance for developing countries. Large sections of people, in India remain poor and marginalised. They continue to be exploited, fail to get value for their labour and do not have the opportunities to escape from the poverty cycle. Information and Communication Technology has great relevance in today's world. E-governance projects are not successful in all parts of India. Thus, government has to take necessary actions to overcome these challenges to implement e-governance in rural areas. Implementation of ICT programmes in simple method and language, which is easily understandable by the rural people, can play a vital role in e-governance. The improved e-governance services will help in the development of rural infrastructure, which in turn would result in improving the living standard of rural masses.

References

Acar, S. (Ed.). (2009, May 12). *Improving Access to Government through Better Use of the Web*. Retrieved July 11, 2015, from w3c Web site: http://www.w3.org.

Bhavneet Dhindsa, M. N. (2013). Benefits And Challenges of E-Governance Portal. *International Journal of Soft Computing and Engineering, 3*(5), 121-123.

Convention on the Rights of Persons with Disabilities. (n.d.). Retrieved Auguest 6, 2015, from United Nations Enable Web site: http://www.un.org.

e-Governance and Modi Government's Ambitious "Digital India." (2015, March 22). Retrieved September 30, 2015, from patheos web site: http://www.patheos.com/.

e-Governance in Developmental Schemes. (2012, December 9). Retrieved 18 september, 2015, from India gov.Archives web site: http://www.archive.india.gov.in.

e-Governance in Rural Agricultural Development. (2012, December 9). Retrieved September 13, 2015, from India Gov.Archive web site: http://www.archive.india.gov.in.

e-Governance in Rural Development. (2012, December 9). Retrieved October 15, 2015, from india.gov.in: http://www.archive.india.gov.in.

e-Panchayats. (2012, December 9). Retrieved September 2015, 17, from India gov.Archive web site: http://www.archive.india.gov.in.

Finance, M. o. (2014-2015). *Mid-Year Economic Analysis*.

Forman, M. (2005, June 15). EGovernment: Using IT to Transform the Effectiveness and Efficiency of Government. United States.

Gates, B. (2005, February 3). *Building Software That Is Interoperable By Design*. Retrieved October 10, 2015, from Microsoft web site: http://www.microsoft.com.

GDP per capita of India. (2015, June 19). Retrieved 9 2015, September, from Statistics Times Web site: http://statisticstimes.com.

Kapoor, D. (Ed.). (2015, March 22). *E-Governance and Modi Government's Ambitious "Digital India."* Retrieved October 19, 2015, from Patheos web site: http://www.patheos.com.

McGuigan, B. (2015, September 25). *What is E-Government?* (N. Foster, Ed.) Retrieved October 20, 2015, from Wisegreek: http://www.wisegeek.com.

National e-Governance Plan. (2015, August 21). Retrieved September 26, 2015, from india gov website: http://www.india.gov.in.

National Informatic Center. (2013, September 2). Retrieved October 2, 2015, from National Informatic Center web site: http://www.nic.in.

Online Land Records. (2012, December 9). Retrieved September 11, 2015, from National Portal of India web site: http://www.archive.india.gov.in.

The Digital Governance Initiative. (n.d.). Retrieved October 7, 2015, from digitalgovernance web site: http://www.digitalgovernance.org.

In: e-Governance in India: Problems, Prototypes and Prospects ISBN: 978-1-63484-830-5
Editors: P. Kumar, R. Sharma and U. Kaushal

Chapter 4

MYTHS AND REALITY ABOUT E-GOVERNANCE IN RURAL INDIA: A CONFIRMATORY TEST

Puneet Kumar*
Assistant Professor, College of Engineering and Technology,
Mody University of Science and Technology, Lakshmangarh, Rajasthan, India

ABSTRACT

Although, there are islands of success in the area of e-governance in India, but, still there are some areas, which are not explored or inadequately explored. This attempt tries to identify major bottlenecks in implementation of e-governance especially in rural areas supported with a rigours primary survey. On the basis of secondary literature review Rajasthan state is identified as one of the leading state in utilization of e-governance services whereas Haryana state is lagging behind. Therefore, these two states viz. Haryana and Rajasthan were identified as course of the study. The presented effort is a kind of confirmatory test performed to demystify the actual visualization of e-governance up to grass root level.

Keywords: rural development, challenges, primary data, awareness level, Haryana, Rajasthan, PRIs

1. INTRODUCTION

In India, there are numerous islands of success in context of e-governance as depicted in various chapters of this book. The central as well as state governments are keeps on sprouting novel e-governance applications for automation of various mundane tasks. The review of literature evidently shows the positive inclination of governments towards rural areas from e-

* Assistant Professor in Computer Science, Department of Computer Application, College of Engineering and Technology, Mody University of Science and Technology, Lakshmangarh, Rajasthan, email: professor.pkumar@gmail.com.

governance perspective. Moreover, the government has also kept automation of PRIs (Panchayati Raj Institutions) as one of the central MMP.

But on contrary to aforesaid, the review of literature revealed that the situation of e-governance is not overwhelming in rural areas. It seems to be more or less pathetic. The seamless effort of the government seems to go in vain. As pointed out by the review, lack of awareness among the PRIs and bureaucrats, lack of connectivity, lack of citizen centric applications, inadequate level of participation of the people, cost ineffectiveness of services, sustainability issues of the CSCs, time consumption in availing e-services, lack of local language support and lack of interoperability among various e-governance applications are the prevailing issues. Whereas, the issues like lack of political will, poverty, illiteracy, etc. are also inadvertently existing in rural areas.

It jiggles the mind of researcher because the governments are acclaiming its success in delivering e-services up to local level, but on the other hand the conducted researches apparently demystifies that the scenario is not overwhelming in rural areas. This state of quandary has incited the researcher to conduct a survey with the intent of identifying grass root realities which may result into mitigation of dilemma aptly.

Therefore, a survey was conducted in selected districts of two states especially focused towards PRIs. The *Rajasthan* and *Haryana* states were chosen as target states whereas Sikar, Churu and Rewari, Karnal were chosen as target districts from both the states respectively. These two states will be having similar type of demographical conditions especially in terms of topography, economy and literacy. The districts from these states were chosen on the basis of their literacy rates because it is evident from various studies that the literacy rate is directly proportional to the level of awareness among people. Further, a pretested interview schedule was used for conduct of the survey. During the survey some personal observations were also made by having discussions with villagers, elected representatives and bureaucrats. And, as a result some interesting results were obtained which are discussed in subsequent sections of this chapter.

2. Review of Literature

The former President of India, Sir A.P.J. Kalam (Kalam, 2008), has visualized e-governance as “A transparent smart e-governance with seamless access, secure and authentic flow of information crossing the interdepartmental barrier and providing a fair and unbiased service to the citizen.” In order to access the level of effectiveness of e-government in any nation the concept of e-government readiness index was coined. According to United Nations e-government survey framework (Affairs, 2012), e-government readiness index indicates capability and the inclination of the public sector towards deployment of ICT for improving knowledge and information in the service of the citizen. The capability embraces: fiscal, infrastructural, social capital, regulatory, bureaucratic and systemic capacity of the state. The inclination indicates towards testament of the government’s commitments in providing information and knowledge for the empowerment of the citizen.

The report (Commission, 2008) has described about seamless initiatives taken by Government of India to accomplish the deployment of e-governance in India. According to this report in 1970, the Government of India (GoI) has established Department of Electronics and subsequently in 1977 GoI has taken first major step towards implementation of e-governance by establishment of National Informatics Centre (NIC). By 1980 most of the government offices were equipped with computers but their role was confined up to word processing. With the span of time and advent of ICT, the GoI has taken a remarkable step for fostering e-governance by launching the National Satellite Based Network NICNET in 1987 followed by District Information System of the National Informatics Centre (DISNIC) and according to (Prabhu, 2012) NICNET was the first government informatics network across the world equipped with facilities like TELNET, FTP, Internet along with database services (GISTNIC and MEDLARS). Up to 1990, NICNET has extended its extent from state headquarters to district headquarters. The GoI has established Ministry of Information Technology in year 2000, and identified minimum 12-points agenda for e-governance. This agenda comprises of providing computers with software to officers, necessary training to officials, adoption of office procedure automation software (developed by NIC) and inclination towards automation of various mundane operations. Finally in year 2006, the GoI has launched National e-Governance Plan (NeGP) and categorizes the initiatives in to three broad categories *viz* G2C (Government to Citizen), G2B (Government to Businesses) and G2G (Government to Government). The report also portrays a brief report about various G2C initiatives like *Bhoomi* project in Karnataka, *Gyandoot* in Madhya Pradesh, *Lokvani* in Uttar Pradesh, *FRIENDS* in Kerla, *e-Mitra* in Rajasthan, e-Seva in Andhra Pradesh, *RACE* in Bihar, G2B initiatives like *e-Procurement* in Andhra Pradesh and Gujarat, *MCA21* and various G2G initiatives like *Khajane* project in Karnataka, *SmartGov* in Andhra Pradesh. It also indicates some key factors responsible for success and failure of any e-governance projects.

The (Chauhan, 2009, Technology, 2014, Times, 2007) has described NeGP, along with its vision, components, implementation strategies and architecture of the plan. Further, it also gives an overview of India from geographical, political, economic, social, and legal perspective moreover; it also discusses the IT aspect of India in context of implementing NeGP. It states that NeGP comprises of 27 mission mode projects and components with the objective of computerization and automation of essential mundane tasks with an estimated outlay of INR 3.3 billion. In year 2011, four new MMPs related to health, PDS, education and post were also added therefore, currently NeGP encompasses 31 MMPs. The SWAN (State Wide Area Network), SDC (State Data Centre) and CSC (Common Service Centre) were also identified as the major components for delivering numerous e-services.

The government is expanding an enormous amount on cultivating the culture of e-governance through NeGP, but despite of that results are not overwhelming. Although there are islands of success in the area of e-governance, but still there are certain areas which are unexplored or inadequately explored. On the basis of the survey; 85% failure rate for e-governance projects has been noticed across the world, whereas in year 2009 alone, the worldwide expenditure on the technology abided by the government was 428.38 billion US dollars (Luna-Reyesa, Melloulib, and Bertotc, 2013). The authors (Mistry, 2010, Dwivedi and Bharti, 2010, Gajendra, Xi, and Wang, 2012, Kumar, Umashankar, Rani, and Ramana, 2010) have identified major impediments and challenges in successful implementation of e-governance in India. According to them inadequate planning, leadership failures, deficiency in finances, lack of motivation and awareness, dearth of citizen centric nature of applications, poor cooperation among bureaucrats and people at local level, lack of trust, miserable technical design which endures lack of interoperability among distinct e-governance applications and underutilization of ICT infrastructure resources are the major obstacles in successful implementation of e-governance in India. It is aptly emphasized by (Rajagoplan and Sarkar, 2008, Guma, 2013, Odat, 2012) that, community centric e-governance applications need to develop after identification of local needs, conditions and demands. The authors (Bhatnagar and Singh, 2010) delineated about parameters for analysing impact of e-governance services and states that quality of service delivered by e-governance and cost abided by the citizen for availing e-services are the major factors responsible for sustainability of any e-governance programme. They also advised that a survey must be conducted for analysing degree of relevance in order to mitigate the occurrence of failure. The impact assessment analysis for every e-governance project has also been recommended and they suggested about incorporation of impact assessment and evaluation module within the application. Furthermore (Savoldelli, Misuraca, and Codagnone, 2013), have also accentuated on impact assessment of e-services and suggested a model for the measurement of e-government and (Stanimirovic and Vintar, 2013) also suggested an indicator model for evaluation of transformation effects, infrastructure investments, political and sociological effect, economic and sustainability impacts with reference to e-governance.

3. District Profiles

Sikar

This district exists in Rajasthan state and according to the 2011 census; Sikar district has a population of 2,677,737 and a population density of 346 inhabitants per square kilometre (900/sq. m). The district is having sex ratio of 944 females for every 1000 males, and a literacy rate of 72.98%.

Churu

According to the 2011 census, Churu district has a population of approximately 2,041,172 and situated in Rajasthan state. The district has a population density of 148 inhabitants per square kilometre (380/sq. m). Churu has a sex ratio of 938 females for every 1000 males, and a literacy rate of about 67.46%.

Karnal

Karnal district is situated in Haryana. According to the 2011 census, Karnal district has a population of 1,506,323. The district has a population density of 598 inhabitants per square kilometre (1,550/sq. m). Its population growth rate over the decade 2001-2011 was 18.22%. Karnal has a sex ratio of 886 females for every 1000 males and a literacy rate of 76.4%.

Rewari

District Rewari is situated in Haryana state having total area equal to 1,594 km^2. According to the 2011 census, Rewari district has a population of 896,129 and a population density of 562 inhabitants per square kilometre (1,460/sq mi). Rewari has a sex ratio of 905 females for every 1000 males, and a literacy rate of 82.2%

4. Description of Sample

It has been already discussed that a survey was conducted to know the problems existing in rural areas at local level. There are four districts in which survey was conducted and the responses from PRIs were collected in the form of interview schedules. The numbers of respondents in the state as well as district are mentioned in the Table 1.

It is clearly evident from the Table 1 that the respondents from each tier were taken into consideration for performing the survey.

5. Awareness about E-Services in Haryana

The Table 2 describes about the level of awareness about e-services and ICT in the state of Haryana. Both the Table and the Figure 1 clearly show that Rewari is having relatively more awareness in comparison with Karnal. However, the awareness trend is found similar in both the districts i.e., the PRIs are least aware about CSCs and most aware about mobile phones.

The Figure 1 reveals that, in district Rewari, 53.4% of the stakeholders are aware about offered e-services, 67.2% are aware of Internet, 43.1% are conscious about call centres, only 50% are having knowledge about NeGP and 89.7% are well versed with mobile phones.

The Figure 1 depicts that in district Karnal, the elected representatives are less aware in comparison with district Rewari i.e., their level of awareness about offered services is 46.9%, about internet is 61.2%, only 34.7% is about CSCs in local vicinity, 44.9% about NeGP and 85.7% about mobile phones.

Table 1. Sample Description

Stakeholder	Tier	State			
		Haryana		Rajasthan	
		Rewari	Karnal	Sikar	Churu
Zila Parishad	III	5	6	5	4
Panchayat Samiti	II	12	8	12	13
Gram Panchayat	I	41	35	42	37
Total		**58**	**49**	**59**	**54**
State wise Total		107		113	
Total Sample Size		220			

Table 2. Awareness about e-Services and ICT in Haryana

Awareness about e-services and ICT in Haryana					
Awareness about	Rewari		Karnal		Average Awareness (%)
	Aware	% aware	Aware	% aware	
Offered e-Services	31	53.4	23	46.9	50.19
Internet	39	67.2	30	61.2	64.23
Mobile Phones	52	89.7	42	85.7	87.68
CSCs	25	43.1	17	34.7	38.90
NeGP	29	50.0	22	44.9	47.45
Call Centres	25	43.1	18	36.7	39.92

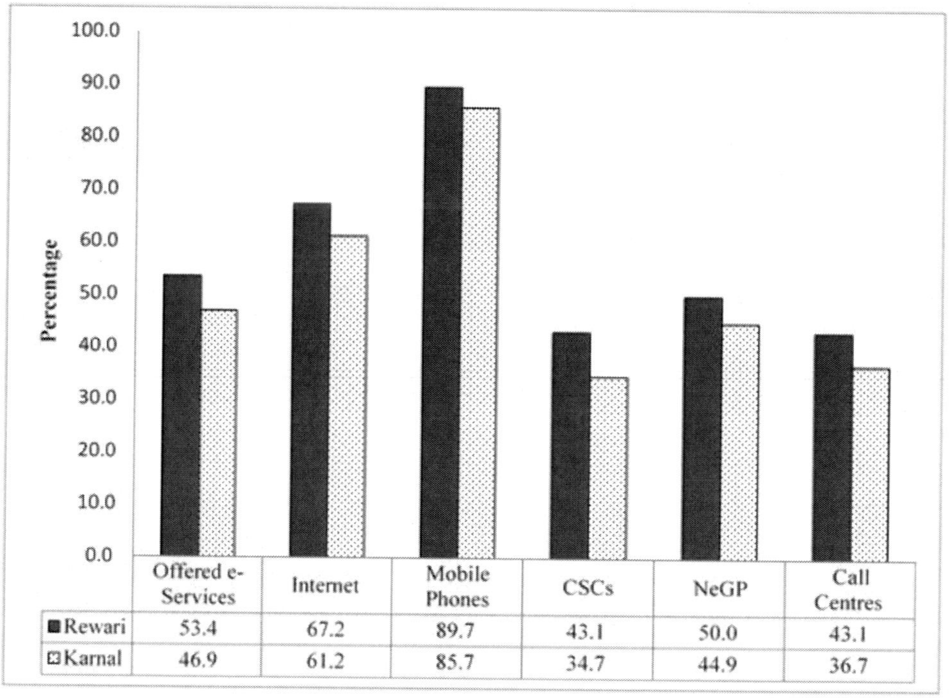

Figure 1. Awareness about e-governance and ICT in Haryana.

The Figure 2 clearly indicate that district Karnal is slightly lagging behind than district Rewari in all observed aspects. But respondents of both the districts are least aware about CSCs and call centres. In the current era, mobile or cellular phone has become protuberant media of communication; therefore as a result the respondents of aforesaid districts are most aware about it. The bar chart (Figure 2) and Table 3 throws some spotlight on obliviousness of elected representatives about offered e-services in context of rural development.

6. Awareness about E-Services in Rajasthan

The Table 4 and Figure 3 elucidates that the awareness level of respondents in Rajasthan is pretty fair in comparison with Haryana. The awareness levels about offered e-services are 61% and 57.4% in district Sikar and Churu respectively whereas it was observed 46.6% and 53.1% in district Rewari and Karnal respectively. Moreover, 74.6% and 68.5% people are well aware about internet in both the districts of Rajasthan correspondingly.

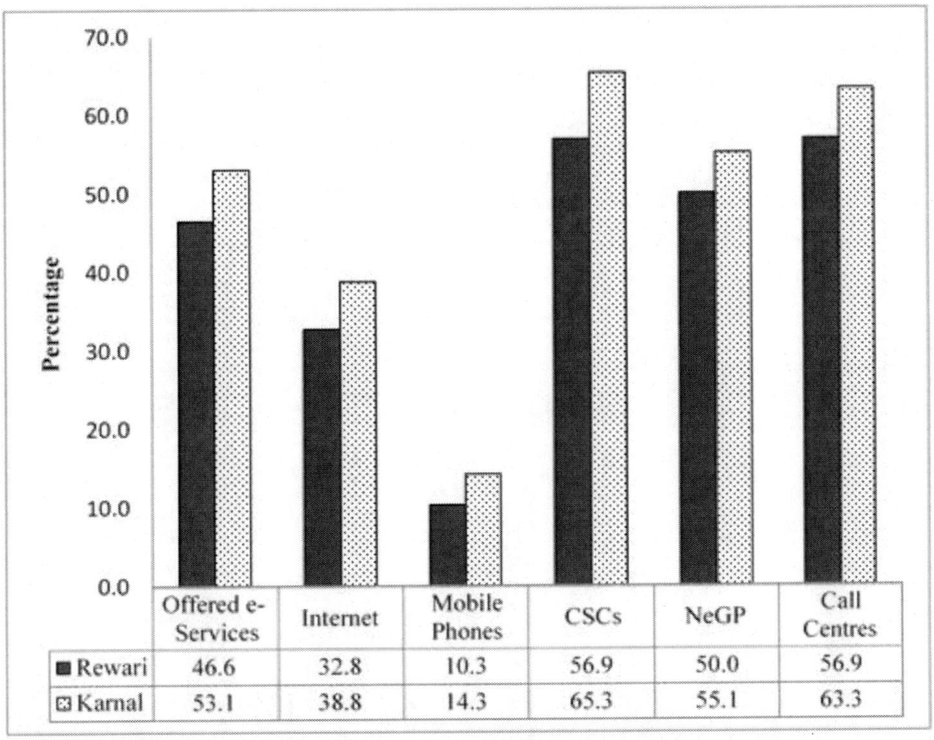

Figure 2. Lack of Awareness about e-Governance and ICT in Haryana.

Table 3. Lack of Awareness in Selected Districts of Haryana

Lack of Awareness about:	Rewari	Karnal
Offered e-Services	46.6	53.1
Internet	32.8	38.8
Mobile Phones	10.3	14.3
CSCs	56.9	65.3
NeGP	50.0	55.1
Call Centres	56.9	63.3

The awareness level about mobile phone is quite high in Sikar (Figure 3) i.e., 91.5% whereas it is 87% in district Churu (Figure 3). Surprisingly 66.1% respondents of Sikar district and 64.8% of Churu know about CSCs. The information about NeGP and call centres is spread among 55.9% and 50.8% respondents of Sikar respectively. Whereas it is observed 51.9% and 50% in district Churu.

It is evident from the graph Figure 4 and Table 5 that the respondents of Haryana are more oblivious in comparison of Rajasthan in almost all aspects.

Table 4. Awareness about e-Services and ICT in Rajasthan

Awareness about e-services and ICT in Rajasthan					
Awareness about	Sikar		Churu		Average Awareness (%)
	Aware	% aware	Aware	% aware	
Offered e-Services	36	61.0	31	57.4	59.21
Internet	44	74.6	37	68.5	71.55
Mobile Phones	54	91.5	47	87.0	89.28
CSCs	39	66.1	35	64.8	65.45
NeGP	33	55.9	28	51.9	53.89
Call Centres	30	50.8	27	50.0	50.42

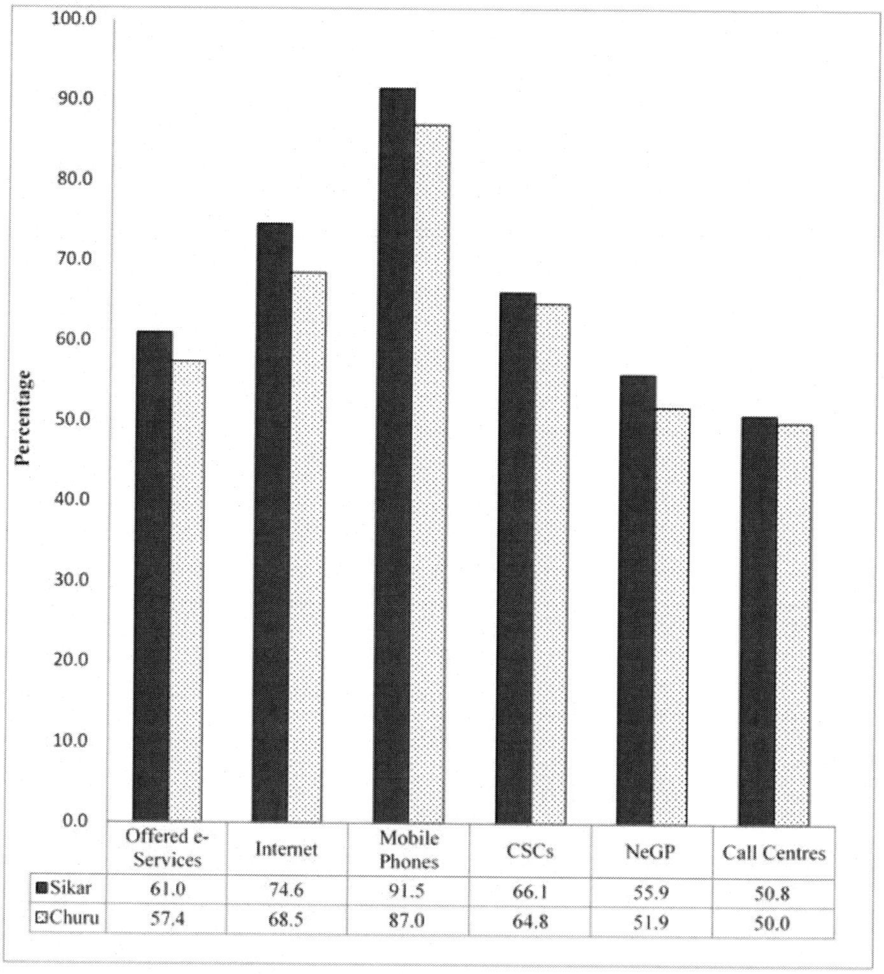

Figure 3. Awareness about e-Governace and ICT in Rajastan.

Nevertheless, a similar type of obliviousness trend is observed about e-services and ICT in Haryana and Rajasthan. The people are least aware about call centres and NeGP in both the districts of Rajasthan whereas most aware about mobile phones and internet.

Table 5. Lack of Awareness in Selected Districts of Rajasthan

Lack of Awareness about	Sikar	Churu
Offered e-Services	39.0	42.6
Internet	25.4	31.5
Mobile Phones	8.5	13.0
CSCs	39.9	35.2
NeGP	44.1	48.1
Call Centres	49.2	50.0

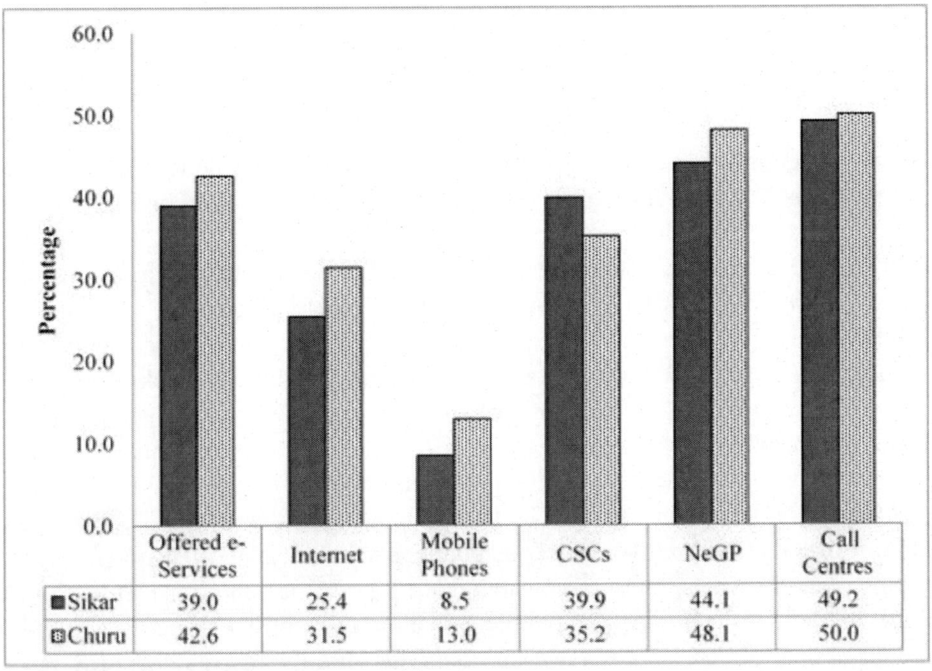

Figure 4. Lack of Awareness about e-Governance and ICT in Rajastan.

The key reason behind this is the inclusion of private partners for dissemination of cellular services. Further in order to enhance their consumers, the private partners have extended their accessibility up to remote areas.

7. Obstacles in Implementation of e-Governance

The review of literature has pointed out major bottlenecks in effective implementation of e-governance in rural areas. In order to identify the intensity of such plausible prevailing factors the survey was performed. The Table 6 and Figure 5 reveals about intensity levels of the factors which are prominently responsible for hindering the growth of e-governance in rural areas.

Table 6. Obstacles in Implementation of e-Governance

Obstacles	Haryana (%)			Rajasthan (%)		
	Karnal	Rewari	Total	Sikar	Churu	Total
Internet connectivity	50.0	38.8	44.9	55.9	53.7	54.9
Lack of capacity building	87.9	93.9	90.7	89.8	90.7	90.3
Lack of interest	86.2	89.8	87.9	86.4	85.2	85.8
Cost incurred in availing e-services	51.7	44.9	48.6	62.7	61.1	61.9
Time consuming	48.3	38.8	43.9	50.8	48.1	49.6
Lack of CSCs	41.4	34.7	38.3	57.6	61.1	59.3
Lack of Centralized call centres	37.9	28.6	33.6	42.4	40.7	41.6
Lack of regional languages	58.6	55.1	57.0	59.3	55.6	57.5

The Figure 5 is showing the trend for both the districts of Haryana and Rajasthan. The Figure 5 indicates that lack of capacity building or awareness is the most prominent factor whereas lack of centralized call centres is least prominent factor among selected districts of Haryana and Rajasthan. The inadequate internet connectivity will be condemned by 54.9% respondents of Rajasthan which encompasses 55.9% from Sikar and 53.7% from Churu respectively whereas a total of 44.9% respondents of Haryana which comprise of 50% from Karnal and 38.8% from Rewari are also in the favour. The lack of capacity building programmes is imputed by 90.7% respondents of Haryana and 90.3% respondents of Rajasthan Haryana which reflects its prime dominance among all. The lack of interest is also a prominent factor which is proclaimed by 87.9% respondents of Haryana and 85.8% respondents of Rajasthan. It is attested by 48.6% and 61.9% respondents of Haryana and Rajasthan respectively that e-services delivered in rural areas are not cost effective. Moreover 43.9% respondents of Haryana and 49.6% of Rajasthan affirm that availing e-services is time consuming. It is aptly observed by 38.3% respondents of Haryana and 59.3% respondents of Rajasthan that lack of CSCs is also a considerable factor responsible for feeble growth of e-governance in rural segment. Although, there is a significant difference of 21.9% in the responses about lack of CSCs but it's not surprising because the respondents of Rajasthan are more aware about e-services in comparison to Haryana. Further, the capacity building programmes and delivered e-services should support regional languages because it has been pointed out by 57% respondents of Haryana and 57.5% respondents of Rajasthan.

CONCLUSION

The intent of the survey was to get acquainted with problems prevailing at grass root level in rural areas. However, the secondary data has aptly pointed out such problems, but in order to analyze their intensity, the survey was necessary. It can be treated as a confirmatory test for the problems suggested by literature review. The results of the survey depicted above absolutely resembles with majority of issues raised by review of literature. Hence, the prominent problems in the rural society are Internet connectivity, ineffective capacity building, lack of awareness, lack of interest and the cost incurred in availing e-services. By undergoing personal observations and discussions with the involved bureaucracy, the problem of interoperability among various e-governance applications and cost of ICT infrastructure were also pointed out. It has been also observed that political will is also playing a crucial role in implementation and utilization of e-governance. The government is acclaiming its success but it seems to go in vain. The problems identified in the course of this study need to be taken care of by the state as well as central governments for successful implementation of e-governance especially in rural areas of the country.

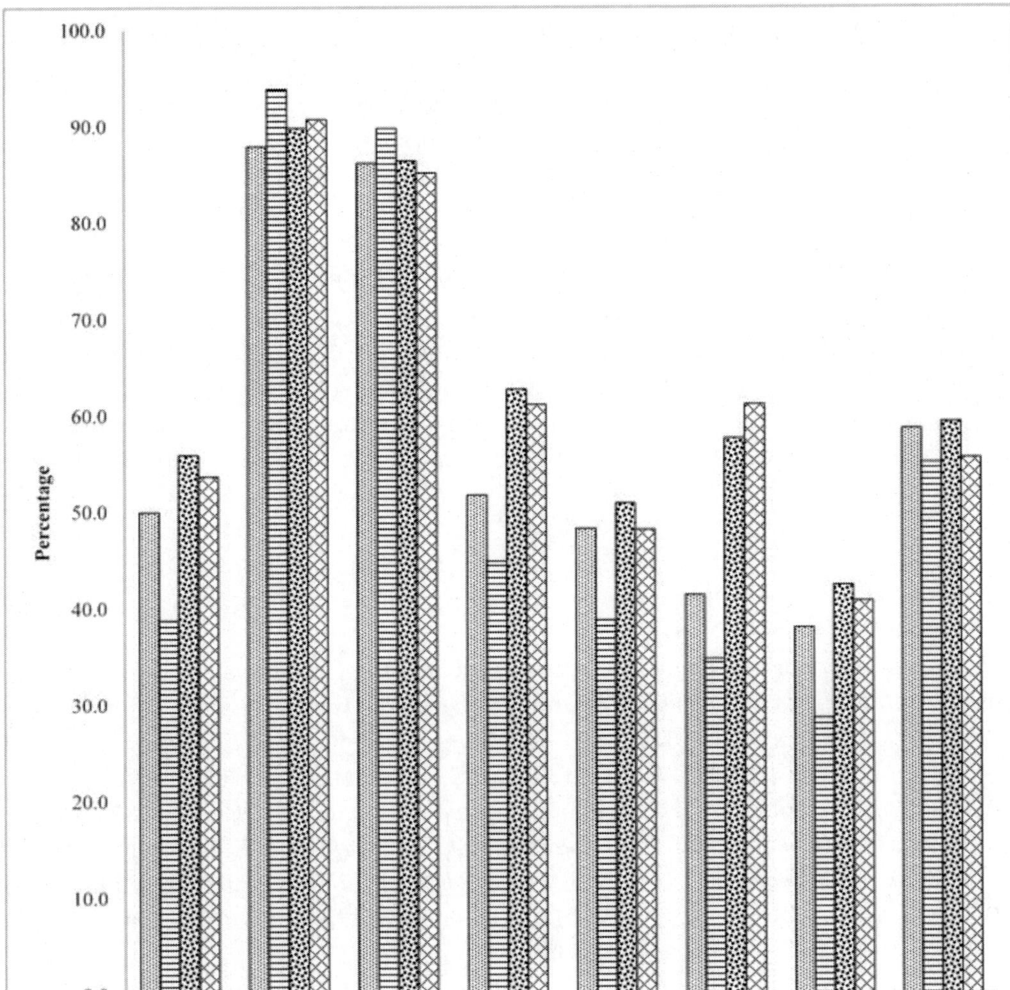

	Internet connectivity	Lack of capacity building	Lack of interest	Cost incurred in availing e-services	Time consuming	Lack of CSCs	Lack of centralized call centres	Lack of regional languages
Rewari	50.0	87.9	86.2	51.7	48.3	41.4	37.9	58.6
Karnal	38.8	93.9	89.8	44.9	38.8	34.7	28.6	55.1
Sikar	55.9	89.8	86.4	62.7	50.8	57.6	42.4	59.3
Churu	53.7	90.7	85.2	61.1	48.1	61.1	40.7	55.6

Figure 5. Major Obstacles in Successful Implementation of e-Governance in both States.

References

Affairs, U. D. (2012). *Country Data View*. Retrieved 2014, from UN Public Administration Programme: http://unpan3.un.org/egovkb/datacenter/CountryView.aspx?reg=ASIA%20~%20Southern%20Asia.

Asadi, J., and Rashidi, H. (2012). E-government with service oriented architecture. *International Journal of Advanced Research in Computer Science*, 91-93.

Bannister, F., and Connolly, R. (2012). Forward to the past: Lessons for the future of e-government from the story so far. *Information Polity*, 211-226.

Bansal, K. L., Sharma, S. K., and S. S. (2012). Impact of Cloud Computing in Implementing Cost Effective E-governance Operations. *Gian Jyoti e-Journal*, 1-12.

Bhatnagar, S. C., and Singh, N. (2010). Assessing the Impact of E-Government: A Study of Projects in India. *Information Technologies and International Development*, 109-127.

Bhattacharya, J. (2012). *e-Gov 2.0: Policies, Processes and Technologies.* New Delhi: Tata McGraw Hill.

Bilbao-Osorio, B., Dutta, S., and Lanvin, B. (2013). *The Global Information Technology Report 2013: Growth and Jobs in a Hyperconnected World.* Geneva: World Economic Forum and INSEA.

Chauhan, R. (2009). *National E-Governance Plan in India.* Macao: United Nations University - International Institute for Software Technology.

Chou, S.-K., and Lin, J.-S. (2012). The Australian e-Government Strategy Development and Outcome. *International Journal of Digital Content Technology and its Applications*, 322-332.

Chuna, S. A., Shulmanb, S., Sandovalc, R., and Hovyd, E. (2010). Government 2.0: Making connections between citizens, data and government. *Information Polity*, 1-9.

Commission, S. A. (2008). *Promoting e-Governance: The Smart Way Forward.* New Delhi: Government of India.

Das, R. K., and Patra, M. R. (2013). A Service Oriented Design Approach for e-Governance Systems. *International Journal of Information Technology Convergence and Services*, 1-11.

Dwivedi, S. K., and Bharti, A. K. (2010). E-Governance in India- Problems and Acceptability. *Journal of Theoretical and Applied Information Technology*, 37-43.

Forum, W. E., and Accenture. (2010). *Exploring The Future of Cloud Computing: Riding The Next Wave of Technology-Driven Transformation.* Switzerland: World Economic Forum.

Gajendra, S., Xi, B., and Wang, Q. (2012). E-Government: Public Participation and Ethical Issues. *Journal of E-Governance*, 195-204.

Guma, P. K. (2013). Public-Sector Reform, E-Government and the Search for Excellence in Africa: Experiences from Uganda. *Electronic Journal of e-Government*, 241-252.

Hada, P. S., Singh, R., and Goyal, D. (2012). Security Engineering in G-Cloud: A Trend towards Secure e-Governance. *International Journal of Computer Applications*, 33-38.

Kalam, A. P. (2008). A Vision of Citizen-centric e-Governance for India. In: R. Bagga, and G. Piyush, *Compendium of eGovernance Initiatives in India* (pp. 3-7). Hyderabad: SIGeGov Publications.

Kumar, N. V. (2011). Service Level Management in e-Governance Projects. In: N. Bhatt, and A. Aggarwal, *E-Governance Policies and Practices* (pp. 209-217). Ahmedabad: Nirma University.

Kumar, S. P., Umashankar, C., Rani, J. K., and Ramana, V. (2010). e-Governance Applications for citizens - Issues and Framework. *International Journal on Computer Science and Engineering*, 2362-2365.

Luna-Reyesa, L. F., Mellouli b, S., and Bertotc, J. C. (2013). Key factors and processes for digital government success. *Information Polity*, 101-105.

Meijer, A., Bannister, F., and Thaens, M. (2012). ICT, Public Administration and Democracy in the Coming Decade. *Information Polity*, 201-207.

Mistry, H. (2010). *e-Governance: Efficiency and Challenges in India.* Mumbai: Mahindra Special Services Group.

Misuraca, G., Alfano, G., and Viscusi, G. (2011). A Multi-Level Framework for ICT-Enabled Governance:Assessing the Non-Technical Dimensions of 'Government Openness.' *Electronic Journal of e-Government*, 152-165.

Odat, A. M. (2012). E-Government in Developing Countries: Framework of Challenges and Opportunities. *Journal of Theoretical and Applied Information Technology*, 1013-1021.

Prabhu, C. (2012). *E-Governance: Concepts and Case Studies.* New Delhi: PHI Learning Private Limited.

Radhakrishnan, C., Kamal, K. K., and Joshi, P. (2012). e-Governance on Cloud: Need and Challenges. *Journal of Information Systems and Communication*, 124-128.

Rajagoplan, R., and Sarkar, R. (2008). Digital Networks and Sustainability: Do we need the Government? *IEEE*, 49-54.

Rao, V. R. (2013). A framework for unified digital government: A case of India. *Journal of E-Governance*, 35-55.

Satyanarayana, J. (2004). *E-Government: The Science of the Possible.* New Delhi: Prentice Hall of India.

Savoldelli, A., Misuraca, G., and Codagnone, C. (2013). Measuring the Public value of e-Government: The eGEP2.0 model. *Electronic Journal of e-Government*, 373-388.

Stanimirovic, D., and Vintar, M. (2013). Conceptualization of an Integrated Indicator Model for the Evaluation of e-Government Policies. *Electronic Journal of e-Government*, 293-307.

Tebib, A., and Boufaida, M. (2013). A Framework Based Protocol for A Better Interoperability Among Services in E-government. *Journal of Theoretical and Applied Information Technology*, 174-180.

Technology, D. O. (2014, March 14). *National e-Governance Plan.* Retrieved March 19, 2014, from Ministry of Communications and Information Technology, Government of India Website: http://deity.gov.in/content/national-e-governance-plan.

Times, T. E. (2007, February 2). *News.* Rs 3,300 cr for national e-governance plan. Bhopal, India: The Economic Times.

In: e-Governance in India: Problems, Prototypes and Prospects ISBN: 978-1-63484-830-5
Editors: P. Kumar, R. Sharma and U. Kaushal

Chapter 5

DEMYSTIFYING E-GOVERNANCE IN INDIA: A COMPARATIVE ANALYSIS WITH DEVELOPED AND DEVELOPING NATIONS

Kumar Sambhav Pareek [1,*] ***and Twinkle Patel*** [2]
[1]Assistant Professor in Political Science,
College of Arts, Science and Humanities,
Mody University of Science and Technology,
Lakshmangarh, Rajasthan
[2]Student- B.A. Second Year, Mody University,
Lakshmangarh, Rajasthan, India

ABSTRACT

"IT Indian Talent + IT Information Technology = IT India Tomorrow", an equation solved by Narendra Modi will surely pave its way to make India experience the power of e-governance.

The booming entry of technology into the cosmos of human life has changed the entire perspective of human perceiving; the working pattern of people, the business agendas and the government services. E-governance makes use of Information and Communication Technology (ICT) to upgrade the system of governance and hence provide better services to the citizens.

E-government uses technology as tool to enhance the access and delivery procedure of government services for the benefit of citizen. Hence, it facilitates the people with convenience, customization and empowerment to aid their desire. Technically, e-governance is the praxis of communication and information technologies to mutate the coherence, accountability and transparency of informational and transitional barter with the organizations and government institutions.

Keywords: Digital India, Security Council, G-4, G-8, G-20, BRICS, ASEAN, NeGP

* E-mail: dr.kumarspareek@gmail.com.

1. E-GOVERNANCE IN INDIA: A KALEIDOSCOPIC VIEW

The National e-governance Plan by Indian government pursues to establish the foundation and proffer motivation for long-term magnification of e-governance in India. The National e-Governance Plan (NeGP) has been formulated by the Department of Electronics and Information Technology (DEITY) and Department of Administrative Reforms and Public Grievances (DARPG). The Union Government approved the NeGP on May 18, 2006((NIC) 2015).

The NeGP aims at improving delivery of government services to citizens and businesses with a very noble objective to "Make all government services accessible to the common man in his locality, through common service delivery outlets and ensure efficiency, transparency and reliability of such services at affordable costs to realize the basic needs of the common man" (Ibid, (NIC) 2015).

E-governance enables the interaction between various stakeholders in governance like G2G (Government to Government), G2C (Government to Citizen), G2B (Government to Business) and G2E (Government to Employees) (Kumar 2013).

2. SCHEMES

There are several projects initiated by Indian government at state as well as national level which aims to spread the services of e-governance in the country. Government to citizen(G2C) initiatives are project like Bhoomi in the state of Karnataka, CARD initiated by state government of Andhra Pradesh, Vahan and Sarathi by the state government of Tamil Nadu, Project FRIENDS in Kerala, e-mitra in Rajasthan, Lokvani Project at Sitapur district in Utter Pradesh and Gayandoot which is an Internet-based Government to Citizen (G2C) service delivery initiative.

Whereas some of the Business (G2B) initiates are e-Procurement Project in Andhra Pradesh and Gujarat, Chadian Project in Karnataka and SmartGov in Andhra Pradesh (DeitY, Pillars of Digital India 2015).

3. DIGITAL INDIA: A NEW WAVE OF TRANSFORMATION

E-governance is all about the use of ICT in the system of governance. It ensures an increase in participation and high involvement of citizen in the governing system. Furthermore, e-governance is a way of participatory approach in contemporary era. It is truly said that technology infrastructure (IT) in the rural area does not provide better delivery of e-services.

It is required to disseminate a culture of e-governance across various ministries and departments, aiming to decentralize the responsibility and power at the central, state and district levels (Kumar 2013).

Digital India is an exclusive program that spreads its arms and covers multiple government ministries and departments. It pools together a massive amount of ideas. Digital

India aims to bring together the entire government which facilitates the coordination of Department of Electronics and Information Technology (DeitY).

Digital India stands on nine strong pillars namely; Broadband Highways, Universal Access to Mobile Connectivity, Public Internet Access Programs, e-Governance: Reforming Government through Technology, e-Kranti - Electronic Delivery of Services, Information for All, Electronics Manufacturing, IT for Jobs and Early Harvest Programs (DeitY, Pillars of Digital India 2015).

1. Broadband Highways: It aims to cover three element i.e., Broadband for All i.e., at Rural, Urban and National Information Infrastructure (NII) (DeitY, Pillars of Digital India 2015).
2. Universal Access to Mobile Connectivity: Along with its main focuses on network insight and perception, this plan aims to fill in the connectivity void in the country (DeitY, Pillars of Digital India 2015).
3. Public Internet Access Programs: This scheme has two integral limbs; Common Service Centre (CSCs), which would be made multi-functional and operable end-points for the delivery of governmental services. The next limb is Post office and multi-service centre which proposes to be covered and transformed into multi service centre (DeitY, Pillars of Digital India 2015).
4. e-Governance: Reforming Government through Technology: This scheme states that a critical transformation is required to bring in more efficiency in the delivery of government service and it is an necessity that it must be implemented by all the ministries and departments (DeitY, Pillars of Digital India 2015).
5. e-Kranti - Electronic Delivery of Services: e-kranti is considered as one of the most significant pillar of the Digital India initiative. It aims to establish e-education, e-healthcare, and technology for the farmers, security, justice, financial inclusion and cyber security (DeitY, Pillars of Digital India 2015).
6. Information for All: This scheme suggests online hosting of information and documents which will be readily accessible for the information as and when required by the citizen. Online messaging, open data platform and social media engagement are some of the basic agendas of this scheme (DeitY, Pillars of Digital India 2015).
7. Electronics Manufacturing: Promoting electronic manufacturing is the agenda of this pillar, with the goal of NET ZERO import by 2020. National policy on Electronics which was launched in 2012 (NPER) (DeitY 2012) which is investor friendly and market driven aiming to attract the global and domestic companies to invest towards the Electronic System Design and Manufacturing (DeitY, Pillars of Digital India 2015).
8. IT for Jobs: This pillar mainly emphasis on facilitating training to the youth in order to empower themselves for the employment opportunities in the IT/ITES sector (DeitY, Pillars of Digital India 2015).
9. Early Harvest Programs: This pillar contains the projects which are to be implemented in a very short period of time. IT Platform for Messages, Government Greetings to be e-Greetings, Biometric attendance, Wi-Fi in All Universities, Secure Email within Government, Standardize Government Email Design, Public Wi-Fi hotspots and such are few programms under this scheme (DeitY, Pillars of Digital India 2015).

4. Methodology

Technology can be used as a powerful source for sustainable development with the element of participation from the side of public. Technically, e-government aims to work as an apparatus for the development of people.

It is through participatory service that governments aim to engage the citizen in an effective manner for the delivery procedure. e-governance for people ensures that the public services are the module which represents citizen centric, socially inclusive and responsive citizen. The evidence base for the latter is strengthened by recent development in e-government in an increasing number of countries where citizens are users as well as co-producers of public services (United Nations Department of Economic and Social Affairs 2012).

The United Nations E-government Survey has generated a holistic view of e-government development resting on three important spheres:

(i). The availability of online services,
(ii). Telecommunication infrastructure and
(iii). Human capacity (Affairs 2014).

In order to understand the quality of e-governance being provided by the country, it becomes important to study the ranking of the major countries of the world as included in UN Report on E-government of 2014.

The striking fact is that the position of India in this report is 118 out of 193 nations (Affairs 2014) while it was 125 in 2012.Though there is a jump of seven positions but still we are far behind and therefore this chapter is an attempt to study the reasons for the same. This is an attempt to trace the reasons and study the progress of e-governance of India in comparison to the major economies of the world, in relationship to the literacy rate, rural and urban population of the country, which is in direct correlation of the net users and success of e-governance.

India is striving hard to provide better e-governance facilities to its citizens. But it becomes equally important to study the level of e-governance and its implications in other countries of the world.

The present work is an attempt to study the level of e-governance of India in comparison to the different countries of the world on the basis of different parameters viz. the rank in the Network Readiness Index in The Global Information Technology Report 2015which includes the study of 143 nations and report of the year 2014 includes the study of 148 nations (Soumitra Dutta, Thierry Geiger, Bruno Lanvin 2015), the literacy rate, urban population, rural population and number of net users in the country. Rather than comparing India with any particular nation, the attempt is to compare India with different groups and associations, namely the five permanent members of United Nations Security Council, G-4, G-8, G-20, BRICS and ASEAN so as to study the issue at global level.

India is one of the biggest democracies in the world and has developed very good stand in international political scenario. India is having close ties with all the nations covered in the paper and therefore it becomes important to study the position of India at world level in the field of e-governance.

5. India's Comparison with Five Permanent Members of UNSC

United States, China, Russia, Britain and France are the five permanent members of UNSC (nations). Together they are also known as Permanent Five or Big Five. The members of UNSC constitute the five great powers which are considered as Victor of World War II (Paul 1995). The permanent members are the proud owner of the veto power, which enables them to abrogate any non-procedural matter via negative vote despite of the international support (Nations).

Table 5.1 is a data based study of India in comparison to these five members of United Nations Security council. It affirms that the literacy rate of all the permanent members of UNSC has strong roots.

According to The Networked Readiness Index 2015, countries like Unites States and China are still holding on to their same position as they were in 2014; on the other hand Britain and Russia have managed to upgrade its rank. France is the only country which has dropped its position, that too only by one rank. Opposite to India has dropped by six ranks in the report. The data also suggests that, increase in urban population will increase the percentage of literacy rate and net users. The hypothesis, that literacy rate is directly proportionate to the net users proves to be true in Table 5.1. It is also spotted that the literacy rate of India is not up to the mark which is eventually affecting the number of net users in the country.

A downfall has been marked in the ranking of India. Moreover, the rural population of India is comparative high in comparison to the Big Five, which is one significant reason of the failure of e-governance in India. India has to travel a long way to attain the dream of establishing e-governance in a perfect sense. However eradicating the problem of poverty and improving the level of awareness will be the first step towards the success of e-governance in India.

Table 5.1. Comparison with five permanent members of UNSC

S.no.	Name of country	Rank (2015)	Rank (2014)	Net users (%)	Literacy rate (%)	Urban Population (%)	Rural Population (%)
1	United States	7	7	86.6	99	81.6	18.4
2	Britain	8	9	89.9	97.5	87.6	17.4
3	France	26	25	85.8	99	79.5	20.5
4	Russia	41	50	59.3	99.7	74	26
5	China	62	62	46	96.4	55.6	44.4
6	**India**	**89**	**83**	**19.2**	**71.2**	**32.7**	**67.3**

Source: The Global Information Technology Report 2015 and the World Fact Book (CIA).

Table 6.1. Comparison with G-4 countries

S.No	Name of country	Rank (2015)	Rank (2014)	Net users (%)	Literacy rate (%)	Urban population (%)	Rural population (%)
1	Japan	10	16	86	99	93.5	6.5
2	Germany	13	12	86.8	99	75.3	24.7
3	Brazil	84	69	53.4	92.6	85.7	14.3
4	**India**	**89**	**83**	**19.2**	**71.2**	**32.7**	**67.3**

Source: The Global Information Technology Report 2015 and the World Fact Book (CIA).

6. India's Comparison with G-4 Countries

The pillars of G-4 countries are Germany, Brazil, Japan and India. The primary aim of G-4 is to attain permanent membership of UNSC (Wikipedia 2015). Moreover, these countries aid support system to one another to secure the objective.

The UNSC includes the developed country and being the permanent member gives them the little of "ultimate powerful."

Table 6.1 reveals that except Japan, every country amongst G-4 has rolled down from their position obtained in2014. In case of Brazil and India, a significant declination in their position has been observed. Since, literacy rate is having a positive correlation with the level of awareness among the people; therefore it directly affects the percentage of internet users in any country. The Table 6.1 elucidates the same fact i.e., all those countries having high literacy rate have more internet users. Also, it spots light on another aspect that, the countries having more urban population are good in technological adaptation. And it is evident in case of India as it is having highest rural population and least percentage of internet users. Among all G-4 countries, the scenario of India is not overwhelming rather pathetic in context of e-governance with probable bottlenecks like literacy rate, poverty, awareness level people and rural population.

7. India's Comparison with G-20 Countries

G-20 represents the following twenty countries: Australia, Argentina, Indonesia, Italy, Mexico, Saudi Arabia, South Korea, South Africa, Turkey, India, Brazil, Canada, China, France, Germany, Japan, Russia, United States, Britain and European Union (Kirton 2010).

It was established to bring together the developing economies with the aim to moot over the key issues and affairs in the global economy. The G-20 countries together represent around 85% of global GDP, 75% of global trade and two third of the world's population (India 2015). The next Table i.e., 7.1 is an attempt to study the position of India in comparison to the member nations of G-20.

Table 7.1. Comparison with G-20 countries

S.No.	Name of country	Rank (2015)	Rank (2014)	Net users (%)	Literacy rate (%)	Urban population (%)	Rural population (%)
1	European Union	*	*	78.5	98.6[2]	90	10
2	South Korea	12	10	91.5	97.9	82.5	17.5
3	Australia	16	18	89.6	96[1]	89.4	10.6
4	Saudi Arabia	35	32	59.2	94.7	83.1	16.9
5	Turkey	48	51	46.6	95	73.4	26.6
6	Italy	55	58	59.9	99.2	69	31
7	Canada	11	17	92.9	99	81.8	18.2
8	Mexico	69	79	41.1	95.1	79.2	20.8
9	Indonesia	79	64	16.7	93.9	53.7	46.3
10	**India**	**89**	**83**	**19.2**	**71.2**	**32.7**	**67.3**
11	Argentina	91	100	59.7	98.1	91.8	8.2

Source: The Global Information Technology Report 2015 and the World Fact Book (CIA).
*Data not available in the report.
**The nine countries (Brazil, China, Britain, United states, South Africa, Japan, Germany, Russia and France) not mentioned in Table 7.1 are already covered in Table 5.1 and Table 6.1.

Table 7.1 imparts that countries like Australia, Argentina, Italy, Mexico and Turkey have improved their rank according to The Networked Readiness Index 2015, whereas the other countries including India has degraded its rank. India immensely lacks behind with the percentage of net users as compared to other G-20 countries. It can clearly be asserted from Table 7.1 that all the G-20 countries hold a good percentage of literacy rates but India seems to lag behind with an average difference of 20%.

On average G-20 countries has more than 50% of urban population whereas India has only 32.7% of urban population, which eventually affects the literacy rate of the country.

8. India's Comparison with G-8 Countries

The Group of Eight (G8) refers to the group of eight highly industrialized nations i.e., France, Germany, Italy, the United Kingdom, Japan, the United States, Canada, and Russia (Laub 2014).

Table 8.1. Comparison with G-8 countries

S.No.	Name of country	Rank (2015)	Rank (2014)	Net users (%)	Literacy rate (%)	Urban population (%)	Rural population (%)
1	United States	7	7	86.6	99	81.6	18.4
2	United Kingdom	8	9	89.9	99	82.6	17.4
3	Japan	10	16	86	99	93.5	6.5
4	Canada	11	17	92.9	99	81.8	18.2
5	Germany	13	12	86.8	99	75.3	24.5
6	France	26	25	85.8	99	97.5	20.5
7	Russia	41	50	59.3	99.7	74	26
8	Italy	55	58	59.9	99.2	69	31
9	**India**	**89**	**83**	**19.2**	**71.2**	**32.7**	**67.3**

Source: The Global Information Technology Report 2015 and the World Fact Book (CIA).

Table 8.1 affirms that all the G-8 countries on an average holds 99% of literacy rate which is in direct correlation with the percentage of net users. According to The Networked Readiness Index 2015, countries like United Kingdom, Canada and Russia have managed to revamp its orientation. India is comparatively marked as inferior in reference to the urban population which is also the cause of low literacy rate in the country, juxtaposed to the G-8 countries. The literacy rate of India is way too less in comparison to the G-8 countries.

Table 8.1 enlightens the fact that all the G-8 countries are highly industrialized and thus possess good technological adaptation phenomena. It is time that India inculcates technology into the mainstream of political and economical agendas in the sector of industry, agriculture; the backbone of the nation to upgrade its level and governmental sector to improve the effectiveness of the services.

9. India's Comparison with BRICS Nations

41.6% of the world population (Publication 2015) and 20% of global GDP is represented by BRICS countries which include; Brazil, China, Russia, South Africa and India (O'Boyle 2014). The members of BRICS are a combination of developing or budding industrialized countries. All the members of BRICS are also the member of G-20 countries which are enumerated in the above Tables. All the BRICS members share similar stage of newly advanced economic development.

Table 9.1. Comparison with BRICS nation

S.No	Name of country	Rank (2015)	Rank (2014)	Net users (%)	Literacy rate (%)	Urban population (%)	Rural population (%)
1	Russia	41	50	59.3	99.7	74	26
2	China	62	62	46	96.4	55.6	44.4
3	South Africa	75	70	46.9	94.3	64.8	35.2
4	Brazil	84	69	53.4	92.6	85.7	14.3
5	**India**	**89**	**83**	**19.2**	**71.2**	**32.7**	**67.3**

Source: The Global Information Technology Report 2015 and the World Fact Book (CIA).

Table 9.1 reveals that all the members of BRICS have more than 90% of literacy rate whereas India's literacy rate is disappointing in comparison to the other four countries. According to The Networked Readiness Index 2015 a significance downfall can be traced in the rank of countries in 2015, only Russia has managed to upgrade its position. The hypothesis that urban population has positive correlation with literacy rate of the country followed by the net users of the respective country proves to be true. It can thus be stated that the reason for rolling down of rank and less number of net users in the country like India is because of the less percentage of urban population which eventually results in lack of awareness.

The administrative structure of India now needs to pay much attention to make the people aware about the activities of e-governance.

10. India's Comparison with ASEAN Nations

The Association of Southeast Asian Nations is an organization of ten countries situated in Southeast Asia. The ASEAN country includes Brunei, Cambodia, Indonesia, Laos, Malaysia, Myanmar, Philippines, Singapore, Thailand and Vietnam.(Secretariat T. A.) The main motive of ASEAN association is to accelerate economic growth, also work for social and cultural development in order to strengthen the foundation of partnership (Secretariat A. 2008).

Table 10.1 reveals that the ASEAN association is a mixture of the country like Singapore with the top ranking according to The Networked Readiness Index 2015, whereas countries like Cambodia and Myanmar immensely lack behind, though Myanmar has managed to upgrade its position. Most of the ASEAN countries hold more than 80% of literacy rate on an average, but India seems to lag behind, which eventually shows effect on the net users of the country.

Thus it can be considered that the literacy rate has direct correlation with the percentage of net users in the country. As Singapore has 80% literacy rate because of nil rural population and 100% of urban population which justifies its top ranking in the data.

Table 10.1. Comparison with the ASEAN countries

S.No	Name of country	Rank (2015)	Rank (2014)	Net users (%)	Literacy rate (%)	Urban Population (%)	Rural Population (%)
1	Singapore	1	2	80.7	96.8	100	-
2	Malaysia	32	30	40.3	94.6	74.4	25.6
3	Thailand	67	67	28.8	96.7	50.4	49.6
4	Philippines	76	78	39.4	96.3	44.4	55.6
5	Indonesia	79	64	16,7	93.9	53.7	46.3
6	Vietnam	85	84	43	94.5	33.6	66.4
7	**India**	**89**	**83**	**19.2**	**71.2**	**32.7**	**67.3**
8	Laos	97	109	5.8	79.9	38.6	61.4
9	Cambodia	110	108	5.4	77.2	20.7	79.3
10	Myanmar	139	146	2.1	84.7	34	66
11	Brunei	Not included*	45	55.6	95.4	77.2	22.8

Source: The Global Information Technology Report 2015 and the World Fact Book (CIA).
*Not included in 2015 report because of non-availability of data. (Soumitra Dutta, Thierry Geiger, Bruno Lanvin, 2015, pp 7).

The literacy rate of India is comparatively low and the incapability of the illiterate to understand the methodology of internet access creates an obstacle in the way to attain the objective of e-governance in the country.

11. Findings

E-governance is surely not a retire, but prominently India has to travel a long way to attain the goal of e-governance in the nation, transforming the nation into e-nation. However, it is integral to work on steps to eradicate the problem of poverty in the country.

1. Liberating technology is a source of "Good Governance" for a developing country like India, which will eventually empower the citizens.
2. It is essential that the administrative service of India pays much attention to make the people aware about the activities initiated by government with the objective of successful e-governance.
3. Inculcating technology into the mainstream of political and economical agendas in the industrial and agricultural sector will upgrade its level and help government sectors to improve its effectiveness.
4. The current scenario of India is not overwhelming in context to the technological infrastructure because of diminishing literacy rate, increasing poverty specially in the rural areas.
5. From the interpretation of the data in the above mentioned tables as well as in the report prepared by United nations on E-Government, it can be affirmed that India is lagging behind in comparison to the other countries.

12. Impediments of e-Governance in India

1. The problem of poverty: The poverty rate of India is 21.9%. There are 220,299,003.7 poor people living in rural area of India ((IFAD)). That eventually suggests that the access of internet in developing country like India is too expensive and unaffordable.
2. Dominance of English language: English is considered as the universal language on the internet. The supremacy of English language on the internet hinders the access of the non-English -speaking population in India. Currently there are 447 living languages in India (Lewis, Simons and Charles 2015) and thus English fails to pave its way. 95.81% of the total population in US is capable of understanding the English language, whereas only 23.2% of the total population is capable of understanding this language in India (Exploredia 2011). Due to such inundate dominance of English language the communication channels, computers and the internet services fails to impart its true efficiency, especially in the rural areas.
3. Lack of awareness and infrastructure: In general there is lack of awareness regarding the advantages of e-governance. Also, the administrative structure does not pay much attention to make the people aware about the activities of e-governance. The paucity of necessary infrastructure elements like electricity, internet, technology and the ways of communication affects the pace and eventually leads to delay in implementation.
4. The problem of inequality: The inequality between the rich and poor, whereby the poor is unable to access the benefits of e- governance because of economic crises. Also, void between the rural and urban committee, where the rural committee fails to

enjoy the advantage reason being the lack of infrastructure. Furthermore, the incapability of illiterate to understand the methodology of internet access creates inequality between the educated and illiterate. Hence, most of the section in society remains deprived of the utility of e-governance.

5. Technological challenges: One of the major characteristics of technology is that, it keeps on upgrading; and our government may not be in an ideal state to buy new server every year. Additionally, interoperability becomes a major challenge as the e-government applications sometimes fails to have this characteristics and thus, the existing application and newly developed application fails to be executed together.
6. Economical Challenges: Due to the unstable GDP (Gross Domestic Product) of the country; India has limited financial resource, hence the implementation and maintenance of the project becomes difficult.
   The success of e-governance requires a good amount of money involved in the operational and evolutionarytask.

13. Suggestions

- Legislation: a stringent law should be legislaed in order to guarantee electronic delivery of services by the government. The Electronic Delivery of Service Bill, 2011, was initiated in the Lok Sabha on 27th December, 2011 by the Minister of HRD and Information Technology, but it lapsed and now the present government has once again initiated it and it should be passed as soon as possible.
- Literacy: The literacy rate of India is worrying. The element of 'technological handicap' can be traced in India and it is the duty of the government to apprise the citizen about e-governance and increase people's awareness towards e-governance.
- Computer literacy: Along with generating awareness through literacy it is equally important that the government should work hard to generate computer literacy awareness specially in the rural population.
- Effective control over government machinery: There is a requirement of continuous evaluation, it is the responsibility of the government to regularly evaluate the headway and virtue to make sure that they are on the right path which will lead to the success of e-governance.
- Development of infra-structure: The administrative structure of e-governance must pay attention to the requirements of proper technological infrastructure which includes electricity, internet and the ways of communication.
- Willingness: Government must ensure that it accomplishes the task of speeding and simplifying the task for better delivery of services.

Conclusion

It is now evident that the government needs to frame law which effectively aims to fully assimilate the budding technology. It is time that we build a strong bridge with the pillars of literacy to go beyond the language barrier and eradicate the dominance of English language.

The concept of e-governance is evolutionary in nature; hence, it will take time to boost up the literacy rate, which will eventually increase the percentage of net users in the country, leading to the success of e-governance. There is a requirement of political will power and social acceptance of e-governance in the nation by both urban and rural areas of the country. E-governance will thus lead opulence of e-learning and e-empowerment. E-governance is a ray of hope for the citizen as well as the government to bring in transparency and increase the efficiency of the governmental services.

REFERENCES

(IFAD), I. F. (n.d.). Rural poverty in India. Retrieved October 29, 2015, from Rural Poverty Portal: http://www.ruralpovertyportal.org/country/home/tags/india.

Affairs, D. O. (2012). United Nations E-Government Survey. New York: United Nations Department of Economic and Social Affairs.

Affairs, D. O. (2014). United Nations E-Government Survey. New York: Department of Economic and Social Affairs.

DeitY, G. (2012, November 19). Policies. Retrieved October 30, 2015, from Depart-ment of Electronics and Information Technology: http://deity.gov.in/esdm/policies.

DeitY, G. (2015, June 16). Pillars of Digital India. Retrieved October 30, 2015, from Digital India: http://www.digitalindia.gov.in/content/programme-pillars.

Exploredia. (2011, February 25). How Many People In The World Speak English 2013? Retrieved October 30, 2015, from Exploredia: http://www.mapsofworld.com/world-top-ten/countries-with-most-english-language-speaker-map.html.

India, T. (2015). What is the G20? India: Bennett, Coleman and Co. Ltd.

Kirton, J. (2010, July 22). What Is the G20? Retrieved October 30, 2015, from G20 Information Centre: http://www.g20.utoronto.ca/g20whatisit.html.

Kumar, P. (2013). e-Governance in India: A Prognosis. *The IUP Journal of Information Technology,* IX(2), 62-69.

Laub, Z. (2014, Laub, Z. 3). The Group of Eight (G8) Industrialized Nations. Retrieved October 27, 2015, from Council on Foreign Relations: http://www.cfr.org/international-organizations-and-alliances.

Lewis, M. P., Simons, G. F., and Charles, D. F. (2015). India. Retrieved October 26, 2015, from Ethnologue: Languages of the World, Eighteenth edi-tion: http:// www.ethnologue.com/country/IN.

Nations, U. (n.d.). Permanent and Non-Permanent Members of UNSC. Retrieved October 30, 2015, from United Nations Security Council: http://www.un.org/en/sc/members/.

Nations, U. (n.d.). Voting System and Records. Retrieved October 30, 2015, from United Nations security council: http://www.un.org/en/sc/meetings/voting.shtml.

O'Boyle, B. (2014, July 11). Explainer: What Are the BRICS? Retrieved October 28, 2015, from Americas Society/Council of the Americas: http://www.as-coa.org/articles/ explainer-what-are-brics?

Paul, J. A. (1995, February). Security Council Reform: Arguments about the Future of the United Nations System. Retrieved October 30, 2015, from Global Policy Forum:

https://www.globalpolicy.org/security-council/security-council-reform/41128-veto-analysis.html.

Publication, B. J. (2015). Rosstat and Statistics of Russia. Retrieved October 30, 2015, from BRICS Joint Statistical Publication: http://www.gks.ru/free_doc/doc_2015/BRICS_ENG.pdf.

Secretariat, A. (2008, January). The ASEAN Charter. Retrieved October 21, 2015, from Association of South East Asian Nations: http://www.asean.org/archive/publications/ASEAN-Charter.pdf.

Secretariat, T. A. (n.d.). ASEAN Member States. Retrieved October 29, 2015, from Association of Southeast Asian Nations: http://www.asean.org/asean/asean-member-states.

Soumitra, D., Thierry, G., and Lanvin, B. (2015). The Global Information Technology Report. Switzerland: World Economic Forum.

Wikipedia. (2015, October 25). G4 Nations. Retrieved October 30, 2015, from Wikipedia, the free encyclopedia: https://en.wikipedia.org/wiki/G4_nations.

In: e-Governance in India: Problems, Prototypes and Prospects ISBN: 978-1-63484-830-5
Editors: P. Kumar, R. Sharma and U. Kaushal

Chapter 6

LINKAGES BETWEEN ICT AND POVERTY: A PARADIGM SHIFT

Rajesh Sharma[1,*], Sushil Kumar Rai[1] and Manish Didwania[2]
[1]Assistant Professor of Economic, Mody University, Lakshmangarh, Rajasthan, India
[2]Associate Professor of Commerce, Mody University, Laksmangarh, India

ABSTRACT

Technological innovations have changed the economic environment significantly. ICT has contributed in mobilizing the economic resources globally. Therefore, the GDP of various countries has increased over the years. As a result, new job opportunities have been created not only in ICT sector but also in other related areas such as banking, NIC, research and development, health and sanitation, education, etc. This work is an attempt to relate the positive impacts of ICT on various economic indicators particularly poverty and GDP growth. Further, paper tries to depict the role of ICT sector in Indian economy.

Keywords: e-governance, GDP, SAARC

1. INTRODUCTION

One of the most remarkable changes observed in the recent past is the advent of technology driven growth, especially in the develop countries. However, the developing countries like India are still struggling with the potential use of technology. For achieving the inclusive and continual growth, public and private sectors have to work with full potential in rural and urban areas together. After 5th five year plan (1974-79), the Government of India has launched many poverty alleviation programmes. These programmes are initiated to generate more employment opportunities in rural areas (Nath, 2013). In order to implement these programmes successfully, efficient and transparent government is required. Therefore,

* Dr. Rajesh Sharma, Assistant Professor, Mody University of Science and Technology, Lakshmangarh, District Sikar, Rajasthan, email: professor.rajeshsharma@gmail.com.

technology driven system is a prerequisite which will help in generating transparency and prompt decision making for the government (Roy, 2011). Success stories of various countries have indicated that, the ICT focused delivery mechanism for dissemination of services has proved more efficient and transparent (Dutta and Geiger, Technology Report 2015). This chapter intends to highlight the successful linkages between ICT's upsurge and GDP increase and poverty reduction at international and national level. Further, paper presents the snapshot of ICT usage among SAARC countries and role of ICT sector in Indian economy.

2. ICT and GDP Growth Linkages: An International Perspective

To achieve the inclusive and sustainable growth, ICT and e-governance have become major policy tools nowadays. The countries having involvement of ICT in the development process have generated growth in terms of GDP, and a positive correlation between both has been observed. Resultant, countries with high Networked Readiness Index have always sustained high GDP growth (Alvarez, 2015, Kumar and Dharminder, 2013). However, besides GDP growth, the development of ICT depends on literacy level and citizen-centric political set-up, which is evident from the success stories of Morocco and Mauritius where respective governments have shown strong will to implement the e-governance plans (Survey 2014). The Centre for Innovation on e-government Development in Colombia and e-government Development Agency in Uruguay are immersed in strengthening the links between public and government by improving ICT and e-government services (Survey 2014). The contributions of agricultural, services and ICT sectors in the Nigerian economy have apportioned 6-8 percent in recent past. And, it is expected that the ICT sector's contribution will surpass other sectors due to the huge investment in this area (ICT Contributions to GDP in Nigeria, 2014).

Likewise, in Asian countries, Republic of Korea, Japan and Singapore have maintained strong telecommunication infrastructure with their strong GDP and national education policy (World Development Indicators database, 2013). Government of Sri Lanka has championed the inclusive growth concept by providing 65 types of e-services through mobile phones. Apparently, GDP growth rate of Sri Lanka remained better than most of the Asian Countries in last decade (Bank, 2015). As a result, literacy rate of Sri Lanka increased to 92.6 percent (Wikipedia, 2015). In order to disburse government services to the stakeholders with transparency and efficiency, six Gulf Cooperation Council countries have launched their online portals recently (Baharain, n.d.).

In terms of GDP growth and employment generation, most of the European countries went through a lean patch in last decade. To achieve the sustainable growth, these countries have launched an ambitious e-governance action plan named as Digital Agenda for Europe (DAE) in 2010. It was estimated that the successful implementation of DAE would be able to increase the GDP growth by 5 percent in next 8 years. Furthermore, it was expected that the successful establishment of ICT infrastructure would be able to create 1.2 million new jobs in various ICT related fields; and, it would leverage the GDP growth of European countries further (Ministry of Statistics and Programme Implementation, 2010, Survey, 2014). Besides high GDP growth, both Australia and New Zealand have remained among top countries in the world in terms of maintaining high E-Government Development Index (EGDI) (Pulletikurthi V. S., 2015, Survey, 2014).

Both, Cross-countries and country-wise researches manifest that the persistent high GDP growth rate helps in diluting the incidence of poverty and opens new avenues for employment. Therefore, policy makers are now immersed in propagating inclusive growth framework, which enables the stakeholders to utilize local resources efficiently and stimulates other economic factors such as investment, infrastructure development, employment opportunities and high Per Capita Income (Solow, 2015, Development, 2008, Krongkaew, Chamnivickorn, and Nitithanprapas, January 2006, Son and Kakwani, 2004, Agrawal, 2008, Bourguignon, 2004).

Table 2.1. Trends in poverty indicators by region, 1990 to 2015 (population in billion)

Region	1990	1993	1996	1999	2002	2005	2008	2010	2015 (forecast)
East Asia and Pacific	926	871	640	656	523	332	284	251	115
Europe and Central Asia	9	14	18	18	11	6	2	3	2
Latin America and Caribbean	53	53	54	60	63	48	37	32	30
Middle East and North Africa	13	12	12	14	12	10	9	8	9
South Asia	617	632	631	619	640	598	571	507	406
Sub-Saharan Africa	290	330	349	376	390	395	399	414	408
Total	1,908	1,910	1,704	1,743	1,639	1,389	1,302	1,215	970

Source: World Bank, World Development Indicators (2014).

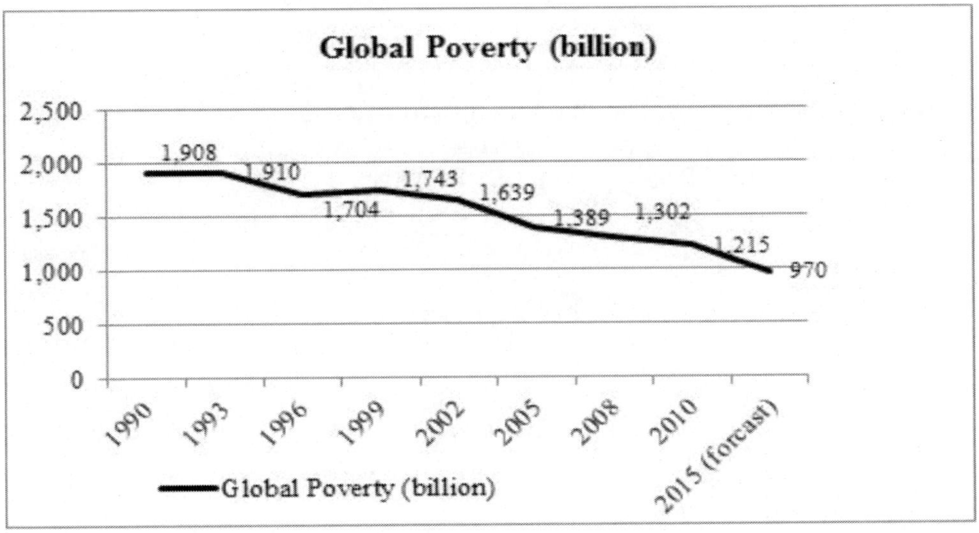

Figure 2.1. Global poverty, 1990 to 2015.

ICT infrastructure development itself is not the guarantee of low level of poverty and high level of GDP growth. For the effective deployment of e-governance services, strong ICT infrastructure, awareness about e-government services, political will and most importantly high literacy rate are the prerequisites (Puneet and Dharminder, 2014). And it is evident from the success stories of previously mentioned countries that, they have been able to nurture these prerequisites successfully. Table No. 2.1 and Figure No. 2.1 narrate about the poverty decline in the various regions in last twenty five years.

It is evident from the trends depicted by Table No. 2.1 and Figure No. 2.1 that the global poverty, since 1990 to 2015 is continuously decreasing and present trend suggests that it would decline in near future also. In 1990, the global poverty was 1908 million, which has been reduced up to 970 million in 2015.

The ICT usage in all spheres of life has increased significantly and the number of ICT users in last fifteen years across the world increased from 40.7 billion in 2001 to 212.8 billion in 2015. Table No. 2.2 and Figure No. 2.2 show the year wise improvement in the ICT users (in billions), which approves the importance of ICT sector in the world economy.

The below mentioned statistical analysis using linear regression equation advocates that the ICT involvement and improvement has helped in reducing the poverty worldwide. In the equation poverty is a dependent variable, and it is negatively related with ICT infrastructure and improvement which means, ICT advancement has helped in diluting the poverty prevalence.

	ICT	POVERTY
ICT	1	- 0.96597152115509
POVERTY	- 0.96597152115509	1

Estimation Equation:

=========================

POVERTY = C(1) + C(2)*ICT

Substituted Coefficients:

=========================

POVERTY = 1732.05890061 - 3.54828730245*ICT

Dependent Variable: Poverty Method: Least Squares Sample: 2002-2015 Included observations: 5				
Variable	Coefficient	Std. Error	t-Statistic	Prob.
C	1732.059	73.92630	23.42954	0.0002
ICT	- 3.548287	0.548534	- 6.468671	0.0075
R-squared	0.933101	Mean dependent var		1303.000
Adjusted R-squared	0.910801	S.D. dependent var		244.4003
S.E. of regression	72.99296	Akaike info criterion		11.70778
Sum squared resid	15983.92	Schwarz criterion		11.55155
Log likelihood	- 27.26944	Hannan-Quinn criter.		11.28849
F-statistic	41.84371	Durbin-Watson stat		2.062743
Prob(F-statistic)	0.007497			

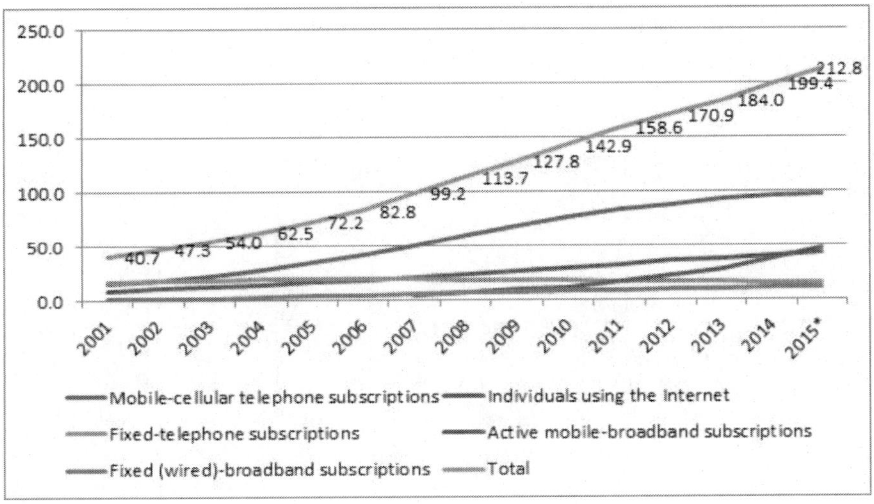

Figure 2.2. ICT users, (in billions).

Table 2.2. Global ICT developments, 2001-2015 (population in billion)

ICT Use	2001	2002	2003	2004	2005	2006	2007	2008	2009	2010	2011	2012	2013	2014	2015*
Mobile-cellular telephone subscriptions	15.5	18.4	22.2	27.3	33.9	41.7	50.6	59.7	68.0	76.6	83.8	88.1	93.1	96.1	96.8
Individuals using the Internet	8.0	10.7	12.3	14.1	15.8	17.6	20.6	23.1	25.6	29.4	32.5	35.5	37.8	40.6	43.4
Fixed-telephone subscriptions	16.6	17.2	17.8	18.7	19.1	19.2	18.8	18.5	18.4	17.8	17.2	16.7	15.9	15.2	14.5
Active mobile-broadband subscriptions							4.0	6.3	9.0	11.5	16.7	21.7	27.3	37.2	47.2
Fixed (wired)-broadband subscriptions	0.6	1.0	1.6	2.4	3.4	4.3	5.2	6.1	6.9	7.6	8.4	9.0	9.9	10.3	10.8
Total	40.7	47.3	54.0	62.5	72.2	82.8	99.2	113.7	127.8	142.9	158.6	170.9	184.0	199.4	212.8

Source: International Telecommunication Union's World Telecommunication/ICT indicators database.

Table 2.3. Countries that have high income level and score more than 66.6 per cent in e-participation

Country	E-information (%)	E-consultation (%)	E-decision making (%)	Total (%)	Income level	Region
Netherlands	96.30	86.36	77.78	89.66	High	Europe
Republic of Korea	96.30	81.82	88.89	89.66	High	Asia
Uruguay	88.89	95.45	66.67	87.93	High	Americas
France	96.30	77.27	77.78	86.21	High	Europe
Japan	85.19	86.36	88.89	86.21	High	Asia
United Kingdom	96.30	77.27	77.78	86.21	High	Europe
Australia	92.59	77.27	77.78	84.48	High	Oceania
Colombia	74.07	81.82	88.89	79.31	Upper middle	Americas

Source: United Nations, E-Government Survey 2014.

Various macroeconomic studies including World Bank Report (2009) have also displayed strong causal relation between ICT development and GDP growth over a period of 26 years (1980 to 2006). This study confirms that, due to 10 percent increase in ICT infrastructure in developed and developing countries the GDP increased by 1.35 and 1.19 percent respectively (Pepper and Garrity, 2015). Invariably, Table No. 2.3 also shows that the countries with high income level have utilized e-services effectively.

Table No. 2.3 highlights that the e-decision making, e-consultation and e-information sharing services utilization have been exploited effectively by developed countries such as Netherlands, Republic of Korea, Uruguay, etc.

3. ICT and GDP Growth Linkages: SAARC Experience

Regional cooperation for economic development for South Asian countries was imperative because these countries were struggling with the high population growth rate (Bishnu Pant, Sushmita Pradhan, and Santosh Gartaula, 2014). However, due to over-population, the use of mobile services in SAARC countries has increased by 19% from 2007 to 2012 (Konuma, 2013). The advancement in ICT services has a positive impact on the market-mechanism of these countries by improving the delivery of information services and widening the scope of markets (Sahoo, 2008). These South Asian countries have achieved a 6% GDP growth rate annually in last 20 years (Amin, 2013). Successively, in SAARC countries the poverty incidences have also declined by 0.034% in comparison to GDP growth rate (Oli and Thapa, 2014). The relation between poverty and ICT use has been depicted by the Table No. 3.1 and Figure No. 3.1.

It is evident from the Table No. 3.1 that in last two decades incidence of poverty in SAARC countries reduced from 48.5 percent to 31.3 percent. In the same period, internet users increased from 0.10 percent to 11.6 percent. Invariably, persistent 6 percent GDP growth of the region has defended this inverse trend between poverty and internet use.

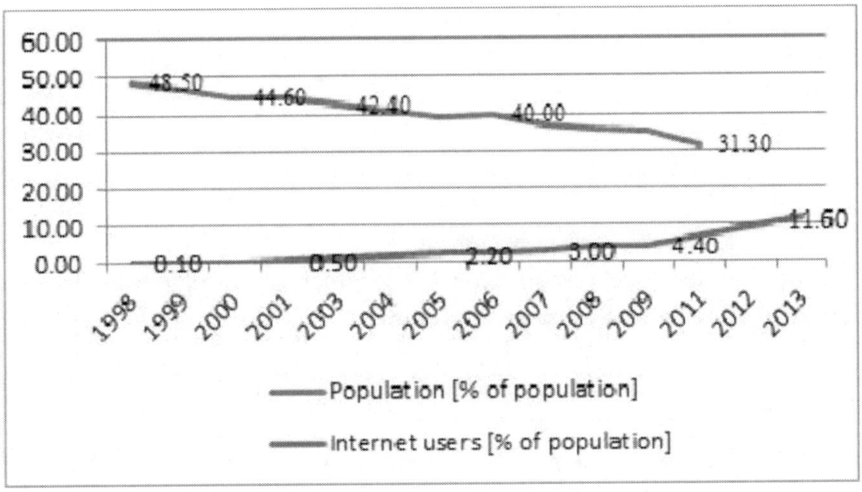

Figure 3.1. The relation between poverty and ICT use.

Table 3.1. Population living in poverty, $1.25 per day in 2005 ppp [% of population] and internet users [per 100 population] for SAARC countries

	1998	1999	2000	2001	2003	2004	2005	2006	2007	2008	2009	2011	2012	2013
Population [% of population]	48.50	47.00	44.60	44.50	42.40	40.70	39.40	40.00	37.10	35.90	35.00	31.30		
Internet users [% of population]	0.10	0.10	0.20	0.50	1.50	1.80	2.20	2.50	3.00	4.00	4.40	7.20	9.40	11.60

Source: Data retrieved from World Bank and SAARC Sites.

Table 3.2. Level of income and EGDI level in SAARC countries

Country	Sub-region	EGDI Level	Level of Income	GNI
Afghanistan	Southern Asia	Low	Low	690
Bangladesh	Southern Asia	Middle	Low	830
Bhutan	Southern Asia	Middle	Lower Middle	2420
India	Southern Asia	Middle	Lower Middle	1550
Maldives	Southern Asia	Middle	Upper Middle	5430
Nepal	Southern Asia	Low	Low	700
Pakistan	Southern Asia	Middle	Lower Middle	1250
Sri Lanka	Southern Asia	High	Lower Middle	2910

Source: United Nations E-Government Survey 2014 E-Government for the Future We Want *GNI (Gross National Income) per capita, PPP (current international $).

Table No. 3.2 reveals that the E-Government Development Index (EGDI) is low in Afghanistan and Nepal because these countries have low level of national income. And the middle income group countries have achieved middle level of EGDI. However, except Sri Lanka, other SAARC Countries have not materialized the prospective use of e-government services. Infect, all SAARC countries need to improve their ICT infrastructure to improve the delivery of e-government services, which would help them to achieve high level of GDP.

4. Indian Experience

Despite high level of population growth, India is one of the fastest growing countries in the world. However, due to global meltdown and structural influences, India witnessed an erratic GDP growth rate in last decade (Sawhney, 2010). On the other hand, incidence of poverty reduced to 21.9 percent in 2011-12 which was 37.2 percent in 2004 (Planning Commission, 2013). Table No. 4.1 and Figure No. 4.1 depict the declining trend of poverty in India.

Various studies suggest that due to ICT infrastructure development, job opportunities in India have increased and it has contributed in generating tax revenue also. Further, Government of India had generated more than Rs. 1 billion from the 3G spectrum auction in 2010 which was around one percent of national income. Invariably, these developments have helped in reducing the incidents of poverty in India (TRAI, 2012). Government of India has recognized the ICT sector's contribution in GDP growth; therefore, expenditure incurred on this sector has increased persistently in last 15 years which is exhibited by Table No. 4.2.

Table No. 4.2 reveals that the expenditure incurred on ICT sector apportioned 3.98 percent of national income in 2011-12, which was merely 1.25 percent of national income in 2002-03 (Figure No. 4.2).

Table 4.1. Percentage of poor estimated in India from expert group methodology (Tendulkar) in last two decades

Year	1993-94	2004-05	2009-10	2011-12
% of Poverty	45.3	37.2	29.8	21.9

Source: Government of India Planning Commission, 2013.

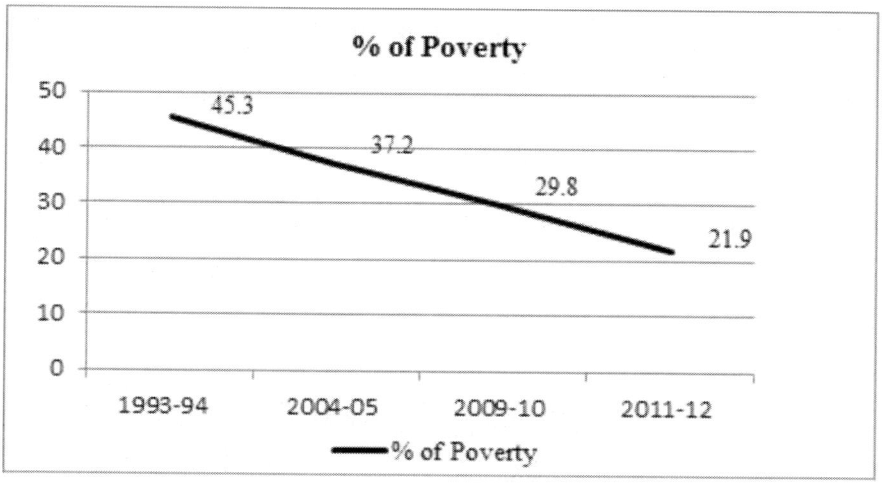

Figure 4.1. The declining trend of poverty in India.

Table 4.2. Expenditure incurred on telecommunication and it infrastructure by Government of India (GDP at factor cost at constant price 2004-05)

Year	2002-03	2003-04	2004-05	2005-06	2006-07	2007-08	2008-09	2009-10	2010-11	2011-12	CAGR
Expenditure on Telec. And IT Infrastructure	32386	40742	49279	60857	75669	93928	117465	154496	188246	209332	21%
% Share in National Expend.	1.25	1.46	1.65	1.87	2.12	2.41	2.82	3.421	3.82	3.98	12%

Source: Ministry of Statistic and Programme Implementation, GoI, 2011-12.

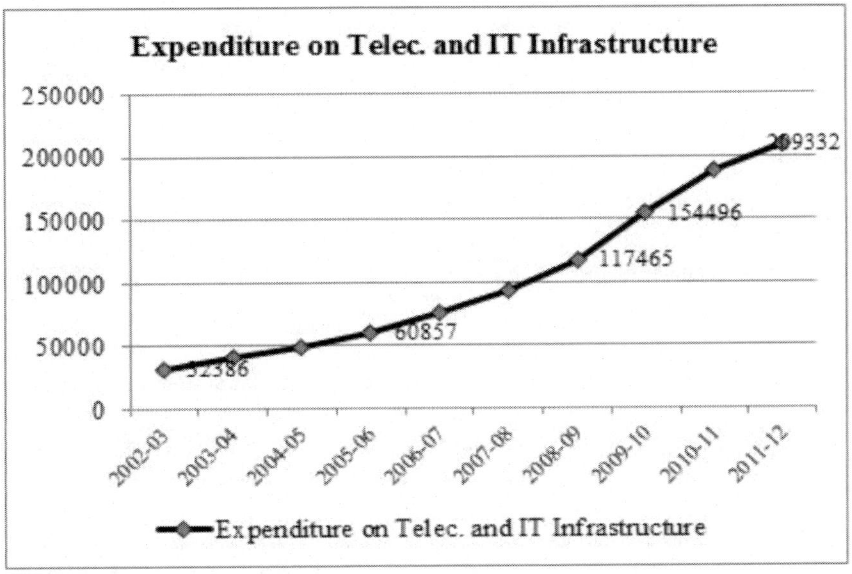

Figure 4.2. Expenditure incurred on telecommunication and it infrastructure by Government of India.

A comparative analysis of Figure No. 4.1 and 4.2 exhibits the same negative relationship between poverty and development of ICT infrastructure as previously investigated by Figure No. 3.1. These linkages, evidently, show that the growth of ICT and e-services has helped in diluting the incidences of poverty and creating new job opportunities in India.

5. The Importance of Telecommunication Sector in India

In order to augment the e-government services and networking infrastructure, Government of India launched National e-governance Plan (NeGP) in 2006 (Bussell, 2012). As a result, in India, ICT infrastructure and services improved considerably, which contributed in generating positive socio-economic impact. The total number of telephone subscribers increased to 943.49 million up to February, 2012, which were merely 28.53 million in 2001 (TRAI, 2012). Table No. 5.1 gives a snapshot of ICT usage in India, which narrates the importance of this sector in Indian economy. Though, in the last decade, telecom services subscribers increased considerably but urban teledensity was 4.4 times more than rural. Whereas, wireless phones or mobile phones controlled the market, and landline phones share was merely 3.4 percent of the total subscribers.

Further, Table No. 5.1 shows that, the telecommunication items export increased from Rs. 135 billion to Rs. 140 billion in 2010-11. This sector has helped in increasing the inflow of FDI which was Rs. 75.46 billion in 2010-11; and Indian telecommunication companies have also started investing in other countries. Consequently, the rate of job creation by ICT sector has remained high in 2000s and it has created around 3.6 million new jobs directly or indirectly (Commission, 2008, COAI, 2005).

The share of ICT sector in Indian GDP has increased over the years and showered net revenue for the government (Bhide, 2010). The ICT sector has mobilized the resources significantly and contributed in generating boosting economic environment (TRAI, 2012). Undeniably, ICT sector has a positive multiplier effect on the other sectors such as banking, NIC, Research and Development, Health and Sanitation, education, etc. These sectors have witnessed new industrial changes and mobilized human resources significantly (TRAI, 2012). As a result other economic indicators such as GDP, job creation, poverty alleviation, rural development and privatization and globalization process observed positive changes (GoI, 2010). That is why, in order to strengthen the long run economic growth and development, modern economists have supported the role of technological advancement in all spheres of life. And ICT driven economic growth has become a major contributor in the Indian economy (Jain, Tuteja, and Raman, 2008).

Table 5.1. A Snap Shot of Indian Telecommunication Sector Till February, 2012

Variable	Data	Status
Teledensity†	February 2012	78.10
Urban teledensity†	February 2012	169.37
Rural teledensity	February 2012†	38.53
Total number of subscribers	February 2012	943.49 million
Total number of wireless subscribers	February 2012	911.17 million
wireline phones	February 2012	32.33 million
Number of Internet subscribers	December 2011	22.39 million
Number of broadband	February 2012	13.54 million
Number of wireless data subscribers	February 2012	431.37 million
Production of telecom equipment#	2010–11	Rs 535 billion* (Rs 510 billion in 2009–10)
Total exports of telecom items#	2010–11	Rs140 billion* (Rs 135 billion in 2009–10)
Total imports of telecom items#	2009–10	Rs 450.3 billion
India's export of telecom consultancy#	2010–11 Rs 12.7 million up to September 2010	(Rs 72.70 million in 2009–10)
FDI in telecom‡	2010–11	Rs 75.46 billion
Gross revenue of telecom services sector	2010–11	Rs 1,717 billion

† Number of telephone subscribers per 100 people. * Projected. # *Annual Report 2010–11*, Department of Telecommunications, Ministry of Communications and Information Technology, Government of India (2011), www.dot.gov.in. ‡ Department of Industrial Policy and Promotion, Ministry of Commerce and Industry, Government of India (http://dipp.nic.in/).

Conclusion

Poverty alleviation has always remained a daunting task for the policymakers. To eliminate the poverty, new strategies and technologies have been evolved. And the results are also soothing, especially in the areas and destinations where ICT usage has been initiated. On the bases of international experiences, it could be manifested that for the consistent economic growth and development of modern economies, use of ICT has become imperative (Bhambhani, 2015). Infusions of ICT and e-governance services have enabled the natural and physical resources to move significantly at global level. The global impact of Indian techno-entrepreneurs has generated huge amount of revenue for Silicon Valley as well as for Indian economy (Chandrasekhar, 2013). These technological changes have generated new opportunities for economic growth. However, in order to achieve sustainable growth, continuous technological innovations are required. These changes would help in igniting development process further (Soumitra Dutta, 2015). The increased utilization of ICT and e-governance services would promote positive spillovers in future.

References

Agrawal, P. (2008). Economic Growth and Poverty Reduction: Evidence from Kazakhstan. *Asian Development Review*, 24(2), 90-115.

Alvarez, L. (2015). *Developing the Network for Growth and Equality of Opportunity.* Geneva: World Economic Forum.

Amin, S. (2013). *Future of Economic Cooperation in SAARC Countries.* Islamabad: Islamabad Policy Research Institute.

Bank, W. (2013). *World Development Indicators database.*

Bhambhani, S. N. (2015, April-June). Role of Information and Technology in Developing Smart Cities. *Journal of Development Management and Communication*, II(2), 119-127.

Bhide, S. (2010). The 3G Auction: What will we do with the extra money? 12(5).

Bishnu Pant, Sushmita Pradhan, and Santosh Gartaula. (2014). Regional Cooperation and Integration in South Asia: Nepal Perspective. *15th Annual GDN Conference*, (pp. 1-11). Accra-Ghana.

Bourguignon, F. (2004). The Poverty-Growth-Inequality Triangle. *Poverty, Inequality and Growth.* New Delhi: e Agence Française de Développement and the EU Development Network (New Delhi: French Development Agency e and the EU Development Network).

Chandrasekhar, C. (2013, October 30). *Information and Communications.* Retrieved October 31, 2015, from United Nations Development Programme: Human Development Reports: http://hdr.undp.org/.

COAI. (2005). *OVUM Report on Economic Benefits of Mobile Services in India: A Case Study for the GSM Association.* New Delhi: Cellular Operators Association of India.

Commission, P. (2008). *Report of the High Level Group on the Services Sector.* New Delhi: Planning Commission, GoI.

Development, D. f. (2008). *Growth Builiding Jobs and Prosperity in Developing Countries.* Retrieved August 2015, from OECD.ORG: http://www.oecd.org/derec/unitedkingdom/40700982.pdf.

Dutta, S., and Geiger, T. (Technology Report 2015). *The Global Information Technology Report 2015.* Geneva: World Economic Forum.

E-government Strategy Baharain. (n.d.). Retrieved August 2015, from http://goo.gl/x6iF8c.

GDP Per Capita. (2015, August). Retrieved from http://data.worldbank.org/: indicator/NY. GDP.PCAP.CD.

Ghosal, R. K. (2012). Growth, Poverty and Inequality Paradox in India—A Panel Data Approach. *32nd General Conference of The International Association for Research in Income and Wealth,* (pp. 1-35). Boston.

GoI. (2010). *Value Addition and Employment Generation in the ICT Sector in India.* New Delhi: Implementation, Ministry of Statistics and Programme.

ICT Contributions to GDP in Nigeria. (2014, September). Retrieved August 24th August, 2015, from http://telecomworld.itu.int/:blog/ict-contributions-to-gdp-in-nigeria/.

Jain, R., Tuteja, A., and Raman, K. (2008). *The Indian ICT industry: Enabling Global Competitiveness and Driving Innovation with Equitable Growth.* Chennai: Confederation of Indian Industry.

Konuma, H. (2013). Information and communication Technologies for sustainable agriculture: Indicators from Asia and the Pacific. In: G. Sylvester, *Information and communication Technologies for sustainable agriculture: Indicators from Asia and the Pacific* (p. iii). Bangkok: RAP Publication.

Krongkaew, M., Chamnivickorn, S., and Nitithanprapas, I. (January 2006). *Economic growth, employment, and poverty reduction linkages: The case of Thailand.*

Kumar Puneet, K. D. (2014). A Framework for Improving e-Services Utilization in Rural Areas. *The IUP Journal of Information Technology*, X(2), 36-46.

Kumar, P., and Dharminder, K. (2013, December). ICT in Local Self Governance: A Study of Rural India. *International Journal of Computer Application*, 83(6), 31-36.

Ministry of Statistics and Programme Implementation. (2010, August). *Value Addition and Employment Generation in the ICT Sector in India.* New Delhi: Government of India. Retrieved from http://ec.europa.eu/.

Oli, D. B., and Thapa, Y. (2014). *Best Practices in Poverty Alleviation and SDGs in South Asia: A Compendium.* Kathmandu: SAARC Secretariat.

Pepper, R., and Garrity, J. (2015). *ICTs, Income Inequality, and Ensuring Inclusive Growth.* Geneva: World Economic Forum.

Planning Commission, G. o. (2013). *Review of Epert Group to Review the Methodology for Estimation of Poverty.* New Delhi: Planning Commission, GoI.

Pulletikurthi V. S., D. L. (2015, January). Achieving Sustainable Development Through Electronic Governance: World'S Success Stories. *International Journal Of Multidisciplinary Educational Research*, 4(1(2)), 34-51.

Roy, M. (2011, Oct-Dec). Promoting E-Governance in Panchayats. *Journal of Rural Development*, pp. 393-410.

Sahoo, S. (2008). ICT Initiative of SAARC Agriculture Centre in the SAARC Region. *ICCSIT* (pp. 923-929). Singapore: IEEE. Retrieved from IEEE Xplore Digital Library.

Sawhney, U. (2010). Growth And Structural Change In Saarc Economies. *International Journal of Economics and Finance Studies*, 2(2), 95-103.

Solow, R. M. (2015, August). *Poverty and Economics Growth*. Retrieved August 2015, from Istitute on Research on Poverty: http://www.irp.wisc.edu/publications/focus/pdfs/foc123a.pdf.

Son, H. H., and Kakwani, N. (2004, August). International Poverty Centre. 2, 1-28.

Soumitra Dutta, T. G. (2015). *The Global Information Technology Report 2015*. World Economic Forum.

Survey, U. N.-G. (2014). *The potential of e-Government development in Latin America*. New York: Department of Economic and Social Affairs.

TRAI. (2012). *Telecom Sector in India: A Decadal Profile*. New Delhi: Telecom Regulatory Authority of India.

In: e-Governance in India: Problems, Prototypes and Prospects ISBN: 978-1-63484-830-5
Editors: P. Kumar, R. Sharma and U. Kaushal

Chapter 7

EMPIRICAL VERIFICATION OF ICT EFFICACY ON MACROECONOMIC INDICATORS

Sushil Kumar Rai[*] and Rajesh Sharma
Assistant Professors, COBMEC,
Mody University of Science and Technology,
Lakshmangarh, Distt. Sikar, Rajasthan, India

ABSTRACT

This chapter examines the impact of information and communications technology (ICT) on macroeconomic indicators such as poverty, inequality, employment and growth rate of the Indian economy in the period from 2001 to 2010, using the ARDL model and cointegration. The chapter finds that the use of ICT is beneficial for reduction in poverty and inequality as well as an increase in employment and growth rate. The result of the paper also supports the initiation taken by the government regarding investment in ICT as return on investment is reflected through desire change in selected macroeconomic indicators.

Keywords: poverty, inequality, employment, growth rate, ARDL model, cointegration

Jel Classification: E20, C2

1. INTRODUCTION

In the last two decades of the 20th century it was realized by the policy makers that process of digitalization is not something that happens after addressing development issues, but rather a key component to tackle those challenges efficiently. In this context, the role and importance of information and communications technology (ICT) attracted the attention of

[*] Assistant Professor of Economics, College of Business Management, Economics and Commerce (COBMEC), MUST, Lakshmangarh, Sikar, Rajasthan, E-mail: sushilrai23@gmail.com.

the Indian Government. In 1985, under the direction of Rajiv Gandhi's, the Indian government decided to enhance the pace of ICT use in the 1990s. In the 1990s India began to apply several communication technology initiatives such as e-governance, telecommunication, e-commerce and community information centers while promoting access to the internet to bring economic benefits to the people. Most of the state governments in India have approved e-governance initiative through the use of ICT and are in the process of enabling their citizens to use the internet too.

Over the past two decades, the usage of information and communications technology has enriched the social and financial conditions of our country and in due process the government has invested a lot in the development of ICT. Assessing the impact of ICT at the country level is critical and complex. However, measurement of ICT impacts at the country level is essential for policy making. Optimal allocation of scarce resources is a major concern and it requires good estimates of the return on ICT investments. The present study is an endeavor to assess the return on ICT investments at country level through measuring impact of ICT on macroeconomic indicators such as poverty, inequality, employment and growth-rate of Indian economy.

2. Review of Literature

In most of the available previous studies on ICT, the main factors noted generally fall into three categories- (a) to develop an appropriate model to measure ICTs impacts effectively, (b) ICT helps to increase efficiency and accountability, and (c) ICT promotes wealth creation and economic development. According to the study of current ICT trends such as e-commerce and e-administration have been quoted as routes to wealth creation and economic development (Ebrahimian, 2003)said that digital technology can promote development activities and connect people in the most remote regions on communal, regional or national levels. The importance of information and communications technology use has been recognized as a key to the transformation of socio-economies of developing countries (M., 2003; S., 2007) (Sumanjeet, 2006)study demonstrates that e-governance focuses in bringing improvements in the service delivery, dissemination of information, transparency, public and private partnership, efficiency and accountability study shows that to measure ICT impacts effectively, the relevant developing areas and their interrelationships should be considered in the model. One of the study mentions that both educational quality and on-the-job training appear to be influential catalysts for the modernization of economies via ICT use by persons, commercial and administration (Rangriz & Basava, 2011) (Prasad, 2012)study reveals that ICT and new media technologies have become inevitable in e-governance, but the motivation of adopting e-governance in developing countries like India is quite different from that in developed countries.

In the light of above, it becomes highly significant to make an attempt to study the impact of ICT on macroeconomic indicators. The present study examines the effect of ICT development on poverty, inequality, employment, and growth rate (macroeconomic indicators) of Indian economy for the period from 2001 to 2010.

3. Methodology

3.1. Objective of the Study

To examine the impact of Information and Communications Technology (ICT) on macroeconomic indicators such as poverty, inequality, employment and growth rate of Indian economy.

3.2. Hypothesis

There is no significant impact of ICT on poverty, inequality, employment and growth rate of India from 2001 to 2010.

3.3. Source of Data

Secondary sources have been used to collect the relevant data. The data has been collected from the official website of the United Nations Economic and Social Commission for Asia and the Pacific (UNESCAP). The definition of considered variables and its components are specified in Table 3.3.1.

Table 3.3.1. Definition and component of variables

Variable Name	Component	Definitions
Information and Communications Technology (ICT)	Mobile-Cellular Subscriptions	Average annual rate of change in Mobile cellular subscriptions.
	Fixed-Telephone Subscriptions	Average annual rate of change in fixed-telephone subscriptions.
	Internet Users	Average annual rate of change in internet users.
	Fixed-Broadband Subscriptions	Average annual rate of change in fixed-broadband subscribers.
Poverty		The population living on less than $1.25 per day, measured in 2005 PPP.
Inequality	Gini Index	Measures the extent to which the income distribution within an economy deviates from perfect income equality.
Employment		All persons above a specified age who, during a specified brief period of either one week or one day, were in paid employment or self-employment.
Growth Rate	GDP	Percentage change in GDP at constant 2005 PPP dollars per annum, and in a period of 5 and 10 years.

3.4. Research Tools

To find out a proper empirical evidence between the measured variables, statistical tools like Unit Root test (to check the stationary of economic variables), Pair wise Granger Causality Tests (to investigate the unidirectional and bidirectional relationship between variables), Cointegration test (to find out stationary of the error term in the regression model and a long-term relationship between variables), correlation and regression analysis have been used. ARDL (Auto-regressive Differentiated Lag) regression model is applied and all the four macroeconomic indicators are regressed individually upon Information and communications technology (ICT) for India. The entire analysis is performed with Eviews 9 and SPSS 20 softwares.

4. The Model

An ARDL is a least squares regression containing lags of the dependent variable and explanatory variables. ARDLs are usually denoted with the notation ARDL (p,q), where p is the number of lags of the dependent variable, q is the number of lags of the explanatory variable.

An ARDL model is written as;

$$Y_t = \alpha + \sum_{i=1}^{p} \gamma_i Y_{t-1} + \sum_{j=1}^{k} \sum_{i=0}^{q_j} X_{j,t-1}' \beta_{j,i} + \varepsilon_t \qquad (1)$$

Explanatory variables with at least one lagged term are called dynamic regressor. Since an ARDL model estimates the dynamic relationship between a dependent variable and explanatory variables, it is possible to transform the model into a long-run representation. The calculation of these estimated long-run coefficients is given by:

$$\theta_j = \sum_{i=1}^{j} \hat{\beta}_{j,i} / 1 - \sum_{i=1}^{p} \gamma_I \qquad (2)$$

5. Results and Discussion

To find out the strength and direction of the relationship between ICT and macroeconomic indicators (poverty, inequality, employment and growth rate) correlation analysis is used. The results of correlation analysis have been shown in Table 5.1. It is revealed from the correlation table that inequality and growth rate has opposite relations with ICT while poverty and employment has identical relations. On the basis of existing associations between variables it is interpreted that with the development of ICT, the value of two macroeconomic indicators (inequality and growth rate) decreases whereas other two macroeconomic indicators (poverty and employment) increases. The value of the correlation coefficient between ICT and macroeconomic indicators are not statistically significant.

Table 5.1. Correlation between ICT and macroeconomic indicators

	Poverty	Inequality	Employment	Growth Rate
Pearson Correlation	.431	-.261	.392	-.034
ICT Sig (2-tailed)	.214	.467	.263	.925
N	10	10	10	10

To examine whether Information and Communications Technique (ICT can be used to estimate the value of macroeconomic indicators or not, the Granger causality test is used. The results of the Granger causality test are given in Table 5.2.

Table 5.2. Pair wise Granger Causality Tests

Null Hypothesis	**F-Statistics**	**Prob.**
ICT does not Granger Cause Poverty	4.80430	0.0359
Poverty does not Granger Cause ICT	1.02124	0.4589
ICT does not Granger Cause Inequality	5.29446	0.0543
Inequality does not Granger Cause ICT	1.03673	0.4547
ICT does not Granger Cause EMPLOYMENT	7.01012	0.0319
EMPLOYMENT does not Granger Cause ICT	3.63776	0.1578
ICT does not Granger Cause Growth Rate	6.28987	0.0472
Growth Rate does not Granger Cause ICT	0.00125	0.9988

The result of Granger Causality test shows that there is a unidirectional relationship between ICT and macroeconomic indicators. On the basis of the above result, in a regression analysis, ICT can be used as a predictor to predict the level of poverty, inequality, employment and growth rate of Indian economy.

To inspect whether the variables are stationary or non-stationary, the Augmented Dickey-Fuller (ADF) test is applied because a non-stationary time series may lead to the phenomenon of spurious and nonsense regression. The results of the test have been shown in Table 5.3.

Table 5.3. ADF Unit Root Test

Variable	Level	Lags	T-statistic	P value	Result
ICT	2nd Difference with intercept	1	-3.532604	0.0493	Stationary
Poverty	2nd Difference with intercept	0	-3.432548	0.0483	Stationary
Inequality	2nd Difference with intercept	0	-3.737498	0.0336	Stationary
Employment	1st Difference with intercept	0	-3.974598	0.0491	Stationary
Growth Rate	1st Difference with intercept	0	-3.456129	0.0419	Stationary

Table 5.3 reveals the result of stationary, which suggest the rejection of the unit root null hypothesis of non-stationary at 5% level of significance for all the variables at first and second difference with intercept. All the observed variables are stationary without lags except ICT that is stationary at first lags.

To assess whether the variables of macroeconomic indicators are affected by its past value or not, each of the macroeconomic indicators are regressed against its own past value. The results of the autoregressive model have been depicted in Table 5.4.

Table 5.4. Autoregression of Macroeconomic Indicators

Dependent Variable	Independent Variable	Coefficient	R-squared	Prob.(F-statistics)
Poverty	D(Poverty)	5.095070	0.579969	0.017107
Inequality	D(Inequality)	0.374572	0.382361	0.454011
Employment	D(Employment)	0.310469	0.241432	0.599388
Growth Rate	D(Growth Rate)	0.535088	0.464081	0.043335

Table 5.4 displays that the value of R-squared (explained variation in dependent variable by independent variable) is fairly acceptable for all the macroeconomic indicators. In case of poverty and growth rate the autoregressive model is statistically significant at the 5% level of significance.

This is precisely the situation for which the Auto-regressive Differentiated Lag (ARDL) regression model is designed for. The result of ARDL regression model between poverty and information and communications technology (ICT) has been represented in Table 5.5(a). In the estimated regression equation ICT is used as a stimulus while poverty is defined as a response. ARDL (1,1) model at first lags of explained and the explanatory variables are selected to demonstrate the causal relationship between variables. It is reflected from Table 5.5(a) that 65% (adjusted R-squared) variation in poverty is described by first lags value of ICT and poverty. The values of coefficients of both the independent variables are statistically significant. The model is free from the problem of autocorrelation as it is shown by the result of D-W test (1.99). The negative sign of the coefficients of ICT is revealing the inverse relationship between poverty and ICT. The selected model is statistically significant as the value of Prob. (F-statistics) is less than .05.

The observed regression equation of the selected ARDL model is:

$$D(Poverty,2) = C + D(Poverty(-1),2) + D(ICT(-1),2)$$
$$=-0.175208+0.448441-0.001383 \quad (3)$$

In Table 5.5(b) cointegration and long run form of the estimated ARDL model has been given. The negative sign of the coefficient of cointegration equation reveals that the error term of the regressed equation is stationary and it is statistically significant also as exhibited by its probability value. The long run coefficient between poverty and ICT with negative sign is statistically significant. It specifies that even in the long run the inverse relationship between ICT and poverty will be continued.

Table 5.5(a). ARDL model between Poverty and ICT

Dependent Variable: D(Poverty,2)				
Method: ARDL				
Number of models evaluated: 3				
Selected Model: ARDL(1, 1)				
Note: final equation sample is larger than selection sample				
No d.f. adjustment for standard errors and covariance				
Variable	**Coefficient**	**Std. Error**	**t-Statistic**	**Prob.***
D(Poverty(-1),2)	0.448441	0.162849	2.753713	0.0505
D(ICT,2)	-0.001025	0.011266	3.854971	0.0308
D(ICT(-1),2)	-0.001383	0.010246	5.612345	0.0112
C	-0.175208	0.057436	-3.050470	0.0554
R-squared	0.827959	Mean dependent var		-0.214286
Adjusted R-squared	0.655919	S.D. dependent var		0.389138
S.E. of regression	0.228262	Akaike info criterion		0.178918
Sum squared resid	0.156311	Schwarz criterion		0.148009
Log likelihood	3.373787	Hannan-Quinn criter.		-0.203105
F-statistic	4.812579	Durbin-Watson stat		1.997391
Prob(F-statistic)	0.044684			

Table 5.5(b). ARDL Cointegrating and Long Run Form

Dependent Variable: D(Poverty,2)				
Selected Model: ARDL(1, 1)				
Included observations: 7				
Cointegrating Form				
Variable	**Coefficient**	**Std. Error**	**t-Statistic**	**Prob.**
D(ICT, 3)	-0.001025	0.000266	3.854971	0.0308
CointEq (-1)	-0.551559	0.162849	-3.386928	0.0429
Cointeq = D(Poverty,2) - (-0.0044*D(ICT,2) -0.3177)				
Long Run Coefficients				
D(ICT,2)	-0.004366	0.002020	2.160987	0.0195
C	-0.317659	0.127269	-2.495973	0.0880

The results of ARDL regression model between inequality and information and communications technology (ICT) have been depicted in Table 5.6(a). ARDL (1,0) model at first lags of explained and with no lags the explanatory variables are selected to explain the causal relationship between variables. It is demonstrated from Table 5.6(a) that 68% (adjusted R-squared) variation in inequality is described by inequality and ICT. The values of coefficients of both the explanatory variables are statistically significant. The model is free from the problem of autocorrelation as it is reflected by the result of D-W test (2.02). The negative sign of the coefficients of ICT is exposing the inverse relationship between inequality and ICT. The selected model is statistically significant as the value of Prob. (F-statistics) is less than 5 per cent.

Table 5.6(a). ARDL model between Inequality and ICT

Dependent Variable: D(Inequaliy,2)				
Method: ARDL				
Number of models evaluated: 2				
Selected Model: ARDL(1, 0)				
No d.f. adjustment for standard errors and covariance				
Variable	**Coefficient**	**Std. Error**	**t-Statistic**	**Prob.***
D(Inequality(-1),2)	0.829364	0.300745	2.757696	0.0503
D(ICT,2)	-0.002400	0.000463	-5.187712	0.0139
C	0.986335	0.389338	2.533364	0.0852
R-squared	0.839799	Mean dependent var		0.014286
Adjusted R-squared	0.679598	S.D. dependent var		0.712808
S.E. of regression	0.403478	Akaike info criterion		1.318170
Sum squared resid	0.488384	Schwarz criterion		1.287261
Log likelihood	-0.613594	Hannan-Quinn criter.		0.936147
F-statistic	5.242167	Durbin-Watson stat		2.022192
Prob(F-statistic)	0.003463			

Table 5.6(b). ARDL Cointegrating and Long Run Form

Dependent Variable: D(Inequality,2)				
Selected Model: ARDL(1, 0)				
Included observations: 7				
Cointegrating Form				
Variable	**Coefficient**	**Std. Error**	**t-Statistic**	**Prob.**
D(ICT, 3)	-0.002400	0.000463	-5.187712	0.0139
CointEq(-1)	-1.170636	0.300745	-0.567377	0.0401
Cointeq = D(Inequality,2) - (-0.0141*D(ICT,2) + 5.7803				
Long Run Coefficients				
D(ICT,2)	-0.014067	0.027109	-0.518901	0.6397
C	5.780345	11.670502	0.495295	0.6544

The obtained regression equation of the selected ARDL model is:

$$\begin{aligned} D(Inequality,2) &= C + D(Inequality(-1),2) + D(ICT,2) \\ &= 0.986335 + 0.829364 - 0.002400 \end{aligned} \quad (4)$$

In Table 5.6(b) cointegration and long run form of the estimated ARDL model has been shown. The negative sign of the coefficient of cointegration equation shows that the error term of the regressed equation is stationary. The long run coefficient between inequality and ICT with negative sign is statistically insignificant that means the observed relationship will be applicable only in short-run.

Table 5.7(a). ARDL model between Employment and ICT

Dependent Variable: D(EMPLOYMENT)				
Method: ARDL				
Number of models evaluated: 2				
Selected Model: ARDL(1, 1)				
No d.f. adjustment for standard errors and covariance				
Variable	**Coefficient**	**Std. Error**	**t-Statistic**	**Prob.***
D(EMPLOYMENT(-1))	0.303098	0.198681	1.525549	0.0466
D(ICT,2)	3.66E-05	0.000492	0.074431	0.0474
D(ICT(-1),2)	0.001771	0.000556	-3.182367	0.0462
C	-1.501359	0.419119	-3.582174	0.0699
R-squared	0.809483	Mean dependent var		-0.357143
Adjusted R-squared	0.428450	S.D. dependent var		0.861892
S.E. of regression	0.651598	Akaike info criterion		2.157031
Sum squared resid	0.849160	Schwarz criterion		2.118396
Log likelihood	-2.549609	Hannan-Quinn criter.		1.679502
F-statistic	6.124441	Durbin-Watson stat		2.090074
Prob(F-statistic)	0.044737			

Table 5.7(b). ARDL Cointegrating and Long Run Form

Dependent Variable: D(EMPLOYMENT)				
Selected Model: ARDL(1, 1)				
Included observations: 7				
Cointegrating Form				
Variable	**Coefficient**	**Std. Error**	**t-Statistic**	**Prob.**
D(ICT, 3)	0.000037	0.000492	0.074431	0.9474
CointEq(-1)	-2.696902	0.198681	-3.507634	0.0525
Cointeq = D(EMPLOYMENT) - (0.0025*D(ICT,2) -2.1543				
Long Run Coefficients				
Variable	Coefficient	Std. Error	t-Statistic	Prob.
D(ICT,2)	0.002488	0.001906	-1.305618	0.0217
C	-2.154333	0.859942	-2.505209	0.1292

The observed regression equation of the selected ARDL model is:

$$\begin{aligned} D(Employment) &= C + D(Employment(-1)) + D(ICT,2) + D(ICT(-1),2) \\ &= -1.501359 + 0.303098 + 3.66E\text{-}05 + 0.001771 \end{aligned} \quad (5)$$

The results of ARDL regression model between employment and information and communications technology (ICT) hacw been represented in Table 5.7 (a). ARDL (1,1) model at first lags of explained and the explanatory variables are selected to estimate the relationship between variables. It is reflected from Table 5.7 (a) that 42% (adjusted R-squared) variation in employment is described by first lags value of ICT and employment. The values of coefficients of both the independent variables are statistically significant. The model is free from the problem of autocorrelation as it is shown by the result of D-W test (2.09). The positive sign of the coefficients of ICT is revealing that with the development of ICT the level of employment also increases. The selected model is statistically significant at 5% level of significance.

In Table 5.7 (b) cointegration and long run form of the estimated ARDL model has been given. The negative sign of the coefficient of cointegration equation indicates that the error term of the regressed equation is stationary. The long run coefficient between employment and ICT with positive sign is statistically significant and suggests that even in the long run the development of ICT will increase the level of employment.

The results of ARDL regression model between growth rate and information and communications technology (ICT) have been depicted in Table 5.8 (a). ARDL (1,2) model is selected to explain the causal relationship between variables. From Table 5.8 (a) it is observed that 87% (adjusted R-squared) variation in growth rate is captured by explanatory variables. The values of coefficients of all the explanatory variables are statistically significant. The model is free from the problem of autocorrelation as it is reflected by the result of D-W test (2.01). The positive sign of the coefficients of ICT is exposing the variables are moving in the same direction. The selected model is statistically significant as the value of Prob. (F-statistics) is less than 5 per cent.

The obtained regression equation of the selected ARDL model is:

$$\begin{aligned} D(\text{Growth-rate}) &= C + D(\text{Growth-rate}(-1)) + D(ICT,2) + D(ICT(-1),2) \\ &\quad + D(ICT(-2),2) \\ &= 0.522097 + 0.385429 + 0.007061 + 0.010958 \\ &\quad + 0.013814. \end{aligned} \tag{6}$$

Table 5.8(a). ARDL model between Growth Rate and ICT

Dependent Variable: D(GROWTHRATE)				
Method: ARDL				
Number of models evaluated: 3				
Selected Model: ARDL(1, 2)				
No d.f. adjustment for standard errors and covariance				
Variable	**Coefficient**	**Std. Error**	**t-Statistic**	**Prob.***
D(GROWTHRATE(-1))	0.385429	0.043033	8.956652	0.0508
D(ICT,2)	0.007061	0.000482	14.64797	0.0434
D(ICT(-1),2)	0.010958	0.000656	16.70372	0.0381
D(ICT(-2),2)	0.013814	0.000519	26.61100	0.0239
C	0.522097	0.101774	5.129961	0.1226
R-squared	0.923974	Mean dependent var		0.500000
Adjusted R-squared	0.869869	S.D. dependent var		3.507136
S.E. of regression	0.608774	Akaike info criterion		1.720170
Sum squared resid	0.370606	Schwarz criterion		1.546636
Log likelihood	-0.160509	Hannan-Quinn criter.		1.025500
F-statistic	41.23606	Durbin-Watson stat		2.010274
Prob(F-statistic)	0.016208			

Table 5.8(b). ARDL Cointegrating and Long Run Form

Dependent Variable: D(GROWTHRATE)				
Selected Model: ARDL(1, 2)				
Included observations: 6				
Cointegrating Form				
Variable	**Coefficient**	**Std. Error**	**t-Statistic**	**Prob.**
D(ICT, 3)	0.007061	0.000482	14.647966	0.0434
D(ICT(-1), 3)	-0.013814	0.000519	-26.611005	0.0239
CointEq(-1)	-1.614571	0.043033	-14.281495	0.0445
Cointeq = D(GROWTHRATE) - (0.0518*D(ICT,2) + 0.8495)				
Long Run Coefficients				
D(ICT,2)	0.051797	0.005500	9.416839	0.0674
C	0.849530	0.175139	4.850614	0.1294

In Table 5.8 (b) cointegration and long run form of the estimated ARDL model has been depicted. The negative sign of the coefficient of cointegration equation indicates that the error term of the regressed equation is stationary. The long run coefficient between growth-rate and ICT with positive sign is statistically insignificant and recommends that only in the short-run the development of ICT will enhance the level of growth-rate.

Conclusion

It has been perceived from the above analysis that information and communications technology (ICT) affect the selected macroeconomic indicators of the present study. The results of regression analysis revealed that the chosen macroeconomic indicators are not only affected by ICT, but also these indicators are affected by its own previous value and between these two determinants ICT is more important.

Limitations

The present study suffers from certain shortcomings such as availability of data for a short period that might affect the quality of the results. Perspective researchers can investigate the effect of ICT on other macroeconomic indicators like real wage rate, exchange rate, inflation rate, etc.

References

Ebrahimian, L. D. (2003). Socio-Economic Development in Iran through Information and Communications Technology. *Middle East Journal, LVII*(1), 93-111.

Kauffman, R. J. and Ajay, K. (2008). Impact of Information and Comunication Technologies on Country Development:Accounting for Area Interrelationships. *International Journal of Elecronic Commerce, XIII*(1), 11-58.

M., B.-L. (2003). An Analysis of The Determinants and Effects of ICT Diffusion in Developing Countries. *Information Technology for Development, X*(3), 151-169.

Prasad, K. (2012). E-Governance Policy for Modernizing Government through Digital Democracy in India. *Journal of Information Policy, II*, 182-203.

R., A. and C., Z. (2001). Value Creation in E-Commercial. *Strategic Management Journal, XXII*(6/7), 493-520.

Rangriz, V. and Basava, R. M. (2011). ICT Impact on Contribution of Human Resource Developent to Economic Growth. *The Indian Journal of Industrial Relations, XXXXVI*(4), 661-671.

S., C. (2007). Promoting Development through Information Technology Innovation:The IT Artefact,Artfulness,and Articulation. *Information Technology for Developent, XIII*(1), 49-69.

Sumanjeet. (2006). E-Governance:An overview in The Indian Context. *The Indian Journal of Political Science, LXVII*(4), 857-868.

In: e-Governance in India: Problems, Prototypes and Prospects ISBN: 978-1-63484-830-5
Editors: P. Kumar, R. Sharma and U. Kaushal

Chapter 8

DIGITAL AND INTERNET MARKETING: CRUCIAL BUSINESS MANAGEMENT LANDSCAPE

Pradeep Kautish*
Associate Professor- Marketing Area, Mody University of Science and Technology, Lakshmangarh, District Sikar, Rajasthan, India

ABSTRACT

The market dynamics is ever changing; there is a well visible decisive shift in the economic, demographic, psychological and psychographic indicators in the market. While the economic turbulence in the form of financial crisis is very much evident around us, the drastic changes in demographic, psychological and psychographic indicators of consumers are not apparent to a larger audience. However, marketers are increasingly getting cognizant of how these factors which are reshaping the business landscape. Today's consumer is a changed consumer; as per Philip Kotler today's consumer is price prone and choice rich consumer Since basic products and services are increasingly getting commoditized, in order to sustain, marketers can only differentiate in terms of quality of service, convenience, responsiveness and speed to market. 'Push strategy' adopted by erstwhile marketers, where products used to be simply pushed to consumers no longer works, there is a need to have 'pull strategy' which creates a pull in the minds of consumers by giving them superior quality of service in least possible time at best possible prices.

Keywords: digital marketing, web marketing, social media, eMarketing

1. INTRODUCTION

Technology enables business to expand quickly and efficiently. With correct technology, business can target a wider customer base and grow to higher performance levels

* Dr. Pradeep Kautish, Associate Professor- Marketing Area, Mody University of Science and Technology, Lakshmangarh, District Sikar, Rajasthan, E-mail: pradeepkautish.fms@ modyuniversity.ac.in.

(Brynjolfsson and Saunders, 2009). Role of technology will have to be looked at from a totally different context as a demand driver and synthesizer (Gleick, 2011). To cater to today's tech-savvy digital consumers, enterprises will have to redesign their IT delivery mechanism and leverage various disruptive technologies (Chui et al., 2010). Different technologies would be required to address different needs of today's consumers. (Khermouch & Green, 2001) Online shopping as preferred medium of purchase and social media as preferred communication channel were not in existence few years back; technology embedded systems for convenience and self-help services have become truth; cloud are ready to be agile forever, scalable, cost effective, and for faster business delivery; big data to understand customer needs in better way, stay relevant in the competitive marketplace and augmented reality to enhance customer experience (Davenport and Harris, 2010, Hubbard, 2010). These technologies are taking the center as well as corner stage in the leading enterprises of today and are likely to have the maximum impact on the way traditional markets were behaving few years back (Drucker, 1999). Transcending the times when customer used to come to the marketer, the current business scenario requires enterprises be in constant virtual touch with their customers (Hubbard, 2010). Therefore, understanding these digital technologies and the way these are being used by some of the leading enterprises worldwide becomes imperative for success and to remain successful.

2. What Is Marketing and Digital Marketing?

Marketing is a managerial process of communicating the value of a product or service to target customers or consumers, for the purpose of selling that product or service and of course by making the exchange or transaction profitable for the company. Marketing is an organizational function and a set of managerial processes for creating, developing, maintaining, delivering and communicating value to customers, and establishing mutually beneficial relationship. Marketing is the science of choosing target markets through effective as well as efficient market analysis and market segmentation, understanding consumer behavior and providing superior customer value. (Naik & Kalyan, 2003)

Marketing's core managerial processes are: (a) opportunity exploration or identification, (b) new product or service development, (c) customer attraction or engagement, (d) customer retention and loyalty building, and (e) profitably order fulfillment on time.

A company manages these entire core processes well will normally enjoy success in the marketplace. But when a company miserably fails at any one of these core processes, it will not survive in the market.

> "Marketing is the management process responsible for identifying, anticipating and satisfying customer requirements profitably." The Chartered Institute of Marketing (CIM)

In other words, the company, the product, the service, the ideas, the brand, how you communicate, the design, develop, print process, measuring effectiveness, market research and the psychology of consumer behavior all count as part of the bigger picture of 'marketing.'

The term 'digital marketing' was first used in the 1990s. In the 2000s and the 2010s, digital marketing became more sophisticated as an effective way to create a relationship with the consumer that has depth and relevance (Scott, 2010). Digital marketing is often referred to as "online marketing", "internet marketing" or "web marketing." The term "digital marketing" has grown in popularity over time, particularly in certain countries. In the USA "online marketing" is still prevalent, in Italy is referred as "web marketing" but in the UK and worldwide, "digital marketing" has become the most common term, especially after 2010.

"If your business is not on the Internet, then your business will be out of business."
Bill Gates

2.1. Digital Marketing Transition

This is very important to note that in 2014 and 2015 statistics showed digital marketing remained a growing field. With half-a-billion internet users by 2018 in India could birth a $200 billion digital economy and rewrite the whole business trajectory in the country. As per the data each 10% rise in internet penetration increases GDP by 1.08%, if internet were a sector its weight in GDP would be greater than that of agriculture or utilities. Increase in internet maturity in the west led to rise in GDP per capita of $500 on average in last 15 years. It took more than 50 years of industrial revolution to achieve the same. (Singh, 2015)

The most important questions today's businesses encounters before approaching target audiences across the globe irrespective physical presence or virtual one in the era of social web technologies:

- Is your company product or service easy to find online for customers?
- How to plan digital marketing, covering how to develop and manage new ways of contacting, engaging and managing digital customers. How to manage different digital channels (e.g., web, mobile, email), overall and in specialist technique areas, e.g., search engine marketing, search engine optimization, developing and managing digital applications (Haythornthwaite, 2005).
- How competitive marketing strategy is affected by the changes digital approaches allow you to make to business models, sometimes providing the ammunition to attack and bring down competitors, as many offline companies have discovered. (Stone, 2014)

  If your customers spend time on social networks then you should absolutely be there, no matter you like it or not and no matter they like you or not. Online presence is something which any business can't afford to ignore (Halligan and Shah, 2010).

  If your customers are not on social networks then you should allocate your substantial marketing budget elsewhere but the possibility of this option you can rule out without an exception. No matter you are able to figure out or not but your customer base is searching you online (Watts, 2004).
- Are you active in all the online channels where your target customers hang out please rest assured hang out doesn't mean they necessarily go there to search product or service to buy every time?

  Where are you likely to find your customers, you should be damn clear about it before you hold your horses for something else? Because any negligence on this front can put you in trouble in terms of your current as well as future business avenues. Do you really know without any exception how to leverage the strengths of each of the assets you plan to invest in for your company marketing initiatives, no matter even if it is a sponsorship campaign, league match or anything which you feel petty for now to consider because you create opportunity for your business?

- Do you have any easy, automated marketing process to engage them, communicate with them and follow up them over time; so it is high time not to sit tight at all because your competitors will have already got edge by the time any communication reach your doorstep?

  What is the desired customer action, where they are moving, where they feel company trying for them not only for their satisfaction but also delightment; mind it you are not going to predict or forecast it for your business it is available in their communication which took place last time? But you are sitting closing your eyes. You must be crystal clear on what this is all about before you begin any marketing initiative internally or externally, it does make visible distinction for your business in time to come. It always happen that many time people, group of people (community) seeing your actions and/or inactions seriously from varied lenses. And those actions and/or inactions make or mar your business.

Finally, can your target consumer connect with you on their own online turf? How marketing strategy for consumers is affected by the use of digital channels, in particular how the drive to use digital to reduce marketing costs may lead to reduced differentiation, even commoditization and consequent competitive weakness and lower margins and even revenues, and possibly to financial exposure because offline costs remain the same. (Stone, 2014)

In the last decade, digital advertising has matured dramatically to keep up with savvier consumers. The latest digital marketing technology yields data that helps businesses gain deeper insight into the performance of their marketing campaigns. Understanding the data and how to act on it to reach your consumers more effectively is the key to success in today's digital marketing (Varian, 2013).

2.2. Web 1.0, Web 2.0 and Web 3.0

Tech savvy people are familiar with Web 1.0 and Web 2.0 terminology very well. The way we use internet is evolving at a fast clip. Over last few years new term web 3.0 is slowly catching people's attention. We are not there yet, but web 3.0 is being discussed quite often in blogosphere and technology sites. Lot of non-techie folks asks what exactly the differences in these approaches. So, here is the simple explanation of each. If you search Google you will find hundreds of different definitions and comparisons, however, the following simple explanation is how we can comprehend it. Everyone has his own take on it. (Wikipedia, 2015)

Web 1.0: The information published on the web in a static manner. It is like your word document on the web with pictures and formatting done neatly. Hyper-linking the web-pages and bookmarking were two of the most important aspect of Web 1.0 world. Even today more than 70% users are only familiar with Web1.0. (Natalie, 2007)

Web 2.0: This term was originally coined by Tim O'Reilly. The information published in web 2.0 world is very different from web1.0. There is a very high importance given on usability and sharing. The information published in Web 2.0 world travels like wild fire, either partially or fully. Web 2.0 world has less clutter coupled with easy retrieval of precise information and furthermore building upon that information and sharing it further. Widgets and Tagging are two important features of Web 2.0. Social media and User Generated Content (UGC) are characteristics of what is called Web 2.0 or the "participative web." Web 2.0 can be seen as a trend or tendency rather than a web epoch. Elements of Web 2.0 have existed since the beginnings of the Internet (Lincoln, 2009). On the contemporary, web, compared to the situation about a decade ago, is becoming increasingly easier for users to create their own online content, with minimum technical knowledge. The contemporary online ubiquity of blogs, YouTube videos, comments on news articles or blogs, and podcasts all demonstrate this aspect. Subject to computer literacy and access, anyone can be a creator of Internet content. A decade ago, web content was created by corporations and relatively small communities of technical enthusiasts and discussion, participation, and virtual communities used to occur on more arbitrary areas of the Internet (Barabasi, 2003). Internet Relay Chat (chat rooms), web forums, multi-user domains, and online games are examples of such content. The participatory aspect of the web is now an everyday reality to many users. When reading the news, internet users can see and rate comments, as well as make comments. Many Internet users interact with overlapping online and offline community over digital social networks like Facebook. (Free Encyclopedia, 2011)

Web 3.0: There are varied perceptions of what Web 3.0 is all about. It is purely a word coined as the next version of Web2.0. One basic thing that everyone accepts is Web 3.0 will be a maze/network of application working together homogeneously. The users can do anything and everything they want from a single source on the web. There is yet a lot of time for Web 3.0 world to arrive.

In the Web 2.0 era, first generation e-commerce tactics are no longer compatible to deliver the winning edge position in the marketplace for choice rich and value prone consumers; the value which they derive in form of money, relationship, passion, action and esteem. Today, organizations are looking for innovative ways to unleash the power of the social web technologies provided by Internet and the next new frontier is the realm of social web media and networking.

Social web media runs the gamut from social networking sites like Facebook and MySpace to micro blogging forums like Twitter, to wikis, virtual communities and shared multimedia. Social media offers great strengths over traditional marketing approaches including collaboration, low barriers to entry (in cost as well as usability), and the ability to edit and revise content in real time to accommodate long awaited profitable interface with target consumers. Because research data says that today 97% of internet users go for online searches; in order to do so they likes, dislikes, comments, opinions etc. on almost all disposed content from consumer centric to community centric, to people centric to organization centric and to society centric to country centric they have enormous issues and concern to express when researching about products or services offered by corporations. They look for all information whether solicited or unsolicited about the company's product or service they buy, consume and suggest to any other potential consumer. We are living in an over communicated society which is not only exciting but also equally challenging for the organizations to accommodate business goals with public concerns.

Web 2.0, virtual customer environments and fast emerging personal communication technology are defining rules of the game for corporations. Web 2.0 activities, such as watching user-generated videos, posting blogs, writing micro blogs and participating in social networks some time with motives some time for enjoyment, are quickly capturing the attention and time online of more and more internet users. Digital technology has revolutionized the way in which people communicate and share information at local, national and international levels. Management professionals now have to grapple with the most powerful and challenging media ever evolve and transformed the business perspectives - word-of-mouth connections that join anybody to everybody in any target market by no more than six links. (Carroll, 2010) After the 'traditional media' and the 'new media,' the next buzz among the management professionals, therefore, is 'social media.' From Facebook, LinkedIn, Myspace and YouTube to blogs, social media on the internet is the most promising new way to reach out your target audiences no matter you talk about consumers who can join your product or service purchasing gang or prospective clients and potential or prospective employees who can join your organization in future.

2.3. Social Media Interface

Social media is a term used to refer to online web based technologies and practices that are used to share opinions and information, promote discussions, forums and build relationships in form of formal and/or informal set up. Social media services and tools involve a combination of technology, telecommunications and some kind of social interactions, sharing ideas and discussing openly about issues which affect all people in varied ways. They can use a variety of different formats, for example text, pictures, video and audio that's why it is part of media revolution. The term 'social media' is applied to the tools in question, their applications and collaboratively developed path propounding best practices for business as well as society.

Wikipedia…Facebook…Flickr…MySpace…RSS feeds…..YouTube… digg.com… blogs- Social media is almost everywhere and we all take part in the growing conversation in one shape or form whether we want to it or not; intentionally or unintentionally we become the part of the whole conversation. As social web 2.0 technology brings the global marketplace within reach of just about everyone, today's businesses are seeing more and more of the value of social media to help reach new markets across the street and around the world. Statistics show, in fact, that a staggering 90% of companies today report that social media is an important tool for growing their customer base and their bottom line which is an encouraging preposition for all stake holders.

Modern digitalized world has given birth to Generation 'C' where 'C' stands for Consumer 2.0 and –

- Connected
- Content
- Community
- Co-creator
- Conversation
- Creative

Table 2.1. Comparison between Web 1.0 and Web 2.0

Platform	Web 1.0	Web 2.0
User's Role	Reading	Writing
Communication Mode	Corporate Communication	Peer Communication
Content	Text Content	Multi Media
User's Online Behavior	Directed Behavior	Browsing
User's Objective	Information	Interaction
User's Interaction	Mass Communication	Personal Communication
Rights/Ownership	Website Owner	You

2.4. User Generated Content (UGC)

UGC refers to content that is created by Internet users, often through content platforms such as BlogSpot, WordPress, Twitter, Facebook, Instagram, Wikipedia, and YouTube. UGC includes blog posts, podcasts, online videos, tweets and status updates. There is no exact definition of the term. According to an often cited definition from an OECD report, UGC is content made publicly available over the Internet, involves a "certain amount of creative effort", and is "created outside of professional routines and practices." UGC usually created by amateurs, rather than professionals and is "undertaken without the expectation of remuneration or profit." Motivating factors for creating UGC include "connecting with peers, achieving a certain level of fame, notoriety or prestige, and self-expression."

In comparison to traditional media content, UGC development and distribution is neither expensive nor technically complex. Content quality is not guaranteed through traditional media gatekeepers. Content curation (selection of content for publishing and dissemination) is not centralized, as it is with traditional or "old media." With old media "relative to the potential supply, only a few works are eventually distributed," while with UGC internet access and computer and web literacy are the only prerequisites for distribution.

In the history of mankind, communication technology remained decisional pivotal force for success or failure of any civilization. It was one of the critical natural instinct which was always compelling and impelling human race to devise new mechanisms for communication processes. This communication desire was the most important factor responsible for development of so many languages around the world. Once language got into existence than it was communication technology which provided motives to communicate as much as possible. Need to mention telephone was the one invention which can be considered as a landmark in communication medium and communication technology. Telephone created some sought of different and interesting communication landscape. But it took almost more than 40 years to reach out common masses, for many years telephone was a commodity or service for classes. A class of consumers used to enjoy the benefits of this product. After many years it reached to the people for their personal disposal. The most significant and path breaking technological advancement that has created the most powerful marketing impact to date is the Internet. Figure 1 shows the dynamics of digital transformations over the years.

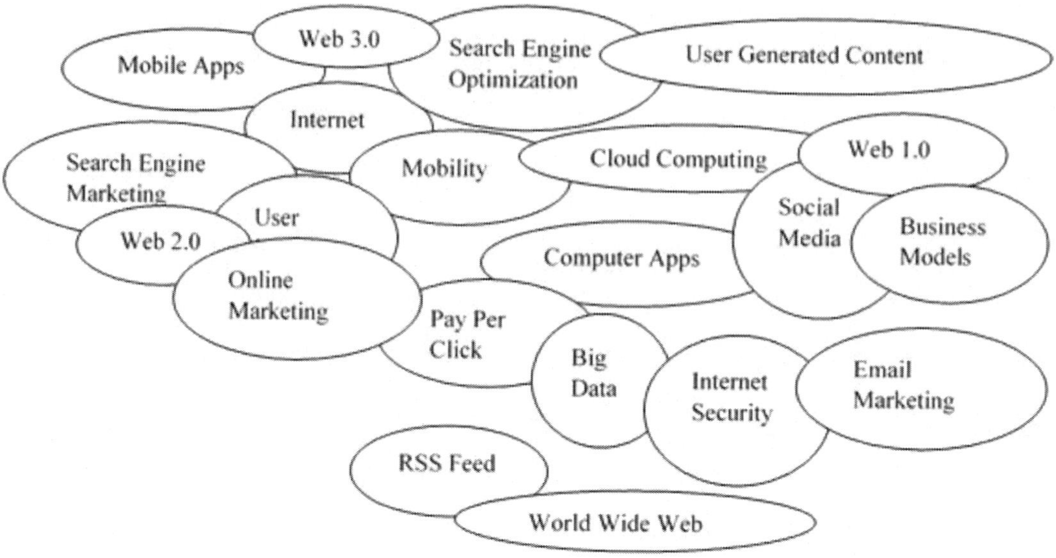

Figure 2.1. Dynamics of Digital Transformations.

When digital marketing revelation started in early 90s, the promise of digital marketing channels was to deliver the intended message to the intended audience at the intended time- a game-changing upgrade over traditional marketing channels. Digital media marketing has become popular as savior of marketing data collection, synthesis, analysis, and measurement that would yield the most efficient, optimized marketing programs. Fast-forward 15 years, and we've learned that achieving that reality isn't impossible but can be far more difficult than it seems at first glance.

Today's digital marketing landscape is more complex than ever before. The continuous and rapid introduction of new platforms, tools, data sources, and media consumption devices (such as mobile devices and tablets) have created an environment that can make any marketer's head spin. The challenge now lies in identifying which unique composition of all those choices is required to produce the outcomes needed to achieve your digital marketing goals and objectives.

Digital marketing is great at creating, developing and maintaining data about consumers, what they like and dislike, and where they have been online. Advance understanding of digital marketing helps company work smarter by providing the managers with the approach and information need to understand and utilize the data that exists across the entire digital landscape. Hopefully the original digital promise that got everyone so excited in the first place will become a reality for you, and you'll have a better understanding of why digital marketing channels continue to draw more investment in time and money away from traditional marketing channels.

The Internet or in other words, World Wide Web is a typically client-server application that provides a graphical user interface for information presentation, dissemination, and demonstration so that interactive communication can take place. In information technology parlance, we can communicate in almost any way imaginable over a network of computers with the help of Internet. And the computers add previously unprecedented functionality to the business situations. As it is the primary goal in marketing communication is to add value to a product in the eyes of a prospective, potential or current customer. Another way to say this is the fulfillment of customer's needs, wants and desires. The Web is an exciting opportunity for all businesses as marketers to add value to products and services and fulfill needs, wants, and even subtle desires through the use of interactive information presentation and business transaction systems. Over a period of time by continuous investment in this sphere, we can build successful marketing relationships with business entities through this evolving process. These kinds of Internet based systems can be highly effective for marketing communications to target markets. (Barnett, 2011)

Business success lies in its effective marketing strategies. The overall marketing strategy involves advertising, public relations, promotions and sales with main aim to create awareness of products among customers and build personalize relationships. Without marketing, business can offer best products or services in an industry, but no potential customers would know about it. Without marketing, sales may crashed and companies have to face loss therefore marketing is an important aspect to increase sales in an organization. Nowadays, there are huge changes in the way marketing strategies are apply; the way sales forces promote and sell the products; the way in which communication with clients, suppliers and our own staff; the way we reach the target market share; the way we make goods available to customers due to evolution of technology and opening of global markets, the information oriented world i.e., customers are educated about products.

Emerging technologies lead to personalize the consumer experience in real time and almost everywhere with a click.

Due digital era, consumer demands focus on four areas:

- Now: anywhere at any time by a click customers wants to interact with fast response.
- Can me: customers want to do new things as kinds of information are available effectively in ways that create value for them.
- For me: The data stored will be personalized to their needs and targeted specifically to them.
- Simply: all interactions need to be easy and simple.
- Quick: they will expect companies to reply as soon as possible as nowadays customers are cash rich and time poor.

Due to on-demand marketing and evolution of technology and increase in availability of information through search technologies encourages the consumers to share, compare different products, and share their experiences as feedback; and add a "wherever" dimension by a click to the digital environment. So digital marketing plays an important role in increasing the overall sales in an organization by providing a direct relationship with customer with transparency and integrity.

Why essentially corporations need to be online and why company has to seriously think about Internet Marketing?

- The target market and competitors are already there so it is inevitable to move with them. If you market and sell products or services to a middle-class clientele, you need to extend your strategy to include the internet.
- Normally, Internet users expect the highest level of convenience and full information at their fingertips. Companies need an attractive website as central point of contact

for customers. If the desired details don't come up in web search, it is for sure your company will get ignored for business.

- Now day's customers are fickle mind. They will not expend a lot of energy to find your company online. Even worse situation will be, if your competitors are easy to find online, your potential customers will happily turn to them without any hesitation.
- Since Indian consumers are using, socializing and buying on the web and especially online advertising spend is growing- now is the high time to move marketing efforts into the online sphere and capitalize on a new and connected audience waiting for your company.
- Audiences want to interact with and converse about your company offerings. Give them the opportunity to do it in a mediated space, become part of the active discussion with them and establish everlasting contact with them.
- Online marketing is almost always cheaper and more targeted than traditional. You can reach the best customers at the lowest price per customer if you compare it.

The Internet is one of the most advanced tools that can be applied to marketing management. Increasingly corporations are incorporating the Internet into their marketing strategies. Growing use of the Internet as a consumer-oriented marketing tool has been common now and has already accepted as a standard marketing tool by the vast majority of businesses. Likewise, the Internet- the web, emails, blogs, social networks, and newsgroups- are being increasingly and widely used for marketing programs. The Internet is an interactive global communications medium that changed the playing field, and language, for marketers everywhere. It has the potential to impact and influence the market as well as marketing dynamics to the extent of strategic implications of the same. (Porter, Competitive Advantage, Creating and Sustaining Superior Performance, 1985) Still very few organizations fully understand the technicality of internet marketing. But it is fact that companies need to have fair understanding of internet marketing methods in-house, in order to understand why certain things need to be done and in which context. Companies can then make this vital decision to either do everything in-house, or manage the process and outsource the technical side to search engine optimization firm.

Growing use of the Internet for business marketers is a modern reality and need of hour. Broadcast media such as television, radio and print media such as newspapers, and other traditional marketing avenues will continue to be used in the market but the corporations who will ignore the Internet will lose the race for sustained competitive advantage. On the other hand, those who have embraced the Internet have demonstrated its power and are innovators. Many trade experts believe that it is only the beginning of a technological leap in future it is going to be even drastic if organizations will not fully appreciate it.

> "The Internet is a worldwide network of computers that provides a highly interactive system for marketing communication. Nothing more and nothing less." Donny Emerick

3. Internet Marketing

Internet marketing is one of the fastest growing, most vibrant and most exciting branch of marketing today. As the world is becoming even more connected, and in order to keep up with web developments and trends has emerged even vital for marketers try out reaching new target audiences- who are more choice prone, discerned, fragmented and cynical than ever. Technology, design and software are changing at such a high rate that it seems almost impossible to keep up with web trends. Products and services are evolving and adapting to the online sphere e.g., we have new avenues for shopping Flipkart and Snapdeal etc. The web is constantly shifting its models, growing with its penetration potential and changing its size-everything is fleeting in order to keep pace with environment. As properly understood, this innovative platform can be harnessed to complement existing marketing practices, extend operations with wider reach, and create new horizon of opportunities. The key lies to successful marketing over the Internet are creating, developing, and applying the strengths of the medium to proven traditional marketing practices in innovative ways. Traditionally the four Ps of marketing given by E. Jerome McCarthy namely, Price, Product, Place, and Promotion, have been considered the cornerstones of a firm's marketing strategy. The use of the Web as a business-to-business or business-to-consumer or consumer-to-consumer marketing tool includes the fifth P of marketing, 'People' and fits pretty well within this traditional marketing framework. It is used as a promotional tool, a distribution channel, sometimes it is the product, and its use may affect price.

What is Internet marketing?

The evolution of the internet has triggered a fundamental and radical change in the way that customers initiate a purchase activity. Substantially large number of consumers now starts their buying process by researching on the internet. That shift in consumer behavior has created a tremendous threat to traditional businesses, and a huge opportunity for newer, smaller organizations.

Afuah and Tucci (2003) enunciate the Internet as *"technology with many properties that have the potential to transform the competitive landscape in many industries while at the same time creating whole new industries."*

Internet marketing is often called online marketing or eMarketing as well but in practice they have some similarities and dissimilarities also, it is essentially any marketing activity that is conducted online through the use of internet technologies. It comprises not only advertising that is usually shown on websites, but also other kinds of online activities like email and social networking also. Every aspect of internet marketing is digital, meaning that it is electronic information that is transmitted on a computer or similar device or gadget like cellphone etc., though naturally it can tie in with traditional offline advertising and sales too. Driven by unending globalization of business operations, fierce competition and even more particularly, new ever evolving consumer trends and technological developments in all spheres, marketing today is no longer what it used to be just few years back. Marketing has changed so much even progressive organizations are struggling for existence. Now the game playing turf got changed so much and old ways of doing business are gone. Businesses have to continuously keep up with new marketing developments in order to stay ahead of the competition. Keeping up to date with changes in demand and using technology to understand, anticipate, reach and satisfy customers are key differentiators. Now Internet is one of the most powerful tools available today to meet, greet, treat target market and reach directly to your customers. Search engine optimization is the tool to implement internet marketing successful. Typically search engine optimizations firms have advanced know how about technical issues, but they don't necessarily understand how to portray your company's business online. They will do what they are told to do as far as the instructional mechanism is concerned, or they will tend to do a very good job of just certain aspects of search engine optimization. However, you know your company businesses best and that's why it is even more important for you to understand what you can and cannot do, or should or should not do, from an internet marketing perspective. Internet marketing is not just SEO rather it is much beyond it but non-technical people do not have much idea about it. Internet marketing refers to advertising and/or marketing efforts that use the Web based technology and email to drive direct sales via e-commerce or e-business. Aside from the necessity of being visible to consumers, the Internet offers the promise of being the "great leveler." It allows smaller and less-known companies to compete effectively with larger and more mature ones on their turf. Internet marketing, which is also called online marketing, is any web based tool, strategy or method of getting the company name out to the public domain. The internet advertisements can take many different forms and/or formats and some internet strategies focus on subtle messages rather than clear-cut advertisements. Advertising agencies helps generating and placing the ad copy, an ad server who technologically delivers the ad and tracks visitor statistics, and advertising affiliates who do independently promote work for the advertiser.

Before the Internet technology landscape, there were many different ways to promote or advertise, with the help of different media such as radio, TV, newspapers, magazines, and some others were telemarketing or pamphlets or leaflets etc. Usually the goal was to make aware the prospective and potential buyers, get a company and/or product name, a statement etc. communicated to as many customers as possible for the smallest price possible to get maximum mileage. In fact if we try to understand the dynamics of modern marketing, the most significant technological advancement that has created the greatest marketing innovation is the Internet. The Internet or the World Wide Web (www) abbreviation continues to radically transform the way we do business in years to come. Most critically, it has turned on its head, the way businesses communicate with the consumer and consumer communicate to the business. The paradigm shift is in the establishment of the dialogue between these two entities. Consumers are now in better control of the reins of purchasing power and they can command over business as never before. Now it is the customers who are calling the shots. And this has become possible, in no small way, because of the Internet only. Business can no longer afford to sell what they produce rather they have to produce what consumer looking for desperately. They have to listen to their customers, understand their needs and produce what they want at best price and value proposition. Businesses need to realize this very fact that in modern wired world, if they are not online, that means they are not on demand no matter their product offerings are good or they offer it in value for money. The Internet offers a vast array of marketing advantages and unmatched opportunities to reach more consumers than ever before. As you are talking one-to-one rather you are one-to-many and in some cases many-to-many. Broadly it includes email marketing, search engine marketing (SEM), social media marketing (SMM), many other forms and/or formats of display advertising (including web banner advertising), and mobile advertising to name a few. Like any other media, online marketing frequently involves both an identified publisher, who integrates advertisements into its online content, and an advertiser, who provides the advertisements to be displayed on the publisher's content. That initial consumer online activity could involve a Google web-search, consulting an industry hub or participating in some social media forum. The point is, if your company is not present in one or more of those online places, the potential consumers don't know that you exist and you are probably excluded from the rest of their buying activity. In modern technology driven world, Internet marketing is growing and vibrant section of marketing because the world has becomes ever more connected, keeping up with latest developments and business trends are vital for marketers. The company offerings in terms of products and services are evolving and adapting to the online sphere of the market. Now the relative importance of Internet for marketing purposes depends upon the nature of its products and services with the behavior patterns of the target audience.

In broad sense, Internet marketing has three basic principles to follow:

1) Immediacy- The web changes are always at a blistering pace and normally online audiences, whose attention spans are so short, expect on-the-minute updates and information which they require for their specific purposes. To keep up the favor, fervor and attention of this elite group of individuals sometime called 'techy,' you must respond to online messages and interact with communities as fast as possible in order to maintain relationship with them.
2) Personalization- Online customers are no longer faceless, nameless entities of a broad target audience they are well informed individuals who want to be addressed personally and want to be provided everything they look on online platforms. This is wonderful opportunity for marketers to use the wealth of personal information available online to company benefit by targeting the relevant people precisely, personally and of course profitably.
3) Relevance- The communication which is taking place online must be interesting, exciting and relevant to the audience; otherwise it will simply be ignored and investment is going to be a waste by the organization. With all the information that is competing for audience's attention, we must find a way to stand out and engage them. The best way to do this is by giving them exactly what they want, when they want it and where they want.

3.1. Digital Marketing

It refers to the use of the internet and digital media capabilities to helps sell your company product or services. It includes both direct response marketing and indirect marketing elements and uses a range of technologies to help connect businesses to their customers. Digital marketing or e- marketing or Internet marketing refers to a set of powerful tools and methodologies used for promoting products and services through the Internet or World Wide Web.

3.2. Conventional Marketing

It refers to any type of promotion advertising or campaign that has been in use by companies for years, methods of conventional marketing can include print advertisement like for e.g., newsletter, newspapers, print advertisement etc. Digital marketing and conventional marketing are different: one focuses on the web and the other focuses on media like print, television, radio, and direct mail. Digital marketing and conventional marketing are used to attract qualified customers and build brand awareness in your market, and they work together to power successful marketing results.

3.3. Symbiotic Marketing

As the traditional site-centric approach continues to be plagued with increased costs and decreased effectiveness, alternatives are being sought. An alternative strategy is the symbiotic marketing approach, which is based on the concept of mutuality. (Lockett & Blackman, 2001)

Symbiotic Marketing assumes that it is not impossible to protect content such as intellectual property and concentrates on what needs to be done in order to build and defend a customer base. The model works under the assumption that by making the service available to a multitude of sites, the probability of new customers finding the service is increased. "This strategy seems to be appropriate for business-to-business markets since the most important site for a service to be referenced is their own company's Intranet site or access page Internet coverage of the service." The symbiotic marketing model has a centralized site, but other sites are asked to incorporate the service on their own sites. "The service is taken to the site the customer wants to use rather than the customer having to go to the service provider's central site." (Lockett & Blackman, 2001) An example of this is Amazon. Amazon encourages other sites to become associates and provides Amazon services on their sites, and the companies have a number of different ways to link to Amazon's site.

The symbiotic marketing model is the best strategy to use when building a customer base if:

(1) "The service is based on changing data;"
(2) "The service is viewed as adding value to the host site and not seen as a competitive threat;"
(3) "The service is simple for other sites to implement;" and
(4) "The feedback from clients can be immediately used to enhance the service."

In addition to the above-mentioned scenarios, the nature of the targeted service market may be a factor in an organization deciding whether or not to use the symbiotic marketing model. (Lockett & Blackman, 2001) highlighted three examples of situations where this model may be the best strategy.

These examples include:

- "Where markets are fragmented and there are no big established dominant players in the industry."
- "Where market segments have had traditionally long product development cycles."
- "Where the customer base is in a business-to-business rather than a consumer context."

One of the disadvantages of this model is that building links requires time, and it may be more time than some companies are willing to commit. In addition, the model may be difficult to implement in a large organization with a well-developed marketing strategy.

4. Importance of Internet/Digital Marketing

There are many reasons as to why internet and digital marketing is so important for business however let we understand a few primaries of them.

4.1. Track Conversions

The best fact about internet marketing is that you can track every single step while you are carrying out an online marketing campaign from a customer's visit to lead generation and to sales. Analytics is a tool that allows you to measure every part of your campaign in online marketing. Whereas on the other hand you can only measure your ROI in the traditional marketing campaign that too though readership and footfall.

4.2. Specific Targeting

Unlike the conventional marketing you can segment your clients base in to different groups and then can target your add accordingly. You can forward your add to the targeted audience based on age, location and various other demographic factors related with your audience. Internet marketing helps you target a particular section of the masses if you need to. Depending on the age, location, demographics you can forward your ads, promote your product or services to the targeted audience.

4.3. Wide Reach

As the word itself specifies internet marketing is marketing over the internet and we all know about the wide reach internet has. Anybody anywhere can see you as in through your ads irrespective of the region and other factors, depending on your campaign settings.

4.4. Economical and Cost Effective

Being one of the most cost effective media for advertising, internet marketing is becoming everybody's first choice when it comes to advertising economically and at relatively faster rate. The cost of starting a website and conducting other online marketing campaigns to establish online presence is minimal when compared to costs of conventional media of advertising. Digital marketing is more cost-effective than advertising in traditional media like television, radio, and print media. It helps to reach a wider audience of qualified customers, generate new revenue, and get the data you need to accurately measure your return on investment.

4.5. Interactive in Design

Being quite interactive in design, online marketing offers users to take the command and browse through wherever they want unlike conventional media where the information is conveyed and it depends on its fate whether you watch it or overlook it as you don't have any other options to interact with it. Users can anytime go ahead and browse through various information on your website as per their needs.

4.6. Augments Customer Engagement and Trust Building

Internet marketing lets the customer to interact and get engaged. Through blogs and other mediums you provide a lot of useful information to the users that lead to great trust building between you and the consumers. We can simply acquire new clients via ex. Social Media channels. When doing so, ensure you segment them into different customer groups according to their interests. Later, we will be able to interact with them and encourage to various actions.

4.7. Online Branding

The main reason to start an online marketing campaign is to increase the product awareness among the audiences. While browsing through the internet people might come across your brand and might become interested in what you are offering.

4.8. Increases Sales

By letting the customer to shop online, internet marketing is becoming everyone's favorite. Besides, online shopping is in and is never going to be out. As per the estimations it will only increase with the passes of time and not decrease bringing more and more revenue for your business through online marketing.

4.9. Measurable

It's not easy to know how many people heard your radio spots or read your newspaper ad. But you can find out exactly how many times your digital marketing messages were displayed to local customers actively researching a purchase, how many times they were clicked, which web pages they visited after clicking, how long they looked around, and more.

4.10. Accessibility

The site should be easy enough for beginners, accessible by those with special needs, and possibly available in other language if needed. E Marketing is easily accessible than other marketing.

So don't delay in thinking whether you should go online or not. Go ahead and plan an internet marketing strategy for your business and implement them as soon as possible. However, if you are unaware with the technicalities of internet marketing either you can hire an internet marketing professional or can get trained in internet marketing yourself to take your business to the next level.

From the mid-'90s, the digital marketing landscape has undergone tremendous change. For a good 10 years there were two dominant media types, although we've relabeled them through the years. The first is paid media, either in the form of paid search (Google AdWords, Google AdSense) or display advertising (DoubleClick banner ads, Pay per Click). Paid media is literally just that—digital marketing channels that a brand pays to utilize for business objectives.

The second is owned media. This is a generic term for any media marketing asset or platform that a company owns, controls, and utilizes to reach a prospective audience. Some of the most common forms of owned media are dot-com brand websites, email marketing to subscribers, and company blogs. For both paid and owned media, clicks still rule as the dominant data to collect and analyze. However, tracking what happens after a user clicks on a link can be useful, but it can't answer all the questions.

In the past several years, there has been the emergence of a third media type, called earned media. Some say it's new; others think it's simply a new label for what public relations professionals have historically called free media, something generated by word of mouth, buzz, or a communication "going viral" (Dye, 2000). But clearly there is transition from Word-of-Mouth (WOM) to Word-of-Mouse (WOM) (Sernovitz, 2006).

The advance data and tools are available today can give the company the marketing insight need to improve digital performance. Now company better understand both the qualitative and quantitative dimensions of a prospective audience for their business. This knowledge can be personalize user experiences and facilitate a real value exchange that meets users' needs and expectations. Simply put, the company never been in a better position to generate the desired outcomes and predict future behavior thanks to the robust ecosystem of marketing data and consumer analytics tools. Each digital marketing type contains several channels that serve a purpose and play a role in overall marketing mix. The data and analytics associated with each helps in determining how much or how little of a role each should play. No digital marketing strategy can succeed based on only one digital media type.

5. Forms of Internet and Digital Marketing

5.1. Search Engine Marketing

It is a crucial part of web commerce. With the help of search engine marketing a particular product or company website will get visualize on search engine particularly

Google. The main focus of this strategy is to place highly searched keywords in particular places of several web pages of a website. It aims to provide useful content to target market, and improve the overall rank of the website on search engines.

- Pay per Click: It refers to the number of users viewed our website. It is a process to drive targeted traffic on website. It is a predictable process as one can calculate the response of the users and can act as a fastest lead generation in a sales organization
- Search Engine Optimization: Is ensuring that our website is ranked higher to the top in a list of digital searches. It can help potential customers to find product and gives an organisation a chance to attract customers for service. The main aim is to increase the visibility of the website on search engine. With keywords that commonly used and easily remembered by user the website of company can attract traffic of potential customers.

5.2. Email Marketing

It is a primary way to build a relationship with customers. Email marketing involves product offers, coupons, customer newsletters or more informational updates. It increase customer loyalty and provide company a method to build relationship with customers.

5.3. Content Marketing

It is a marketing process of acquiring customers through sharing the content on media. The main focus of organization to communicate the information to users or potential customers, create awareness about new products and service and about customers. The content marketing has four aims:

- Shared information about new product or service.
- Discussion helps an organization to start communication with potential customers.
- Sales generation as prospects is easy to convert into sales through communication.

So content marketing is a powerful tool of digital marketing to get maximum number of potential customers.

5.4. Social Marketing

It is a process of attracting customers through social sites. Businesses establish a presence on social networks like Face book, Twitter, LinkedIn and Google+ in order to engage their digital audience, building followers and to drive traffic back to their website or blog. Nowadays social media is used to promote content marketing techniques. Making digital company profiles on social networking sites is free that is the best thing about social media marketing as it not require heavy investment,.

5.5. Video Marketing

YouTube is the second largest search engine and the third most visited site by the users all over the world after Google. So video marketing can be another way to promote the products and generate sales in an organization. By using video, an advertisement can go viral on Internet lead to version of Word Of Mouth marketing. (Dobele, David, & Michael, 2005) To gain attraction of right customers within less time a single commercial video is enough.

5.6. Article Marketing or Blogging

It is platform where articles are written about specific topics and the articles build backed to website or direct traffic toward a product. Blogging are actually viewed as sharing personal experience to the world which can act as feedback for an organization. Blogs tend to get high trust ratings from people especially if the writer is known to be someone in a specific field.

Table 5.1. Traditional Marketing versus Digital/Internet Marketing

Factors	**Traditional marketing**	**Digital/internet marketing**
Communication	In traditional marketing, the communication takes place in one direction, with one person communicating with a large group of potential customers.	But in digital marketing multi-directional communication means communication with the consumers by company and any consumers can communicate their problems directly on company website and response to them easy quick and easy.
Scheduling and planning	Traditional marketing is well-planned out involves a campaign covering a long length of time and following a specific schedule.	While digital marketing can attract large number of customers through a video or a blog in less time.
Availability	With the traditional marketing, a person can respond to customers in a specified time period.	with digital marketing at any given moment, a customer request or complaint will get a response within a day or two as it requires no physical contact as it can be done anywhere at any movement by clicks and act as a feedback for company.
Scope	Traditional marketing uses less resources and reach less number of customers which result in specific targeting of customers.	Through Digital marketing the content is largely available to the public as a whole and anyone can access the content through a click, which increasing scope of business irrespective of target audience.

Table 5.2. Advantages and Disadvantages of Digital/Internet Marketing

	Advantages	Disadvantages
1.	Extremely low risk as less investment involved for promotion.	Technology oriented.
2.	Reduction in costs through technology automation and use of electronic media	Security, privacy issues.
3.	Faster response to queries of customers and helps to build strong relationship.	Lack of trust of users.
4.	Increased ability to measure and collect data as data can be tracked digital and helps to predict the sales patterns and behaviour of users.	Higher transparency of pricing.
5.	Increased interactivity.	Transparencies of information as consumers are educated.
6.	Boundless universal accessibility.	Maintenance costs of software's and hardware's.
7.	Increased exposure of products and services	Lack of managerial skills
8.	Opens the possibility to a market as extensive coverage of media.	

5.7. Affiliate Marketing

Someone else products or services is promoted by third party and receiving a fee for the referral. Affiliates market their own products, such as through a web site, and have links to other unrelated websites, but have common interest for consumers. They are rewarded with bonus or incentives for the number of times someone links from their site to the targeted site.

5.8. Digital and Internet Marketing Strategy

The use of the Internet is exploding; people spend a lot of time on the Internet because there is a wealth of information to be found. In addition, many consumers feel comfortable purchasing online and value the Internet's capacity for providing information about different products and services. As a result, Internet marketing has blossomed and become a key part of many companies' advertising efforts.

The Internet has reduced costs associated with starting and running a small business, which allows these companies to have an Internet presence because the medium is affordable. Companies have also found the Internet to be an effective communication tool for customers, potential consumers, and other businesses, and the advent of social media further enabled companies to connect and interact directly with consumers.

As a result, marketing has experienced significant changes in how it operates. The Internet poses both opportunities and threats to the field of traditional marketing. When creating a marketing plan, organizations must determine:

(1) If the tool is useful for marketing their products,
(2) Which products can benefit from Internet marketing?
(3) When it is best to use traditional marketing, Internet marketing, or a combination of both, and
(4) What pitfalls need to be avoided so organizations do not experience failure when using Internet marketing.

Internet marketing research has provided years' worth of valuable findings.

5.9. Important Considerations for Successful Digital and Internet Marketing

In case of Internet marketing in Indian context, it is always advisable to keep certain realities and risks in mind before any heavy investments in this business.

- Relatively few people are online from rural areas as compare to urban markets, and those who are usually have limited data and slow connections which is a reality. Anything that you put online has to be accessible to the lowest common denominator in order to get benefit.
- Many Indian consumers browse the web on their cellphones so the content should not be too bulky to download on small devises. Keep your marketing campaign mobile friendly whenever possible.
- Indian consumers are cautious browsers if you compare them with western counterparts; they are very unlikely to make online impulse purchase decisions or to trust a new brand or product that they find online.
- Though India is the country which produces maximum computer engineers in the world at the same time we should always remember that still in India basic computer skills are generally quite limited, so online content has to be clear and easy to use; otherwise, customers will simply give up.
- We need to adhere to legal and ethical codes of conduct, not doing so can lead to harm to our brand image at best, or severe legal sanctions at worst. Make sure you are informed about the latest laws regarding electronic communication.
- As more human interaction is done online, virtual communication becomes tiring and disconnects people from the real world; any interaction online must be personal and supported by offline marketing efforts like after sales services offered by the company.
- Privacy or its slow erosion is a big concern for web users. As the borders between public and private life begin to blur, customers are wary of giving out personal data.

5.10. Opportunities for Digital and Internet Marketing

The Internet opened many new avenues for companies to market new products and provided opportunities to restructure how they were marketing their established products. Benefits of the Internet include its ability to market globally, provide a free market without regulations and barriers to entry, and determine which products sell well in an online format. Companies can decide which products are best to sell online. In addition, they can determine whether they want to sell on their own site or sell products through online retailers such as Amazon. The Internet provides opportunities and challenges for the four Ps of marketing (price, promotion, product, and place) by being an unpredictable distribution channel, a powerful marketing communication and promotional tool, an effective marketing research tool, and an efficient tool for segmenting and targeting consumers and customers.

The Internet can be considered an integrated marketing communication tool. It has the capability to combine the efforts of direct marketing, advertising, and public relations.

5.10.1. Direct Marketing

Companies can communicate and promote products and services to a target market by using e-mail, customized pages, and promotional systems. For example, a company can offer a free product if members of a target market go to a particular survey link to answer questions. The feedback can be used to customize a promotional opportunity to that particular market. However, if the company uses e-mail as a mechanism, the company must ensure that its promotional e-mails are not considered spam—unwanted marketing messages—by their recipients.

5.10.2. Online Advertising

Companies can target global markets and make sure their ads are seen by consumers who will buy their products. Organizations are able to track the effectiveness of their advertising campaigns by tracking how many people see their ad and how many people visit the site based on a particular ad. In addition, the cost of online advertising is typically cheaper than traditional advertising methods such as print or television advertising. In some cases, a company may pay for an advertisement only when a user clicks on it; this system is known as pay-per-click (PPC) advertising.

5.10.3. Public Relations

Companies may also use the Internet to provide corporate information about the organization and its products. Potential customers will be able to find information such as names and background of the senior management team, investor information, history, and product information. Through the use of social media, companies can respond to complaints or other customer concerns quickly and effectively, thus managing their online reputation and establishing rapport with consumers.

The success of the Internet as a medium for marketing depends upon how well the system outperforms any alternative systems. The features of the Internet must be better than any of these alternative systems, and consumers must be able to benefit. Studies have indicated that the Internet is, in fact, one of the best venues for marketing products and services. Many consumer studies include one that distinguishes online and traditional retail formats with regard to the costs and benefits for consumers and another that illustrates how the Internet shares some of the same characteristics as other mediums but also offers new and unique features. Some of the unique features of the Internet are:

- Ability to store larger amounts of data and information at lower costs
- Ability to provide information that is interactive and can be customized for business needs
- Provision of power and inexpensive ways to search, organize, and distribute information
- Provision to perceive (i.e., 3D image and video preview)
- Capability to serve as a transaction and distribution tool for certain products and services
- Establishment of a presence at a low cost model

5.11. Development of Digital and Internet Marketing Strategies

Developing a successful Internet marketing strategy is necessary if an organization wants to make an impression online. A successful strategy should include a great product, a web site designed to sell, and an outstanding marketing strategy. All three of these areas are important and must be developed. If one area fails, chances of success may be reduced. There is three-step process for ensuring the success of an internet marketing strategy.

- Step 1: Develop Product Offering - A company should create a unique product that gives potential customers what they want. The product should fill a void in order to overcome the threat of competition. The company must also develop a target market. Researching the market is key factor for success in this business. The company will need to find out what people want in order to develop a unique, quality product presentation.
- Step 2: Develop Appealing Website - The web site should be designed to sell the product(s). The purpose of the website is to convince the consumer to buy the product. Therefore, words become important. Although graphics are impressive, words mean more. Consumers seek information and want to find out about the product and whether they should buy it
- The objective of this step is to create a website that provides information to potential customers that would lead them to purchase the product.
- Step 3: Develop Sound Marketing Strategy - The marketing strategy is the final step in the process and should include short- and long-term planning. The purpose of short-term strategies is to temporarily boost traffic to the site. Some examples of short-term strategies are purchasing advertising and optimizing the site for search engines. The purpose of long-term strategies is to bring a steady flow of targeted traffic over a period of time. Examples of long term strategies include opt-in e-mail lists, free gifts, and content.

5.12. Building a Customer Base on the Internet

Having an Internet presence does not guarantee a successful business venture. There has to be a significant number of people visiting the site and buying the product/service. In order to achieve success, the organizations must be able to attract customers and establish a solid customer base.

"If the organization website exists in a market-space that is so diverse that mere existence is not a sufficient condition for achieving prominent traffic and the development of a viable Internet venture requires customers, the building of a solid and stable customer base becomes a key component of any company's marketing strategy toward the Internet."

"In addition, the development of a sound customer base will benefit other business functions in the marketing process such as market research, consumer research and sales testing." Therefore, having an Internet customer base is essential for an Internet marketing strategy.

Developing an online customer base can be done through two approaches: site-centric and symbiotic marketing. The two models can be viewed as opposite approaches; however, some organizations have used techniques from both approaches point of view. The site-centric model relies upon the use of a central site that offers a specific product and solicits traffic. The auction site eBay is an example of a website that uses the site-centric model. If a consumer is looking for a particular product or service, he or she may search for that using a search engine such as Google. One search result may be a link to eBay if the product is available on that website.

In the site-centric model, customers are interested in a particular organization's brand that meets their requirements. The central site focuses on attracting and retaining customers, so it invests in building strong brand recognition for the organization. The site-centric approach utilizes an umbrella strategy that has a variety of techniques. All of the techniques have the same theme — attract customers to the company's own web site. According to (Lockett & Blackman, 2001), some of the techniques include:

- Portal Websites - A portal site is either the first site a user sees when logging in or a search engine used to identify other sites. The default portal site may be operated by the Internet service provider (such as AOL) or the provider of the browser (such as Google, provider of Chrome, or Microsoft, provider of Internet Explorer). Examples of search engines include Google and Bing. Companies may develop their own portal links and purchase prominent links in existing key portal sites.
- Purchase Advertising - After the customer purchases the product from the central site, a direct link is provided so that the customer can pay immediately at the organization's site. The large portal sites have advantages in selling targeted advertisements. Some of these advantages include:
  1. Keywords can be used to select an appropriate banner advertisement
  2. Advertisements can be presented on Internet pages with related topics
  3. Regional-specific advertising can be provided on regional-specific search engines
  4. Detailed information can be collected in order to assist buyers with determining the success of specific banner advertisements.
- Direct e-mail - Registered users or subscribers to e-mail services — Customers can agree to receive regular emails or newsletters when the company has new products.
- Direct e-mail - Junk mail or spam-mail.

CONCLUSION

The Internet will continue to play a significant role in the field of marketing. Many will need to further their studies on the benefits and drawbacks of Internet marketing. Theorists may gain new ideas about the Internet and evaluate whether existing marketing theories can continue to be applied to the study of the Internet. Practitioners may continue to conduct market research to determine what consumers want, and policy makers must address topics such as security, consumer protection, intellectual property rights, and privacy issues. As the field of Internet marketing explodes, there still will be a need for traditional advertising. Internet marketing does not threaten the existence of traditional marketing techniques. Rather, it complements the efforts. Although Internet marketing provides valuable assets such as an increased awareness of brand names, traditional marketing efforts still can address some of the disadvantages of online shopping. For example, traditional marketing efforts can promote brick-and-mortar shopping experiences based on the opportunity for social interaction and allow consumers to actually see and physically touch a product before purchasing. Two popular Internet marketing strategies are site-centric and symbiotic marketing. Although the site-centric model has the central site as its foundation and base, the techniques can be expensive and unaffordable for small businesses. The symbiotic marketing strategy is more cost effective and provides organizations with an avenue to develop "a presence on the key portal sites in the business-to-business market." (Lockett & Blackman, 2001) However, it has its downside, especially for large organizations. There tends to be a need for a longer lead time, and it may require more persistence than the site-centric model.

Modern organizations should better serve their customers and usually their bottom line by functioning is to make maximum profits rather it should be more as a focus of resources than as an owner of resources. Outsourcing of non-core functions like Web Site Maintenance, Web Analytics support, SEO and the use of professional Internet business consultants provides many companies with enhanced levels of service at a much lower cost and can help business compete in today's highly competitive marketplace. Global competition in all facets has intensified with the advent of new technologies. Those who can professionally and fully exploit this gamut of opportunities provided by new technology will win the game and others who can't, will definitely loose it. Internet marketing enables company no matter small or big to be responsive, innovatively fast, and build confidence within the company to compete internationally. Throughout its history, the internet has reinvented itself many times and the changes are far from over. The current web is dominated by socializing, cooperation, collaboration, sharing and personal entertainment. An entirely new space created for life activities i.e., work and play it is now an essential tool for virtually every modern business and the go-to repository for all forms of media culture products. People in marketing world called consumers, of all ages are spending more and more time online, and are turning to the internet for better services, convenience and life-enhancing tools: just consider how people use online shopping, online banking, web communities that cross all boundaries, instant news and updates, social networks and chat, self-expression and any of the dozens of other things that the web makes possible. In fact 2014 was the first year where online advertising spend overtook the amount of money spent on newspaper advertising. It was the same year that online readership overtook traditional newspaper readership, which illustrates just how large an impact the internet has had on the marketing and advertising industry. Despite of its seeming ease and accessibility, internet marketing is not something that just anyone can do without formal training or without taking help from specialized professionals from the industry. The online space got cluttered with cultural, legal and financial pitfalls which sometime get overlooked by the companies. Some of the suggestions are like; traditional strategies usually don't translate directly onto the web performance. Customers have diverse, different and challenging expectations. The way that you spend money and schedule your company marketing campaigns works very differently. And with the plethora of new developments, tools, protocols, strategies and approaches, it is impossible to keep up with everything on one's own so one has to take advises from many experts. Keeping yourself educated and informed is the only way to ensure that you stay relevant and innovative.

REFERENCES

Afuah, A. and Tucci, C. L. (2003). Internet- Business Models and Strategies: Text and Cases. McGraw Hill.

Ainscough, T. L. and Luckett, M. G. (1996). The Internet for the rest of us: marketing on the World Wide Web. Journal of Consumer Marketing, 2, 36-47.

Arnott, D. C. and Bridgewater, S. (2002). Internet, interaction and implications for marketing. Marketing Intelligence and Planning, 20(2), 86-95.

Barabasi, A. L. (2003). Linked: how everything is connected to everything else and what it means. New York: Plume.

Barnett, S. (2011). Making sense of audience segmentation. Strategic Communication Management, 8, 36-38.

Bauer, H. H., Grether, M. and Leach, M. (2002). Building customer relations over the Internet. Industrial Marketing Management, 31(2), 155-163.

Bayne, K. (1997). The Internet Marketing Plan. New York: Wiley.

Borgeon, M. (1999). International Trade Forum Magazine. Linking the Internet to Your Marketing Strategy(1), p. 17.

Brynjolfsson, Erik and Saunders, Adam (2009) Wired for innovation: How information technology is reshaping the economy, Cambridge, MA: MIT Press.

Carroll, C. E. (2010). Should firms circumvent or work through the news media? Public Relations Review, 36(3), 278-280.

Chaffey, D. (2000). Achieving Internet marketing success. Marketing Review, 1(1), 35-60.

Chaffey, D. (2000). Internet Marketing. Pearson Education.

Chui, Michael; Löffler, Markus and Roberts, Roger (2010) "The Internet of things," McKinsey Quarterly, March, pp.1-9.

Daryl, T. (2001). Branding in the Digital Age. Journal of Business Strategy, 22(3), 14-18.

Davenport, Thomas H., and Harris, Jeanne G. (2010) Analytics at work: Smarter decisions, better results, Cambridge, MA: Harvard Business Press.

Deighton, J. (1996). The future of interactive marketing. Harvard Business Review, 151-162.

Dobele, A., David, T. and Michael, B. (2005). Controlled Infection! Spreading the Brand Message through Viral Marketing. Business Horizons, 48(2), 143–149.

Drucker, Peter F. (1999) *Management challenges of the 21st century*, New York: Harper Business, 1999.

Dye, R. (2000). *The Buzz on Buzz. Harvard Business Review,* 139–146.

Edelman, B. (2014). *Mastering the intermediaries: Strategies for dealing with the likes of Google,* Amazon, and Kayak. Harvard Business Review(June), 86-92.

Eid, R., Elbeltagi, I. and Zairi, M. (2006). Making business-to-business international Internet marketing effective: A study of critical factors using a case-study approach. *Journal of International Marketing,* 14(4), 87-109.

Free Encyclopedia, o. E. (2011, 11 2). Internet Marketing - History Of Internet Marketing. Retrieved 2015, from Free Encyclopedia of Ecommerce: http://ecommerce.hostip.info/pages/708/Marketing-Internet-HISTORY-INTERNET-MARKETING.html.

Gabrielsson, M. and Gabrielsson, P. (2011). Internet-based sales channel strategies of born global firms. *International Business Review,* 1, 88-99.

Gay, R., Charlesworth, A. and Esen, R. (2007). *Online Marketing: A Customer-led Approach.* New Delhi: Oxford University Press.

Gleick, James (2011) *The information: A history. A theory.* A flood, New York: Pantheon Books.

Guay, D. and Ettwein, J. (1998). *Internet commerce basics. Electronic Markets,* 8(1), 12-15.

Halligan, B., and Shah, D. (2010). *Inbound Marketing: Get Found Using Google, Social Media, and Blogs.* New Jersey: John Wiley and Sons.

Haythornthwaite, C. (2005) Social networks and Internet connectivity effects. Information, Communication, and Society, 8(2), 125-147.

Hoffman, D. L. and Novak, T. P. (1997). A new marketing paradigm for Electronic Commerce. *The Information Society,* 13(1), 43-54.

Hoffman, D. and Novak, T. (1996). Marketing in hypermedia computer-mediated environments: conceptual foundations. *Journal of Marketing,* 60(July), 50-68.

Hubbard, Douglas W. (2010) *How to measure anything: Finding the value of intangibles in business,* New York: Wiley.

Khermouch, G. and Green, J. (2001, July). *Buzz Marketing. Business Week,* 50-58.

Kiang, M. Y., Raghu, T. S. and Shang, K. H. (2000). Marketing on the Internet: who can benefit from an online marketing approach? *Decision Support Systems,* 4, 383-393.

Kiani, G. (1998). Marketing opportunities in the digital world. *Internet Research: Electronic Networking Application and Policy,* 8(2), 185-194.

Kotler, P., Armstrong, G., Saunders, J. and Wong, V. (2001). *Principles of Marketing.* Harlow: Pearson Education Limited.

Lincoln.S. R.. (2009). Mastering Web 2.0, Kogan Page, London and Philadelphia.

Lockett, A. and Blackman, I. (2001). Strategies for building a customer base on the Internet: symbiotic marketing. *Journal of Strategic Marketing,* 9(1), 47-68.

Macdonald, E. K., Wilson, H. N. and Konus, U. (2012). *Better customer insights- in real time.* Harvard Business Review(September), 102-108.

McDonald, M. and Wilson, H. (1999). *E-marketing: Improving Marketing Effectiveness in a Digital World.* Harlow: Financial Times/Prentice Hall.

Melewar, T. C. (2003). The Internet revolution: some global marketing implications. *Marketing Intelligence and Planning,* 21(6), 363-369.

Naik, P. A. and Kalyan, R. (2003). Understanding the Impact of Synergy in Multimedia Communications. *Journal of Marketing Research,* 40(4), 375-388.

Natalie, A. (2007, January 28). A Brief History of Internet Marketing. Retrieved 2015, from Internet and Businesses Online: http://ezinearticles.com/?A-Brief-History-of-Internet-Marketing&id= 434488.

Pitta, D., Franzak, F. and Fowler, D. (2006). A strategic approach to building online customer loyalty: Integrating customer profitability tiers. *Journal of Consumer Marketing, 23*(7), 421-429.

Porter, M. E. (1985). *Competitive Advantage, Creating and Sustaining Superior Performance.* New York: The Free Press.

Porter, M. E. (2001). *Strategy and the Internet.* Harvard Business Review(March), 62-78.

Scott, D.M. (2010). *The New Rules of Marketing and PR,* New Jersey: John Wiley and Sons, Inc.

Sernovitz, Andy (2006). *Word of Mouth Marketing: How Smart Companies Get People Talking.* Chicago: Kaplan Business Publishing.

Singh, S. (2015, February 27). How 500 million internet users transform India. *The Economic Times,* p. 14.

Stone, M. (2014). Building digital skills through training. *Journal of Direct, Data and Digital Marketing Practice, 16*(1), 3-14.

Tiffany, W. (2009, October). *Masters of Design 2009.* Retrieved 2015, from Fast Company: http://www.fastcompany.com/magazine/139/node/1353534.

Varian, Hal (2013) "The value of the Internet now and in the future," The Economist, March 10, http://www.economist.com/blogs/freeexchange/2013/03/technology-1.

Watts, D. (2004). *Six degrees: the science of a connected age.* New York: Norton and Co.

Wikipedia. (2015, September). History of the Internet. Retrieved 2015, from Wikipedia: https://en.wikipedia.org/wiki/History_of_the_Internet.

Yucelt, U. (2007). Online consumers around the globe. *Journal of International Marketing and Marketing Research,* 32(1), 17-24.

In: e-Governance in India: Problems, Prototypes and Prospects ISBN: 978-1-63484-830-5
Editors: P. Kumar, R. Sharma and U. Kaushal

Chapter 9

E-GOVERNANCE AND WOMEN IN INDIA: ASSESSING THE PRESENT, LOOKING TO THE FUTURE

Sanjay Kumar Pradhan*[*,1] and Geetanjali Dutta[2]
[1]Assistant Professor in International Relations,
Pandit Deendayal Petroleum University, Gujarat, India
[2]Analyst on women issues, and Visiting Faculty, at, City Pulse Institute of Film and Television, and Pandit Deendayal Petroleum University, Gandhinagar, Gujarat, India

ABSTRACT

Democracy, along with good governance, is popularly characterized with the features of rule of law, participation, transparency, accountability and efficiency for service delivery and service integrity. If the system of e-governance is peeped up under these criteria, this opportunity is not only complements the attributes of good governance but also works for the cause of marginalized and weaker sections of the society such as women. The issue of gender equity is a supplement to development, where e-governance poses central to gender justice under new age technologies. The e-governance initiatives are theoretically comprehensive and aimed at inclusion of every citizen. However, without a gender perspective, a huge gap is bound to remain between the theory and practice of e-governance in India. Despite many e-governance initiatives in India, the existing gender gap restricts women to be equal partners and beneficiaries of the e-governance initiatives. Hence, it is imperative to look at the emerging innovation with a serious outlook and critical interpretation. The chapter is intended to analyze the importance of e-governance in India with particular reference to women; find out different policies and programmes of the government to empower women electronically; focuses problems associated with the implementation of e-governance on the women context; and possible intervention to make e-governance objectives (for women) effective and result-oriented.

* Corresponding author: sanjaypradhanjnu@gmail.com

1. Introduction

The electronic governance or e-governance has been one of the developments that countries across the globe, both developed and developing, have recognized it. It is a potential driver and enabler in the way governance can be reinvented to address problems in an efficient and effective way, and to deliver the services in a more responsible manner. As a means of governance, incidentally, it brings an exclusively positive vocabulary in making things better. There is a firm realisation among countries that e-governance is not just a government i.e., government on the internet, but beyond it as well. It is a new mode of delivery of governance. A good start has been made in Europe, the United States and other developed countries in the world. In the developing countries, like India, a modest beginning is discernable and in near future, the political leaders of developing countries may find e-governance as a fast and politically rewarding alternative to traditional mode of governance and in its connotation, it is a fundamental aspect of democracy and relationship between the civic community and government officials.

The e-Governance also includes re-organizing government's internal work structure for greater efficiency and effectiveness. It can mean more productive use of resources, and therefore, greater impact, including welfare of women-the target group and using of the same resources. The widespread use of new technologies at workplaces have important gender implications today. It promotes government job opportunities for women in many ways; easier on-job skill enhancement training, education, e-networking, tele-working, etc. It priorities 'new ways of organizing work for well-being' and promoting 'tele-working to increase job opportunities for women.'

Women in general, and rural women in particular, need special attention under e-governance policies due to socio-economic conditions and existing stereotypical notions of the Indian society. India is a country dominated by rural population, and introduction of panchayatiraj system and devolution of power have given ample opportunities to the rural women to participate in the mainstream of local self-government, but unfortunately, they are far behind to the local politics. So far, even with 33% reservation, the women Sarpanches have not been able to equally participate in the process of rural governance. The patriarchal character of the society and unequal participation and involvement of women, accompanied by lack of political awareness of women over their rights, duties and responsibilities, have posed great challenges to women emancipation in the rural areas of India, where governance is still dominated by male counterparts.

2. Access to Information through e-Governance

The women have traditionally been excluded from the external information largely due to factors prevailing to their disadvantage such as lack of freedom of movement or low levels of education. But, the ICT has opened up a direct window for women to the outside world. Information flows to them without any distortion or censoring. This leads to the broadening of perspectives, greater understanding of their current situation, causes of poverty and initiation of interactive processes for information exchange. Access to ICTs for e-governance is crucial for rural women, where it is a means for women's economic empowerment. It is important not only to establish physical facilities such as communication networks or computers, but to ensure that these facilities are utilized by their users to the greatest possible extent. The e-Governance can deliver potentially useful information, such as, market prices for women in small and micro enterprises. For example, use of cellular telephones illustrates how technology can be used to benefit women's lives by saving travelling time between the market and suppliers by allowing women to call for product prices and by facilitating the constant juggling of paid and unpaid family activities. In this regard Gyandoot is an intranet project in Dhar district of Madhya Pradesh which connects 21 rural cyber cafés located on the roadsides of central villages. (Pradhan, ICTs and its Impact on Rural Women in India, 2012)

The term 'empowerment' can be understood as, participation in the decision making processes that impacts the social, political and economic conditions of the society. In India, women's involvement in political actions, social projects or economic activities, processes of dialogue, critical reflections and community involvement are all fundamental leveraging tools for advancing women equality and influencing policy outcomes. To nurture and support women's participation, it will be necessary to establish an enabling environment, which in the context of e-governance is characterized by state-sponsored policies and infrastructures that promote gender equality and women's empowerment. Therefore, e-governance advocates a retreat from the welfare state's publicly funded commitments to equality and social justice.

On the onslaught of information and communications technologies (ICTs), the burgeoning popularity of the internet and the ideology behind the new information economy has coalesced into a force that is fundamentally reshaping the contours of Indian political landscape. This reorganization of the state will profoundly impact on women's opportunities to participate and alter conventional notions of identity. The establishment of e-government and the implications behind the development of the cyber state are the promises and attempts to revolutionize Indian governance and its traditional understandings of democracy. There is the political possibility of shaping the emerging cyber state as a vehicle of empowerment for women and other marginalized sections of the society.

3. E-Governance and Implications

There are three major aspects of e-governance: firstly, the IT, which is enabling the government functions - something similar to back-office automation; secondly, web-enabling government functions so that the citizens will have a direct access; thirdly, improving government processes so that openness, accountability, accuracy, speed of operations, effectiveness and efficiency could be achieved. (Kumar and Sharma, 2012) The role of ICTs to improve governance and strengthen democracy and citizen empowerment is largely visible in the country. It can help to foster more transparent governance by enhancing interaction between government and citizens, revitalizing civic institutions and public debate, promoting equity and equality, and empowering minorities specifically women. It can be particularly powerful in providing a voice to women in rural areas who have been isolated and invisible. In recent years, e-governance has become a priority area of many governments resulting in the implementation of programmes that apply ICTs for e-governance in delivering government services and promoting transparency and accountability. Beyond delivery of government services and information to the public using electronic means, e-governance focuses on using these new technologies to strengthen the public voice to revitalize democratic processes, and refocus management, structure and oversight of government to serve public interest better. Through the electronic forums, bulletin boards and e-mail, government could enable its citizens to participate in public discussions and report any malpractices of the government officials, and voice complaints about government service irregularities. Apart from this, e-governance is significant for the exercise of citizenship and direct public participation in government activities, both of which are key elements in women empowerment, and achievement of gender equality. The gender-responsive governance involves the active and meaningful participation of women in all levels of decision-making and ensuring greater transparency and accountability in government. Information technology can contribute to increasing women's networking for social and political advocacy, strengthening women's participation in the political process, supporting the work of elected women officials, and increasing women's access to government and its services. In this context, the Gyandoot project has been recognized as a breakthrough in e-government, winning the Stockholm Challenge IT Award 2000 in the areas of public service and democracy. The project gives marginalized tribal men and women in central India their first-ever chance to access knowledge electronically.(Pradhan, ICTs and its Impact on Rural Women in India, 2012)

4. Initiatives by the Government

Women literacy is the important part of economic growth and development in India. The education of women is particularly valuable as a strategic investment in the human resource management. The education of women and girls has an impact not only on their own development but also on that of their families and countries. According to the Census of 2001, the percentage of female literacy in the country has increased from 18.33 percent in 1951 to 65.38 percent. The female literacy rate has also increased from 8.86% in 1951 to 54.16%. It is noticed that the female literacy rate during the period 1991-2001 increased by 14.87% whereas male literacy rate increased by 11.72 percent. Hence the female literacy rate actually increased by 3.15% compared to male literacy rate. (Kumar and Sharma, 2012) Different strategies and policies have been adopted by the government for increasing female literacy in the country. The main strategies adopted by the government for increasing female literacy in the country include: National Literacy Mission for imparting functional literacy, universalization for elementary education and non-formal education.

A few instances of India's e-governance initiatives at the district administration or police administration levels bear out the importance of IT as an important agenda of public administration in India. In Tamil Nadu Police uses e-governance to address the problems and the distinctive feature of this experiment of e-governance is that the stakeholders are mainly women, and in a sense, this is an outstanding example of e-governance- 'for' the women and 'by' the women.(Network, 2005) Major objectives of the project include: firstly, develop web-based training in dispute resolution, interviewing techniques, and use of computer programmes for data entry and analyses. This training would be for women officers deployed in all-women police units; secondly, deliver training to a total of 30 women officers from all three women police units located in metropolitan cities; and thirdly, evaluate the outcome of the training which have been provided online.(Network, 2005)The significant outcomes of the project include: firstly, the project is an apt example of how the IT can be used as a medium to address serious problems by involving key stakeholders; secondly, e-governance project has proved itself evolutionary, although, the constraints and tension tends to be different at different stages; thirdly, planning and management have turned successful with the implementation of IT; and involvement of officers at different key levels in the process have made e-governance more structured. Due to overwhelming performance of Tamil Nadu government with e-governance techniques, the state has been awarded with Queens Award Project by the British government.

The e-commerce website (2005) in Tamil Nadu has been designed to sell products made by rural women's cooperatives and the non-governmental organizations (NGOs). The Dhan Foundation (2004) and Swayam Krishi Sangam (2004) are using ICTs, such as handheld devices and smart cards, to improve microfinance projects to empower poor rural women (Jain, www.ifuw.org). The Self Employed Women's Association (SEWA, 2004) has several ICT projects for women, including community learning centres, a school of Science and Technology for self-employed women, and the Telephone project, which provides mobile phones to women in the informal sector. The self-help groups (SHGs) of rural women in Andhra Pradesh have been so successful in marketing their products at home and abroad that the major MNCs want to use their selling skills.

Chhattisgarh, although socio-economically backward state, performing tremendously in the sector of e-governance. The major e-governance initiatives in this regard include:

4.1. Bhuiyan: All land records are computerized under the scheme and with a nominal charge, land records and related information can be obtained and downloaded. This facility is implemented in all Tehsil (Block) headquarters of the state at present, and intended to extend to all the villages in the state.

4.2. The E- Sangwari scheme has been implemented with an objective of providing 7 services to common citizen. Launched in Bilaspur district, the scheme includes the facilities for getting death, birth and caste certificates, availing of F-16 Form, income tax return, Khasara (land record), Income certificate, Domicile certificate and other related documents.

4.3. The e-Kosh scheme has been launched to computerize all treasury transactions of the District Head Quarters.

4.4. The e-Panchayat (local self-government unit) programme has been executed through *Janpad Panchayats* (local self-government units). Each *Janpad panchayat* is provided with two computers, which will be linked to the other computers through satellite. It is sought to be an informative programme, aimed at informing the rural people about the development and welfare schemes and policies of the government and making the application forms available online. It is sought to be interactive in due course of time.

4.5. The Video Conferencing programme is aimed at an interactive interface between the government agencies and people by making it possible for the heads of various government departments to answer the questions asked by the common citizens through video conferencing.

4.6. The Feedback facility is aimed at enabling most of the departments of the government to get a feedback through the web. Apart from this, any citizen of the state can register complaints or suggestions related to any of the schemes or government officials through the internet facilities. In the process, the complaint is directly forwarded to the concerned department or officials online for their attention. The status of the application can also be tracked online.

4.7. CHOICE (Chhattisgarh Online Information for Citizen Empowerment) deals with online disbursement of government services to the citizens.(Saxena & Subramanian, 'E-governance: Initiatives in an Indian State: Some Observations from a Gender Perspective, 2006; Calgary, 2010)

In Karnataka, the State Women's Development Corporation (KSWDC) is giving training to 250 women who are members of different self-help groups under the banner of e-Mahile. The e-Mahile is conceptualized to provide all possible services to the rural public through rural women.(Jain, 2014) Women, particularly members of women self-help groups, who have a minimum qualification of Secondary School Leaving Certificate (SSLC), are given comprehensive computers education. They are taught, how to access the Internet for collecting information and use it for various works. Thereafter, each trained woman who is called village service provider, will be given a laptop, printer, UPS, soil testing kit, LCD projector, digital camera, e-Mahile dual language software educational CDs and internet connection to speed up services for the rural women. The Project Jyoti, a community technology skills programme organized by Microsoft Partners and NGOs in India, provides training to the women to make the trainees employable and enhance their earning potential by imparting basic computing skill. The project Jyoti primarily targets women to improve their abilities to learn about computers, use the Internet, explore new careers, facilitate education and awareness, participate in community activities and develop technological skills through the community learning technology centres. (Sikdar, 2012; Pradhan, ICTs and its Impact on Rural Women in India, 2012)

5. PROBLEMS

5.1. There are instances where women sarpanches have not been able to participate equally in rural e-governance. The 33% elected women representatives at the panchayat level are those who have been basically elected from the women-reserved seats, not from the unreserved seats.(Saxena, Rural e-governance: Exploring the gender gaps and its impact on women(A case study of e-gram suraj scheme of Chhattisgarh State of India), 2010)

5.2. The percentage of women who are actually using the simputers and thus participating in rural e-governance is much less than the male sarpanches. Gender gaps are quite visible and women rarely have transferred the data.

5.3. A large number of male sarpanches are using or have used simputers for their personal works like playing games, calculating, listening to songs etc. (Saxena, Rural e-governance: Exploring the gender gaps and its impact on women(A case study of e-gram suraj scheme of Chhattisgarh State of India), 2010)

5.4. In India, women's ability to participate in the country's rapid progress towards e-governance is impeded by the low status ascribed to them in the Indian societal set ups. This is reflected in the gender disparity in many sectors, where women are in a disadvantaged position. Along with, the extreme poverty and poor IT infrastructure in rural areas, where the majority of Indian women resides, restrict women's access to education and information technology. Such an iniquitous position of women has contributed enormously to the slow pace of development in India.

5.5. Many telecommunication regulatory agencies, both in the North and in the South, have given insufficient attention for gender-based analysis of e-governance.

5.6. Most of the e-governance initiatives have been designed without recognizing the fact that women and men everywhere have different patterns of interaction with computers and the Internet. Women use it mostly for practical purposes, i.e., to find specific information or to shop. In some cases, women are less likely than men to use the Internet because they do not have access, they do not have skills, they do not have disposable income or they do not have time or interest. Therefore, the notion that the ICTs can be a vehicle for making government services and public participation more widespread is flawed by the simple fact that men and women have different user patterns. From this perspective, the move towards digitization of government services for the women may get little materialized.(Rathgeber, 2006)

5.7. Many regulatory agencies have focused on universal access and rural communications services, but few have looked at the basic issues of availability, accessibility and affordability from a gender perspective.(Rathgeber, 2006)

5.8. Male domination in the public domain is a very important factor and there are clear indications that women are getting better representation but are not getting due justice while performing their responsibilities. There is proxy involvement of family members in the duty performance of women. This proves the fact that representation of women not necessarily leads to empowerment.

5.9. The 'patriarchal culture' of restricting women to family domain restricts their access to new technology. The unequal participation of women sarpanches in rural e-governance is the result of prevailing socio-cultural discriminations against women.(Calgary, 2010)

5.10. Local languages and local contents make internet less attractive to women in India. Since women are often less educated than men (particularly in rural India), they are less likely to be able to access the Internet in English, French or any such other languages. Some local languages are now being transcribed into the internet, but there are often problems with standardization. Moreover, the difficulties related to the use of sounds and characters cannot easily be recognized by the computer.(Rathgeber, 2006)

6. Roadmap

6.1. The union and state governments of India should create women portals, which would be able to provide and facilitate women-centric information, policies and activities of the government.

6.2. The government should act more effectively, and become more committed to expand the number of public kiosks in safe locations where women will not be harassed, intimidated, abused and exploited. These locations may include government institutions, libraries, NGOs/SHGs offices, educational and research institutions, shopping complexes, community centers and places of worship.

6.3. Identify critical areas of focus, address digital divide, and intervention thereupon.

6.4. Engaging women's organizations and their SHGs/NGOs to educate and implement e-governance schemes effectively.

6.5. A strong partnership among the state, private and public sectors, women's organizations and SHGs/NGOs must be established to advance, support and implement the strategies in a holistic and effective way.

6.6. For the real empowerment of women through the means of e-democracy, the local people should have the opportunity for input and feedback on government policies and this feedback must be integrated into the further policy making and policy execution.

6.7. Formulation of women-specific schemes and policies by the government to educate and train women on the importance of e-governance and access to software technologies.

CONCLUSION

Analysis of women issues is crucial and it is the foremost step to ascertain critically and evaluate constructively to find out how responsive government services are delivered to the needs and priorities of men and women in the different social and economic stratas of the society. In the process, the e-governance initiatives have faced with a number of challenges. Though there are many emerging programmes and initiatives on e-governance in India, yet, it is generally believed that it would take at least another one decade for the infrastructures to be built adequately, the policies made result-oriented and the interoperability made easier. Driven by the twin forces of globalization and technological advance, India faces a series of opportunities alongside challenges. The process of digital restructuring in India shapes domestic rules and technological advancements for modernization of the India society. The vision of ICT revolution for women empowerment would not impair the developing worlds' pursuits; rather, extends support and solidarity through the promotion of socio-economic and political values like equality and equity within the society. The system of e-governance guarantees that all the citizens have the right to communicate as they prefer both online and offline and the government decision-making reflect the civic voice. Women's participation in these evolving forums and activities is imperative for all the members of society to ensure that e-governance expands the political processes and create a state that is representative and accountable to all the stake holders of the society. As the digital restructuring process of government is still evolving, there exists a general consensus among political actors and the popular media that e-governance is a new panacea for reviving democracy, overcoming political disengagement, and bridging science-society gap. However, the real success of virtual government is not possible without addressing the longstanding challenges associated with the Indian women. Hence, with the ascendancy of the digital state and e-democracy, the e-governance poses a number of challenges and a plethora of opportunities for women and marginalized sections of the society. Overcoming the existing challenges is not only the responsibility of the government and women, but also the responsibility of all the citizens, sections and organizations of the society. In pursuance to these sincerities and commitments, the e-governance initiatives and progress will definitely develop a revolutionary step for gender justice and women empowerment in India.

REFERENCES

Calgary. (2010, February 11). *Rural e-governance in India: Women struggle to take part.* Retrieved September 2015, from Association for Progressive Communications: https://www.apc.org/en/node/9923.

India's simple computer for the poor, http://news. bbc.co.uk/2/hi/sci/tech/1560771.stm.

Jain, S. (2014, January). *ICTS and Women Empowerment: Some case studies from India.* Retrieved September 2015, from Graduate Women International (GWI) http://www.graduatewomen.org/wp-content/uploads/2014/01/jain.pdf.

Karthik, D. (2001, September 24). *India's simple computer for the poor.* Retrieved September 2015, from BBC News: http://news.bbc.co.uk/2/hi/sci/tech/1560771.stm.

Kumar, R. and Sharma, M. (2012). Impact of ICT for women literacy in Indian rural areas of e- governance. *Journal of Information and Operations Management, 3*(1), 194-195.

McNutt, K. (2007). Will e-Governance and e-Democracy Lead to e-Empowerment ? Gendering the Cyber State. *Federal Governmance A Graduate Journal, 4*(1).

Network, E. N. (2005, Jan 01). *Women and e-Governance.* Retrieved September 2015, from Asia's First Monthly Magazine on e-Governance:http://egov.eletsonline.com/2005/01/women-and-e-governance/

Palathingal, A. (2008). *Gender Responsive E-governance: Exploring the Transformative Potential.* New York: UNDP.

Pradhan, S.K. (2012). ICTs and its Impact on Rural Women in India. In P. Gupta, *Rural Opportunities in India* (pp. 14-17). New Delhi: Ardent Publications.

Pradhan, S. K. and Kumar, P. (2009). e-Governance in India: A Case Study of Haryana. *South Asia Politics, vii*(11), 20-23.

Rathgeber, E. (2006, May 8). *Engendering E-Government in Developing Countries.* Retrieved September 2015, from The Information Daily Public Policy Matters: http://www.theinformationdaily.com/2006/05/08/engendering-e-government-in-develo ping-countries.

Saxena, A. (2010). *Rural e-governance: Exploring the gender gaps and its impact on women(A case study of e-gram suraj scheme of Chhattisgarh State of India).* Retrieved September 2015, from The Journal of Community Informatics: http://ci-journal.net/index.php/ciej/article/view/539/519.

Saxena, A. and Subramanian, M. (2006, December 10). *'E-governance: Initiatives in an Indian State: Some Observations from a Gender Perspective.* Retrieved September 2015, from GENDERIT.ORG Feminist Peflection on Internet Policies: http://www.genderit.org/sites/default/upload/India_E_Governance_Gender.pdf.

Sikdar, S. (2012, April 18). Bridging the Opportunitiy Divide with Technology. The Hindu.

In: e-Governance in India: Problems, Prototypes and Prospects ISBN: 978-1-63484-830-5
Editors: P. Kumar, R. Sharma and U. Kaushal

Chapter 10

A CASE STUDY OF AUSTRALIAN MODEL OF E-GOVERNANCE AND CONCEPTUALIZATION OF A PROTOTYPE FOR REJUVENATION OF E-GOVERNANCE IN INDIA

Puneet Kumar** and Kumar Sambhav Pareek
Assistant Professors, Mody University of Science and Technology,
Lakshmangarh, Sikar, Rajasthan, India

ABSTRACT

It is evident from numerous studies that e-governance in India was initiated in a haphazard manner. At the time of evolution of e-governance in India, various provinces have shown their autonomy in development of various e-governance applications. As a result numerous number of applications were developed across the nation to accomplish similar or distinct objectives of various states. But, the scenario of deployment of e-governance is still not overwhelming because India has not envisioned any centralized, futuristic approach in deployment of e-governance. The majority of applications are severely lacking in interoperability, standardization of data and having ample redundancy of data which increases vulnerability of data or information. In order to eradicate such perplexing scenario this paper undergoes the case study of Australian model of e-governance because Australia is one of the pioneer in establishing e-governance with 89% satisfaction ratio among Australians. Further, this paper suggests a prototype to get revived from this situation. It also delineates about prospects of proposed framework after its adoption.

Keywords: framework, model, interoperability, consolidation, virtualization, ICT

* Department of Computer Application, CET, Mody University of Science and Technology, Lakshmangarh, Sikar, Rajasthan, 332311, India, E-mail: professor.pkumar@gmail.com.

1. Introduction

The technological era in India ascends with the advent of ICT; as an inescapable tool for communication and dissemination of information; and as a result the idea of e-governance was coined. E-governance is a fusion of governmental tasks with communication technologies moreover it also brings more accountability and transparency in the system and hence can be treated as an inevitable tool for mitigating corruption. (Mistry J. J., 2012; Agangiba & Agangiba, 2013) As a result numerous e-governance applications were sprouted across the nation. These applications were either department centric or office centric or purpose centric or state centric and very few applications were designed by keeping national perspective nevertheless their success ratio is not overwhelming. Further, each autonomous application is maintaining their data exclusively therefore a single data will get replicated. This replication of data obstructs data consistency and validity. In such circumstances the lessons should be learned from pioneer countries in e-governance across the world. This chapter is an attempt to describe about methodology of Australia about e-governance and its deployment.

2. Review of Literature

On the basis of the survey; 85% failure rate for e-governance projects has been noticed across the world whereas in year 2009 alone the worldwide expenditure on the technology abided by the government was 428.38 billion US dollars. (Luna-Reyesa, Melloulib, & Bertotc, 2013) The documents (Mistry H. , 2010; Dwivedi & Bharti, 2010; Gajendra, Xi, & Wang, 2012; Kumar, Umashankar, Rani, & Ramana, 2010) identifies major impediments and challenges in successful implementation of e-governance in India. According to the report inadequate planning, leadership failures, deficiency in finances, lack of motivation and awareness, dearth of citizen centric nature of applications, poor cooperation among bureaucrats and people at local level, lack of trust, miserable technical design which endures lack of interoperability among distinct e-governance applications and underutilization of ICT infrastructure resources are the major obstacles in successful implementation of e-governance in India. The study (Asadi & Rashidi, 2012) advocated the use of service oriented architecture in e-governance for data management, consolidation of numerous offered services, plummeting the cost of IT infrastructure by integrating services, enhancing reusability and facilitating interoperability among various e-governance applications. The research (Das & Patra, 2013) has identified challenges in designing e-governance applications mentioned as ability to handle heterogeneity of applications, ability to achieve interoperability to accomplish seamless exchange of data, skill to handle scalability so that new applications can be used as an addendum in the existing systems and can handle growing number of users, ability to attain high level of data abstraction to maintain privacy of data.

This present state of knowledge aptly affirms that India is having inadequate e-governance implementation strategies and policies. The adopted methodology for deployment of e-governance is lacking in futuristic ideology. Therefore, the modus operandi adopted by world leaders, who have excelled in e-governance deployment should be analyzed and imbibed.

3. Case Study of the Australian Model of e-Governance

The Global Information Technology Report (GITR), 2013 reveals that the countries like United Kingdom, Netherland, Australia, Japan, Sweden and Australia are the leaders in implementing e-governance across the world. (Bilbao-Osorio, Dutta, & Lanvin, 2013) The Australian model of e-governance abides with various stringent objectives with adequate strategies to accomplish them in order to establish as well as implement strong electronic governance.

3.1. Objectives and Strategies

1.1.1. Building capability
- 1.1.1.1. Improving the use of existing technology capability
- 1.1.1.2. Integrating technology and policy
- 1.1.1.3. Improving program delivery capability
- 1.1.1.4. Developing ICT workforce and skills

1.1.2. Enabling better services
- 1.1.2.1. Delivering easy to use online services
- 1.1.2.2. Greater use of personalized services
- 1.1.2.3. Simplifying government websites
- 1.1.2.4. Increase automation of services

1.1.3. Creating knowledge
- 1.1.3.1. Building business intelligence
- 1.1.3.2. Using location based information
- 1.1.3.3. Developing analytical tools
- 1.1.3.4. Releasing public sector information

1.1.4. Collaborating effectively
- 1.1.4.1. Strengthening external networks
- 1.1.4.2. Building collaboration across government
- 1.1.4.3. Creating the necessary channels

1.1.5. Investing optimally
- 1.1.5.1. Improving investment governance
- 1.1.5.2. Developing a portfolio approach
- 1.1.5.3. Extending coordinated procurement
- 1.1.5.4. Sharing computing resources and services

1.1.6. Encouraging innovation
- 1.1.6.1. Fostering innovation in ICT
- 1.1.6.2. Delivering better ICT- enabled services
- 1.1.6.3. Increasing awareness and early adoption
- 1.1.6.4. Adopting new and emerging technologies

4. Australian e-Governance Architecture (AGA)

To accomplish aforesaid intents, the Australian government has adopted a robust framework comprises of five reference models.

4.2. Performance Reference Model (PRM)

It facilitates the government in planning, management and evaluation of governmental activities. Its prime objective is to analyze and develop a measurement between inputs to government and impact of outcomes. Further, it also consolidates existing measurement systems and process frameworks to reduce the implementation and operational burden on agencies. It encompasses five measurement domains viz inputs domain (deals with the type of input), work domain (identifies the type or nature of work), outputs domain (related with the types of output), usage domain (deals with the types of usage like product consumption, service delivery etc.) and outcomes domain (identifies the types of outcome).

4.3. Business Reference Model (BRM)

BRM further extends the concepts of PRM by linking the government business through to the business processes to derive desired performance outcomes and business objectives. It also incorporates the business-focused enterprise architectures and the management processes of agencies to accomplish the objective of e-governance.

4.4. Service Reference Model (SRM)

It deals with functional and business driven framework which classifies various services in order to meet business and performance objectives. It also identifies investments associated with ICT and assets. To enhance the ability of sharing and reusability of business services, applications, application capabilities and components it is organized across horizontal service areas which are independent of the business functions.

4.4. Data Reference Model (DRM)

The prime objective of DRM is to perform standardization of data. It facilitates information sharing and enhances reusability of data by the Australian government. It incorporates the standardization in three areas firstly data description; which ensures uniform description of data along with its discovery secondly data context; which undergoes standardization of category of data according to taxonomies and lastly data sharing; which facilitates exchange and access of data.

4.5. Technical Reference Model (TRM)

It is a component-driven, technical framework which categorizes the standards and technologies to support and enable the delivery of services and capabilities. Further, it also ensures reusability and standardization of technology along with its components from governmental perspective. (Australia, 2008)

Australia is one of the pioneers in e-governance because majority of the people prefer to use internet as a media of communication with the government; prevailing over other modes of communication. Moreover people are highly satisfied with the services received by the government and have highest level of satisfaction i.e., 89%. It undergoes the use of e-mail, SMS, mobile web applications, phone calls over internet, social networking sites and instant messaging as a media of communication. (Office, 2011) Further, the Australian e-governance model emphasizes on skill development and improving service delivery mechanism along with better quality of services.

5. The Proposed Framework

In India, e-governance was evolved in a haphazard manner without undergoing any centralized policy as a result; majority of e-governance applications in the current scenario are department or state centric. Moreover, these sprouted applications are having lack of interoperability and having enormous data redundancy. The proposed framework depicted in Figure 5.1 is an attempt to eradicate such problems. The *modus operandi* is explained as under:

The link L1 indicates the interaction between users and numerous e-governance applications. After interaction with the interface, the data will be standardized (L2) in order to give a single identity to a single person across all e-governance applications. In current scenario multiple applications have their own interfaces and maintain their separate databases which lead to severe anomalies in data like single person with multiple identities. To wipe off such problems the standardization of data is essential which provides uniqueness to the data on the basis of name, date of birth, geographic location, biometric details etc. and enhances consistency of data. The framework proposes that a central repository of the data should be maintained with all possible kind of information about any individual and link L3 indicates towards addition or updating an existing data in it. Nevertheless individual e-governance applications are managing their data efficiently but to conquer the objectives of interoperability an establishment of centralized data repository is essential. The government data centers should fetch the data and information from established as well as maintained data repository (L4). These GDCs should be synchronized periodically with centralized database. Every e-governance application should fetch basic required information from central repository (L5) or GDCs. It will reduce replication of data and diminishes storage requirements. Furthermore it also improves availability of data. The L6 link indicates towards numerous interoperable e-governance applications functioning under distributed environment. The interoperability among applications is stances on the edges of central repository of data along with inclusion of technologies like virtualization and consolidation.

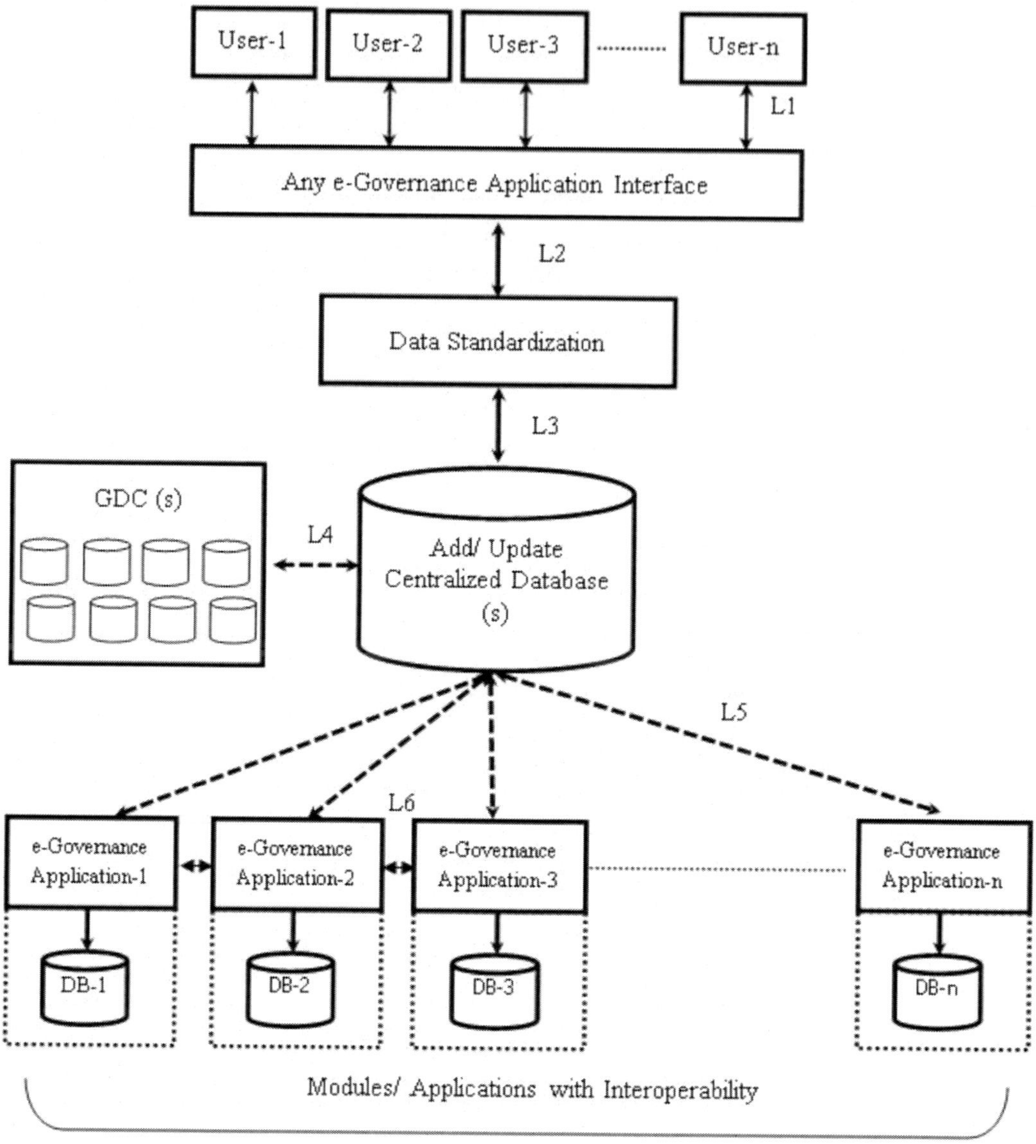

Figure 5.1. Proposed e-Governance framework for India.

6. The Prospects

The fringe benefits after adoption of proposed framework are enlisted as under:

6.1. It is evident from numerous studies that data redundancy causes data inconsistency therefore the proposed framework if adopted will minimize the data redundancy and hence will improve data consistency.

6.2. The malpractices caused by multiple identities and lack of intra department coordination will be hampered which result into more transparent governance.

6.3. It also encourages green governance because hardcopy of bridge documents will not be required. For example in present scenario if anybody wants to transfer a motor vehicle from one state/province to another state/province then he/she has to take NOC (No Objection Certificate) from one state/province. Then the obtained NOC will be submitted into relocated state/province in order to get motor vehicle registered. There are numerous other examples also asserting the same scenario where variety of hardcopy documents are required only for the sake of communication between same or different departments of same or different states/ provinces. After adoption of proposed framework it will be needless to generate such type of intermediate documents and an enormous amount of paper utilization can be reduced.

6.4. The data storage requirements associated with variety of e-governance applications will be reduced because majority of information will be maintained centrally. Furthermore the technologies like virtualization and consolidation will also be used in deployment of applications therefore the framework will be cost effective also in terms of hardware and software costs.

6.5. It will expedite the flow of work also because inter/intra department communication time will be reduced at a great extent.

6.6. Framework will also facilitate government in designing new policies, fetching complex information, performing time series analysis about any particular scheme or group of schemes, trend analysis etc.

6.7. The adoption of proposed framework will certainly reduce the financial losses incurred due to failure of any e-governance application because there will be no special hardware and software requirements for any new e-governance application.

CONCLUSION

The aforesaid case study reveals that all e-governance applications should be operable under a single umbrella. It aptly enhances the level of satisfaction among citizens about e-services. Therefore, the Government of India should ponder, on reviving current e-governance deployment methodology. The proposed framework in this paper concentrates on standardization of data as well as advocates the establishment of centralized repository for data. However, the task is cumbersome but it will certainly expedite the flow of work, along with apt transparency and negligible anomalies, which certainly leads towards a better future of India.

REFERENCES

Agangiba, W. A. and Agangiba, M. A. (2013). E-governance XE "governance" justified. *International Journal of Advanced Computer Science and Applications, 4*, 223-22.

Asadi, J. and Rashidi, H. (2012). E-government with service oriented architecture. *International Journal of Advanced Research in Computer Science, 3*, 91-93.

Australia, C. O. (2008). *Reference Model Overview*. Retrieved December 2013, from Australian Government: website: http://www.finance. gov.au/policy XE "policy" -guides-procurement XE "procurement" /australian-government-architecture-aga/aga-rm/2-reference-model-overview.

Bilbao-Osorio, B., Dutta, S. and Lanvin, B. (2013). *The Global Information Technology Report 2013: Growth and Jobs in a Hyperconnected World*. Geneva: World Economic Forum and INSEA.

Das, R. K. and Patra, M. R. (2013). A Service Oriented Design Approach for e-Governance XE "e-Governance" Systems. *International Journal of Information Technology Convergence and Services, 4*, 1-11.

Dwivedi, S. K. and Bharti, A. K. (2010). E-Governance XE "E-Governance" in India XE "India" - Problems and Acceptability. *Journal of Theoretical and Applied Information Technology, 17*, 37-43.

Gajendra, S., Xi, B. and Wang, Q. (2012). E-Government: Public Participation and Ethical Issues. *Journal of E-Governance XE* "E-Governance" *, 35*, 195-204.

Kumar, S. P., Umashankar, C., Rani, J. K. and Ramana, V. (2010). e-Governance XE "e-Governance" Applications for citizens XE "citizens" - Issues and Framework. *International Journal on Computer Science and Engineering, 2*, 2362-2365.

Luna-Reyesa, L. F., Melloulib, S. and Bertotc, J. C. (2013). Key factors and processes for digital government success. *Information Polity, 18*, 101-105.

Mistry, H. (2010). *e-Governance XE* "e-Governance" *: Efficiency and Challenges in India XE* "India" . Mumbai: Mahindra Special Services Group.

Mistry, J. J. (2012). The Role of eGovernance in Mitigating Corruption. Accounting and the Public Interest. *Accounting and the Public Interest, 12*, 137-159.

Office, A. G. (2011). *Interacting with Government*. Australia: Department of Finance and Deregulation.

In: e-Governance in India: Problems, Prototypes and Prospects ISBN: 978-1-63484-830-5
Editors: P. Kumar, R. Sharma and U. Kaushal

Chapter 11

AN INTEGRATED CLOUD COMPUTING BASED FRAMEWORK FOR NEW APPLICATION AND DEPLOYMENT MODEL OF E-GOVERNANCE FOR HIGHER EDUCATION IN INDIA

Urmani Kaushal[1,*] and Rajesh Sharma[2]
[1]Department of Computer Appliation, CET,
Mody University of Science and Technology,
Lakshmangarh, Sikar, Rajasthan, India
[2]COBMEC, Mody University of Science and Technology,
Lakshmangarh, Sikar, Rajasthan, India

ABSTRACT

E-Governance is the process of reforming the pattern of, working of the government, information and service delivery to the various segments of the society, business communities and the government itself. Functionalities reformation of government must be the ultimate vision of e-governance. The prime objective behind starting e-government projects is to integrate the scattered set of operations, simplification of complex processes at end user level and increasing the accessibility and transparency in the delivery of services. In India both public as well as private partners participates in facilitating the society through education. In this chapter new cloud computing based e-governance framework has been suggested to centerally govern and monitor the activities of higher edcuational institutes like admissions, technology licensing, learning management, resource development, grant management, etc. In the framework, a novel concept of "Government University Cloud" is coined. Furthermore, in order to make "Government University Cloud" more functionally effective, a new dedicated application model G2U "Government to University" need to be implemented.

---

* Department of Computer Application, CET, Mody University of Science and Technology, Lakshmangarh-332311, Sikar, Rajasthan, India. E-Mail: urmani10kaushal@gmail.com.

Keywords: e-governance, Government University Cloud, G2U (Government to University), accessibility, transparency

1. Introduction

The development of any country depends upon the advancement of higher education. And intellectual and economic transformations of any society depend on the collaboration and contribution of various stakeholders such as universities, government, industries, researchers; students etc. Now, most of the universities in India have started to invest on Research and Development which is the need of the hour. (Shahid, Golam, Shaiful, Md. Zakir, and Fariha, 2010) These universities use IT infrastructure as the foundation for their educational activities and research. The technological evolution has provided the facility to migrate the traditional educational services to the cloud-based services. In order to strengthen the educational services, strong ICT infrastructure is required. The development of ICT infrastructure enables the large number of users to access the educational services. The inclusion of e-governance in higher education could help in generating positive environment at university level. And, higher education growth generates favorable environment for research and development (Pardeshi, 2014).

The countries those who have invested more money on higher education have achieved high EGDI (E-Government Development Index). The Republic of Korea and Japan have high GDP growth rate and strong national education policy. As a result, these countries have achieved high EGDI index which is an indicator of the development of ICT infrastructure. In Australia, 99 percent populace is literate and its EGDI index ranked 2nd best in the world. In 2014, Government of Australia spent 5.9 percent of GDP on education which shows that the Australian Government gives due importance to this sector (Noonan and Burke, 2015). As compare to these countries, Indian literacy rate is 74.02 percent and investment on higher education was 4.29 percent of GDP in 2012-13 shown in Figure 1. (UNITED NATIONS E-GOVERNMENT SURVEY 2014, 2014; GoI and Development, 2014) The EGDI of India comes in middle group countries (Between 0.25 and 0.50) shown in Figure 2. Therefore, the present scenario in India, in terms of ICT usage and literacy improvement is not overwhelming. Indian research institutes have developed their curriculum on the bases of available ICT infrastructure and not vice-versa. Moreover, the existing ICT infrastructure available at research institutes is not utilized properly. Most of the universities and research institutes are not having enough software and hardware infrastructure to fully automate their system and the means to communicate with the government at each level (Sharmila Devi, 2012).

Considering the present perplexing situation, present chapter is an attempt to generate a cloud computing based framework of e-governance for higher education. This framework implication would help government to generate additional revenue.

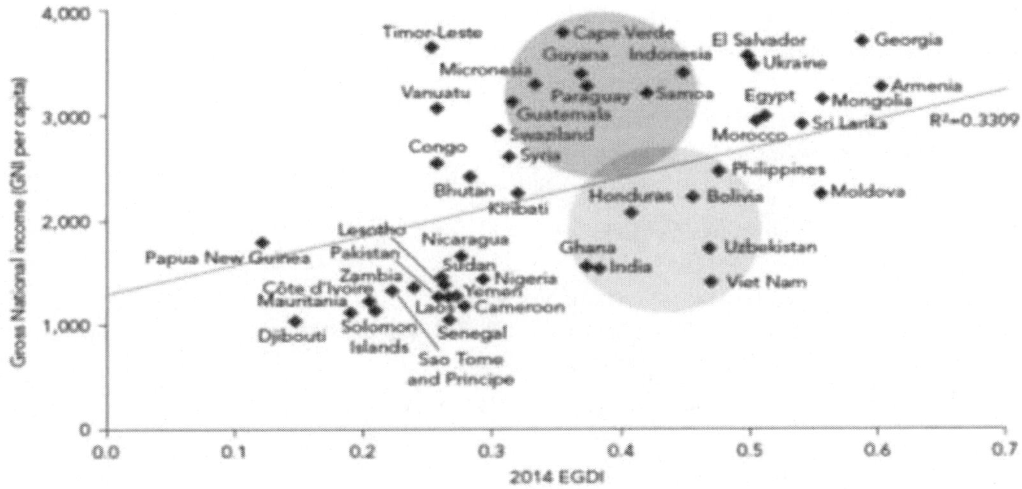

Source: United Nations E-Government Survey 2014.

Figure 1. Relation between EGDI and national income (GNI per capital), lower-middle income countries.

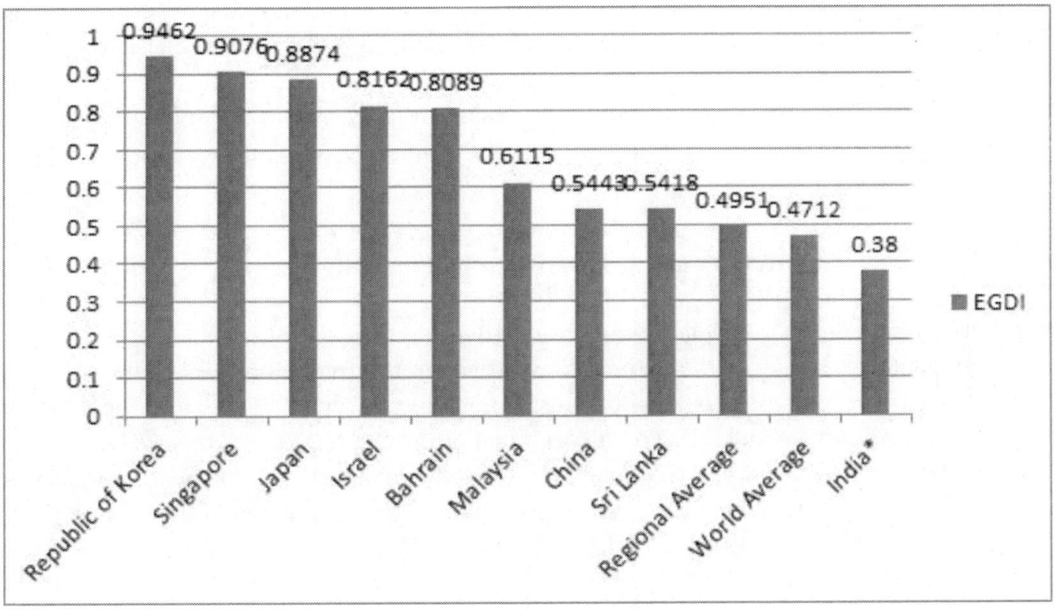

Figure 2. Comparison EGDI.

2. Need of New Model

Various applications of the government have been performed by the participation of different bodies like government, enterprise, business or consumer (Saugata and Masud, 2007). Based on the nature of participating body following e-Government models were framed: The categories are Government to Government (G2G), Government to Citizens (G2C) and Government to Business (G2B) (Siau and Long, 2005) (Yildiz, 2007). Further, the categories can also include Government to Civil Society Organisations (G2CS) and Citizens to Citizens (C2C) (Yildiz, 2007). The four categories are summarized as follows:

1) G2G (Government to Government)
2) G2E (Government to Employee)
3) G2B (Government to Business)
4) G2C (Government to Consumer)

In the aforesaid models of e-governance, the educational or research institutes were not included as prime component while education and research is the most important pillar of a country (Ercan, 2010; Lowendahl, 2012).

Investment of money, efforts, creativity to furnish operational segment in education sector will lead the country toward poverty reduction, improved state of economy, batter health, less corruption, healthy mental status of society and many more (Education|Global Partnership for Education, 2015) (Importance of Higher Education in Developing Countries, 2015).

In India, higher education is being provided by government as well as private sector. Therefore, it is essential to form a new e-governance model for enhancing the participation among higher educational or research institute or universities and the government. The driving factors of e-governance may be driven by technical, economic, social and cultural reasons. So in this chapter, new application model of e-governance G2U (Government to University) has been proposed to avoid unnecessary replication of IT infrastructure and services.

3. Why Cloud Computing?

Cloud Computing is competent enough to provide practical and sustainable solution to variably escalating IT needs with the limitation of budget. It provides on demand configurable computing resources like servers, applications, storage as a services in effective and efficient manner. It can be adopted and utilized with minimal effort and less administrative burden. All the resources can be used by end terminal having internet connectivity. Because computation takes place on a remote server, the user's hardware and software requirements are much lower than they would be otherwise. Adoption of cloud computing will reduce both cost and maintenance requirements (Pardeshi, 2014) (Varma, 2010).

According to UN E-Government Survey 2014, India has clearly advanced e-government despite of relatively lower national income. So running in the same direction, as a step ahead we should modify the way of implementation of e-government for higher education. As discussed above cloud computing may be cost effective and efficient tool for the implementation of e-government in India.

4. Challenges with Traditional Infrastructure

The issue of availability, licensing and support, scalability, accountability, modifiability and physical security is with the existing implementation of e-Governance in education (Varma, 2010).

4.1. Availability: Replication is needed to provide the high availability which in turn will make the process of development cumbersome for individual e-Government project.

4.2. Software Licensing and Support: In existing implementation, each application and data centre require separate licensing. But in cloud implementation it requires only one license for it.

4.3. Scalability: Variable demand of applications and ICT infrastructure cannot be fulfilled by the traditional infrastructure.

4.4. Accountability: Accountability and central authority is not available with applications in traditional infrastructure.

4.5. Modifiability: Changing requirement of applications or infrastructure incurs more cost in traditional infrastructure. For example moving from 200 users to 1000 users will be more costly and time consuming.

4.6. Physical Security: If computing equipment's are installed locally, it became necessary to provide safe environment for information processing activity. Prevention of unauthorized access and physical security must be maintained which quite difficult to maintain.

5. Proposed Framework

The prime objective of the framework proposed in this chapter is to integrate the scattered set of operations, simplification of complex processes at end user level, increasing accessibility and transparency. In the proposed framework which is shown in Figure 3, integration of cloud computing has been done to achieve objective of optimal utilization of budget and generation of the revenue for the government by providing standard and efficient services to all (government and private) universities, higher educational institutes or research institutes. To achieve this goal government has to deploy "Government University Cloud." This government university cloud will provide all type of services to universities or research institutions. The grant released for the research by the different bodies of the government includes certain IT infrastructure as the mandatory head to conduct the research. This IT infrastructure could be provided to all research projects in shared fashion. This initiative will stop the unnecessary replication of IT infrastructure and save the budget which could be used to improve the quality of education.

According to Gartner research (2000) study titled "Gartner's Four Phases of e-Government Model," deployment of e-government must have four distinct phases which will serve as a reference for the proposed framework.

5.1. Presence: "This stage is classified by a simple information-providing Web site of a passive nature, sometimes described as "brochure ware," indicating the same level of functions as a paper brochure" (Pardeshi, 2014). In the proposed model "University Portal" will provide all information related to a university or institute. This university portal will be provided by government as a service to all institutions separately which is highly customizable in nature. Every institution would be able to customize this portal with interference of the vendor.

The users like students, applicants, alumni, faculty, administration, staff and extended members will access whole information about the particular institute or university from this university portal.

5.2. Interaction: At this stage it provides interactions between government and citizen (G2C), government to business (G2B), or government agency to government agency (G2G). In the proposed framework (G2U) government to university model has been proposed. By using this model universities and government with interact with each other. Applications provided by SaaS layer of cloud implementation will interact with users. At this stage government and the universities will interact with each other in every sense. SaaS layer of cloud will provide the interaction software to the universities and government for academic, administrative or research purposes. Highly customizable software's will be provided to all universities and institutions for admissions, learning management, resource development, facilities, grant management, libraries, finance, HR, budget and president's office as a services. These softwares provided by application service provider will be hosted by provider itself which runs and interacts through web browser, hosted desktop or remote client. The softwares/applications provided to universities or research institutes need not to be installed and run on local computer. In this way the process of maintenance and support could be simplified. The process of maintenance will be taken care by the provider. Now the SaaS enabled universities are not burdened with the time-consuming and costly task of managing software updates, security patches and a host of other administrative duties for on premise software solutions (Pardeshi, 2014). These tasks would be managed by the provider efficiently and affordably on the back-end in a time mannered fashion.

5.3. Transaction: In this framework, it is proposed that the government will work as a service provider of software, platform and infrastructure. The universities will use the services as per their requirement and pay as per their uses of IT infrastructure. Students, applicants, alumni, faculty members, administrative members, staff and extended members would be able to perform required monetary transaction with the help of applications provided to the universities. Universities can acquire extended requirement (User Licensing, Technology Licensing, Increased requirement of memory, CPU, Databases etc.) at any instance of time by making less technical and administrative efforts. IaaS and PaaS service model of cloud computing will provide above required services. And universities have to pay only for what they are using. In the case of government funded research project government can allocate the required IT infrastructure for the required duration. This practice will save the budget of replication of the IT infrastructure and the saved fund could be utilized to improve the quality of education.

5.4. Transformation: In the proposed framework, it is suggested that the government must develop its own cloud services. For this government has to develop new deployment model "Government University Cloud" which can be implemented by specified application framed in this research namely G2U (Government to University). By this cloud computing implementation, the government can effectively govern all educational institutes. G2U application and "Government University Cloud" deployment model will formulate the new effective and efficient way of governance. By the implementation of proposed framework, the government will be able to manage and control the functions of universities effectively.

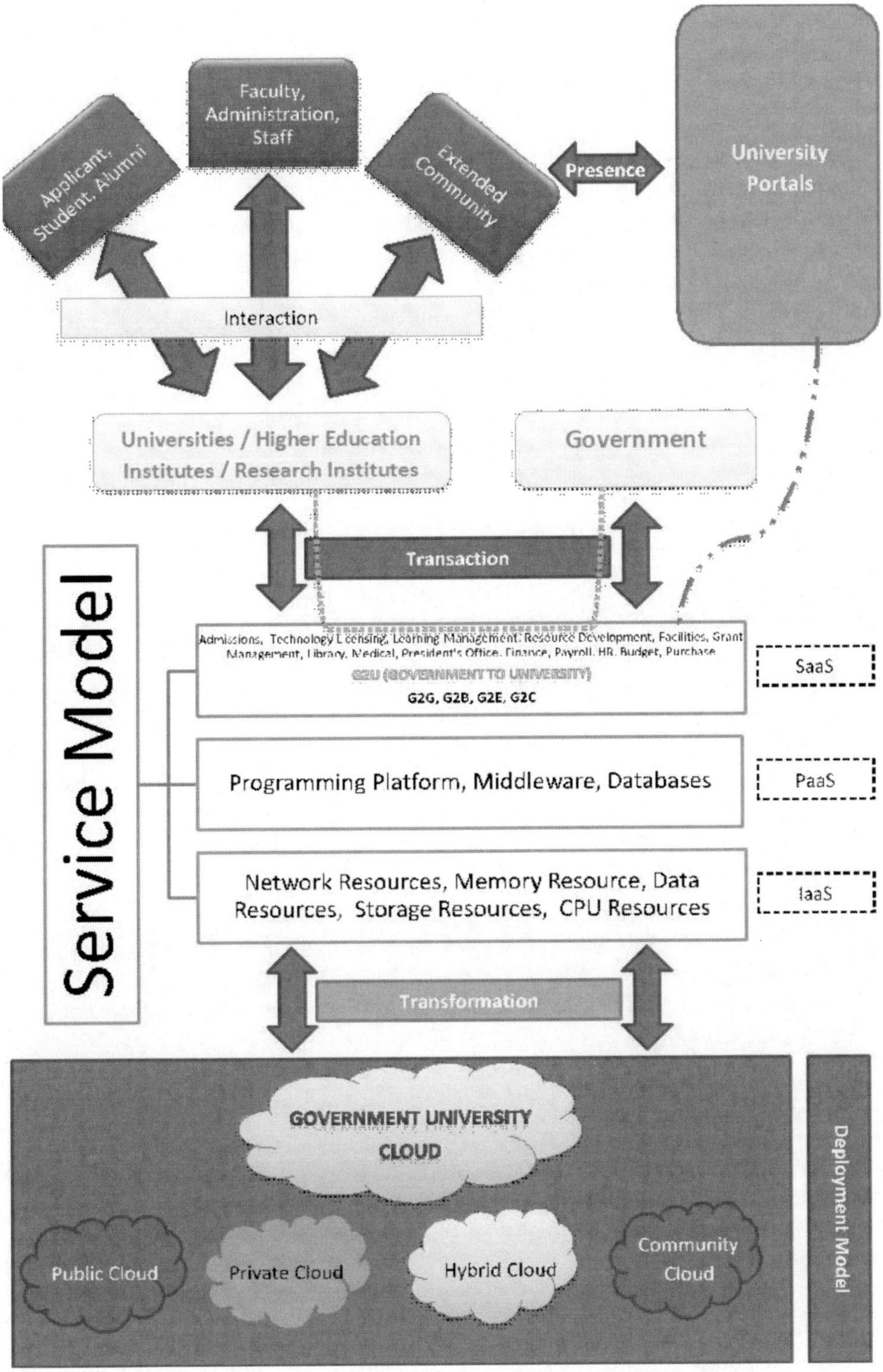

Figure 3. Cloud Computing Based E-Governance Framework for Higher Education.

Conclusion

Currently the operational mechanism of government to handle operations of universities/research institutes/higher educational institutes is not as good as it should be. One government body is not having the interaction with the other to verify operations of universities and research institutes. By the implementation of the proposed framework the government would be able to visualize the information of all the universities at the single place which will help the government in policy making. The deployment of the government university cloud will help the government to stop the replication of the IT infrastructure which will save the wastage of budget. This saved budget could be utilized to improve the quality of education and research. In the same fashion, the proposed G2U application model should be deployed by the government for the smooth functioning of universities and to utilize the services provided by the government itself. As a services provider of infrastructure, platform or software, the government will earn huge revenue.

References

------- (2014). *United Nations E-Government Survey 2014.*

Education|Global Partnership for Education. (2015). Retrieved November 19, 2015, from Global Partnership for Education: http://www.globalpartnership.org/education.

Ercan, T. (2010). Effective use of cloud computing in educational institutions. *Procedia Social and Behavioral Sciences* (pp. 938-942). Elsevier.

GoI, and Development, M. o. (2014). *Educational Statistics at Glance.* New Delhi: Department of Higher Education.

Importance of Higher Education in Developing Countries. (2015, March 13). Retrieved November 19, 2015, from Physical Education Need and Importance: http://www.szemun.eu/importance-of-higher-education-in-developing-countries/.

Lowendahl, J.-M. (2012). A Quick Look at Cloud Computing in Higher Education. *2012 Gartner, Industry research.*

Noonan, P. and Burke, G. (2015). *Expenditure on education and training in Australia.* Melbourne: Mitchell Institute.

Pardeshi, V. H. (2014). Cloud Computing for Higher Education Institutes: Architecture, Strategy and Recommendations for Effective Adaptation. *Procedia Economics and Finance 11 (2014)* (pp. 589-599). Elsevier.

Saugata, B. and Masud, R. (2007). Implementing E-Governance Using OECD Model(Modified) and Gartner Model (Modified) Upon Agriculture of Bangladesh. *10th international conference on Computer and information technology 2007* (pp. 1-5). Dhaka: IEEE.

Shahid, A. N., Golam, M., Shaiful, A. C., Md. Zakir, H. and Fariha, T. J. (2010). A Proposed Architecture of Cloud Computing for Education System in Bangladesh and the Impact on Current Education System. *International Journal of Computer Science and Network Security, 10*(10), 7-13.

Sharmila Devi, M. R. (2012). ICT for Qulaity of Education in India. *International Journal of Physical and Social Sciences*, 542-554.

Siau, K. and Long, Y. (2005). Using social development lenses to understand e-government development. *Journal of Global Information Management, 14*(1), 47-62.

Varma, V. (2010). *Cloud Computing for E-Governance.* Hyderabad: IIIT, Hyderabad.

Yildiz, M. (2007). *E-government research: Reviewing the literature, limitations and ways forward.* Government Information Quarterly.

In: e-Governance in India: Problems, Prototypes and Prospects ISBN: 978-1-63484-830-5
Editors: P. Kumar, R. Sharma and U. Kaushal

Chapter 12

"MOBILE Q": A TINY STEP TOWARDS e-GOVERNANCE IN INDIA

Rajneesh Kumar Srivastava*
Department of Electronics and Communication,
University of Allahabad, Allahabad, India

ABSTRACT

An SMS based software "Mobile Q" using GSM technology has been developed by the author of this chapter with an objective, certainly very much aligned with objectives of e-Governance in India, to relax and make more productive a common man of India by reducing his waiting time in long queues in a cost effective and easy to use manner. "Mobile Q" has been in public domain since last three years but neither "Mobile Q" nor any other "Mobile Q" like queue system has been reported in use in India. This chapter is an attempt to throw light on motivation behind development of "Mobile Q", its salient features and applications as well as challenges faced by the author while attempting to get it in use having a lot more common with challenges e-Governance in India might face.

Keywords: e-Governance, m-Governance, queue, SMS, application software

"The vision of electronic Governance or e-Governance has been over half a century in the making. Electronic governance or e-Governance is the application of information and communication (ICT) for delivering government services, exchange of information communication transactions, integration of various stand-alone systems and services between government-to-customer (G2C), government-to-business (G2B), government-to-government (G2G) as well as back office processes and interactions within the entire government framework. (Saugata & Masud, 2007) Through e-Governance, government services will be made available to citizens in a convenient, efficient and transparent manner. The three main

* Corresponding author: Department of Electronics and Communication, University of Allahabad, Allahabad -211 002, E-mail id: rkumarsau@gmail.com.

target groups that can be distinguished in governance concepts are government, citizens and businesses/interest groups. (Garson, 2006) In e-Governance, there are no distinct boundaries and objective of e-Governance is to use technologies to help both who governs and who are governed. (Garson, 2006; Pierre & Finger, 2007) The advantages of e-Governance include increased access to information, simplicity and convenience, quality service for citizens, efficiency, speed, transparency, accountability, and expanded realm and role of governance.

Taking into account the advantages of e-Governance, Government of India, on May 18, 2006, approved the National e-Governance Plan (NeGP) aiming at improving delivery of Government services to citizens and businesses with the following vision: "*Make all Government services accessible to the common man in his locality, through common service delivery outlets and ensure efficiency, transparency and reliability of such services at affordable costs to realize the basic needs of the common man.*" While envisioning the paths to achieve the goals of e-Governance, Government of India recognized the technology of mobile communications as a fast and easy access to electronic services for citizens through mobile phones. Today, the mobile phone is not just a communication tool to instantly communicate or send and get text and voice messages. Rather, it has emerged as the most suitable technology to bridge the digital divide between urban haves and rural have-nots. Within two decades of its launch in India, mobile phone has reached remote rural areas and has emerged as a delivery channel for different kind of services despite a number of obstacles including poor connectivity, lack of electricity and low level of literacy. Government of India aims to utilize the massive reach of mobile phones, to harness the potential of mobile applications to enable easy and round-the-clock access to electronic services especially for common man and to create unique infrastructure as well as applications development ecosystem for m-Governance, a sub domain of e-Governance, in the country. As a result of this visionary initiative, citizens of India are now able to access services related to health, education, agriculture, bank, infotainment, etc. on their mobile phones. (Mobile Governance, 2015)

India, a country of diversity, is having population of more than 1.2 billion…second in the world! The huge population of India could be a boon if the available human resource is used more productively, thereby, contributing more to GDP of the nation. A common man of India, irrespective of whether he belongs to a metro city, a city, a town, a village or a forest, faces daily a big problem of waiting for his turn in long queues for different services and that of reaching at the place of service much earlier to the start of service just to get a token. Be it

- to consult a doctor in government hospitals or private clinics,
- to procure items through Public Distribution Systems (PDSs)
- to get tickets or reservation at railway stations
- to get admission or deposit fee at counters of schools, colleges or universities
- to cast votes,
- to pay bills
- to get tickets in cinema halls, exhibitions or fairs
- to deposit a form
- to order snacks or meals in restaurants, etc. … … … long queues are awaiting everywhere.

Long queues affect productivity of the nation; women, children and elders face a lot of difficulties; common man gets more stressed and frustrated; chaos occur, corruption flourishes and many times long queues become source of accidents and conflicts. In addition, organizations and administrations need to invest more resources to manage the long queues.

Certain problems associated with long queues could be understood by considering the case of a patient and a doctor. If a patient needs to consult his doctor at his clinic or in a government hospital, one of his attendants would have to travel to the clinic just to get a token and to return back to the patient. Then that fellow would have to bring the patient at the clinic and wait for his turn in the long queue. The attendants and the patients get stressed. Many times the attendants get frustrated waiting in long queues and lock their horns with staff of the clinic. Often, mismanaged long queues result in stampedes and break down of law and order. At the same time, facilities provided by the doctor for patients and attendants seem to be insufficient due to crowd in form of a long queue. As a result, patients and attendants face a lot of difficulties and inconveniences.

In case of public distribution systems, which are basically meant for providing food grains and other essential items to vulnerable sections of the society at reasonable (subsidized) prices by governments, poor citizens face a rampant problem of waiting in long queues at the expense of losing chance of earning their wages for that duration and many times getting denied their dues due to ignorance about their turns as a result of non-transparent PDSs.

Similarly, women, elders as well as differently abled persons find it very difficult to get the services in long queues as they are required to be present physically in the queues for long durations facing problems of eve teasing, queue jumping, thrashing and theft, etc.

In above mentioned examples, the situation could have been better for the patients and their attendants as well as for the doctors and their staffs (including poor citizens, women, elders and differently abled persons) provided

1. The patient could get a token while staying at his home.
2. The patient could be informed while staying at his home about the arrival time of the doctor.
3. The patient could be informed while staying at his home about the current token being served by the doctor and the expected time after which his turn may arrive.

With the above mentioned facilities, the scenario would be quite conducive

1. As attendant of the patient is not required to travel to the clinic just to get a token. This would be quiet convenient and time saving for the patient's attendants. At the same time, this would have positive impact on environment as a result of saving in consumption of fuel and carbon emission as the attendants need not to travel to get a token.
2. As the patient is informed about the expected time for arrival of his turn, he could decide to move from his place to the clinic just by an amount of time sufficient for him to reach at clinic before arrival of his turn. As a result he would have to wait for a minimum amount of time in queue.
3. Very limited number of persons including patients and attendants would be physically present in queue at a time. As a result, it would be possible and affordable

for the doctor to provide better facilities for the patients and attendants. Certainly, the doctors would have interest in doing so.

As of now, it is evident that a cost effective, simple to use and readily available to common man solution for reducing the effort to be part of a queue and waiting time in long queue is warranted to fulfill the "make citizens' lives better" objective of e-Governance.

Let us, now, analyze the factors responsible for problems associated with long queues including different strategies in use to counter these problems including their limitations. "Queues are formal and informal arrangements made to regulate behavior, to recognize the priority of early-comers, and to inhibit the growth of conflict. Ideal queues are supposed to provide place-keeping privileges, sanctions against pushing in, and rights of temporary absence from the waiting line. (Mann, 1969)

A number of ways of formation of queues are described as follows:

1. Queue-A: The user comes at the point of service physically and adds itself to the last user in the queue. The service is provided on the basis of first come - first served basis. The user in queue waits until his turn comes.
   Limitations: The user is required to be present physically to be part of the queue. The user in queue is required to stand and wait physically until his turn comes. No estimated waiting time is informed to him, he can just guess. He gets stressed and many times even frustrated. The user in queue remains non-productive for a significant proportion of time. He cannot afford to move out of the line of queue even for a while. No tokens are being issued and pre queue may be formed before start of the service.
2. Queue-B: The user comes at the point of service physically, gets himself registered at the counter to get a token, gets seated, remains informed about current token being served by some announcer or token display systems.
   Limitations: The user is required to be present physically to be part of the queue. No estimated waiting time is informed to him, he can just guess. He gets stressed and many times even frustrated. The user in queue remains non-productive for a significant proportion of time. Tokens are being issued manually which may result in formation of pre queue.
   Improvements: The user in queue is somewhat relaxed as he is not required to stand in the queue while waiting and can afford to move a while.
3. Queue-C: The user comes at the point of service physically, gets a token himself using a token vending machine, gets seated, remains informed about current token being served by some announcer or token display systems.
   Limitations: The user is required to be present physically to be part of the queue. No estimated waiting time is informed to him, he can just guess. He gets stressed and many times even frustrated. The user in queue remains non-productive for a significant proportion of time.
   Improvements: The user in queue is somewhat relaxed as he is not required to stand in the queue while waiting and can afford to move a while. Tokens are being issued by a machine which may preempt formation of pre queue.

4. Queue-D: The user gets a token number by calling the counter staff on telephone and comes to the point of service at the time of beginning of the service, gets seated, remains informed about current token being served by some announcer or token display systems.
   Limitations: Tokens are being issued manually on telephone lines which may result in formation of pre queue if there are a large number of requests at a time. No estimated waiting time is informed to him, he can just guess. He gets stressed and many times even frustrated. The user in queue remains non-productive for a significant proportion of time.
   Improvements: The user is not required to be present physically to be part of the queue. He becomes part of the queue by getting token number on telephone which saves effort and time of travelling to get a token. The user in queue is somewhat relaxed as he is not required to stand in the queue while waiting and can afford to move a while.
5. Queue-E: The user first comes at the point of service physically and gets registered at the counter to get a token. During registration, user's telephone number is entered by the counter staff in the register and user returns back to his place. When user's turn is about to arrive, user is informed about arrival of his turn through a telephone call a certain amount of time earlier. The user arrives at point of service before his turn arrives.
   Limitations: The user is required to be present physically to be part of the queue. Tokens are being issued manually which may result in formation of pre queue. No estimated waiting time is informed to him and he would have to wait for a call from the counter staff. The user in queue remains non-productive only for a non significant proportion of time.
   Improvements: The user in queue is very much relaxed as he is not required to wait for a long time in queue and saved time could be utilized by him for other productive activities.
6. Queue-F: The user first comes at the point of service physically and gets a token using a token vending machine or token kiosks, gets seated or moves out of the point of service for other scheduled activities. When user's turn is about to arrive, user is informed about arrival of his turn through SMS or e-mail a certain amount of time earlier. The user arrives at point of service before his turn arrives.
   Limitations: The user is required to be present physically to be part of the queue.
   Limitations: No estimated waiting time is informed to user and he would have to wait for an SMS or e-mail. The user in queue remains non-productive for only non-significant proportion of time.
   Improvements: Tokens are being issued by a machine which may preempt formation of any pre queue. The user in queue is very much relaxed as he is not required to wait for a long time in queue and saved time could be utilized by him for other productive activities.

A comparison of above discussed queue systems is presented in Table 1.

Table 1. Comparison between various types of queues

	Queue-A	Queue-B	Queue-C	Queue-D	Queue-E	Queue-F
The user is required to be present physically to be part of the queue	Yes	Yes	Yes	No	Yes	Yes
Token is being issued	No, token is issued implicitly	Yes, manually	Yes, using token vending machines	Yes, on telephone line by counter staff manually	Yes, manually	Yes, using token vending machines
Speed of token issuance	Fast	Slow	Fast	Slow	Slow	Fast
Pre queue May be formed	Yes	Yes	No	Yes	Yes	No
The user in queue is required to wait physically until his turn arrives	Yes	Yes	Yes	Yes	Yes but for a significantly reduced amount of time	Yes but for a significantly reduced amount of time
Token being served is displayed or announced	No	Yes	Yes	Yes	Yes	Yes
Estimated waiting time is informed to user	No	No	No	No	No	No
Estimated waiting time is guessed by the user	Yes	Yes	Yes	Yes	No	No
Waiting time in queue	Very Long	Very Long	Very Long	Very Long	Short	Short
Stress-level of user due to waiting in queue	Extremely High	Very High	Very High	High	Low	Low
User gets frustrated	Yes	Yes	Yes	Yes	No	No
Non-productivity in queue	Extremely High	Very High	Very High	High	Low	Low
Can user afford to move out of the line of queue	No, Even not for a while	Yes, for a while	Yes, for a while	Yes, for a while	Yes, for most of the time	Yes, for most of the time

Out of the six types of queue discussed above, queue type F i.e., Queue-F is having improvements of reduced stress, no frustration, improved productivity and freedom of being on move for the user over other types of queue. Nonetheless, Queue-F suffers from one serious drawback of user not being updated about the current status of the queue and the expected time for arrival of his turn. As a result, in case of non-arrival or absence of many front users of the queue at a time, non-arrival of the users following them in the queue might take place as they would not have sufficient time to reach at the point of service due to not being informed by a certain amount of time earlier. In addition, the user would have to abandon his present activities suddenly and he would have to rush to the point of service which makes user stressed as well as results in reduced productivity of the user during the saved waiting time as the user could not plan for optimally scheduled activities in anticipation of such a sudden alert.

In an improved queue system, say, Queue-X, devoid of the above discussed limitation of Queue-F, a user may get token remotely and be updated quite frequently about current status of the queue, the token number being served and the expected time for arrival of his turn automatically and this is the type of queue which has been implemented in the software "Mobile Q."

A number of organizations have been offering Queue-E and Queue-F systems across the globe since last decade e.g., Q'soft, WaitKnowMore, NemoQ, SMS'Q,' Fraunhofer HHI, Ticktok, Supalocal, Smartqueue, Queue Mobile, etc. but all of them are mostly aiming at serving the privileged sections who could afford high cost smart phone and tablet like devices as well as high cost data services. All of these systems are either Web based or call center based wherein a user could get token remotely followed by being informed about sufficiently accurate arrival time of his turn through SMSs, calls or e-mails. These queue systems connect the service provider and the service users via Internet to form queue and are very efficient, user-friendly and revenue generating. Though, exactly these queue systems do not seem suitable for a common man of India, such types of queue system must have been already in place in India in spite of their being privileged sections oriented.

Few years back, the author of this chapter perplexed by long waiting time in queues in hospitals and doctors' clinics as a common man conceived the idea of "Mobile Q" and developed it for a common man of India taking into account following issues and facts:

- Problems of long waiting time in queues being faced by a common man
- Availability of easy to use, and cost effective conventional mobile phones
- Deep penetration of mobile communications services across the country
- Huge mobile subscriber base
- Comparably very economical and readily available SMS services
- Small foot print of Internet, high cost data services and high cost smart phones/tablets in India demanding learning curve for users

Salient features of "Mobile Q" are as follows:

1. The software "Mobile Q" developed by author of this chapter was brought in public domain in the year of 2012 and the author got its copyright in the year of 2013. (Software Registration Number: SW-6873/2013 dated 02/08/2013)

2. "Mobile Q" is an SMS based software using GSM technology contrary to prevalent queue systems which are based on Internet, Web and smart phones/tablets.
3. "Mobile Q" is a Java based software using AT commands, RXTX - a native interface to serial port in Java and freetts – a text to speech conversion software.
4. No mobile subscriber is required to install "Mobile Q" on his mobile phone.
5. This software is required to be installed on the computer system of the service provider only equipped with a USB port compatible GSM modem e.g., computer systems of Doctors, Counter Clerks, etc.
6. The service provider can set the time of start of the service, size of the physical queue, maximum size of the queue, average service time per token, how frequently a user be informed, etc. in the setting of "Mobile Q."
7. A mobile subscriber can request remotely for a token through SMS sent to "Mobile Q."
8. "Mobile Q" on the computer of a service provider sends information regarding token number, time of start of the service, the present token number being served and the expected time after which the turn of the concerned mobile subscriber may arrive through SMSs sufficiently frequently.
9. Mobile subscriber moves to the service place by a time which would minimize his waiting time in queue taking into account the present status of the queue. The saved time could be utilized by him for other productive activities.
10. Mobile subscriber himself can make query any time regarding status of the queue through SMS to "Mobile Q."
11. If the service is required to be discontinued in certain situations, the service provider can inform to and regret to the mobile subscribers waiting in "Mobile Q" just by clicking a 'sorry' button in "Mobile Q" and entering an appropriate token number so that the users, having token numbers equal to or greater than the entered token number in 'sorry dialog box' would receive sorry messages.
12. Even the user who is not having his own mobile phone but can take help of a mobile phone of one of his friends or relatives could get a token from the service place by going there physically. Further information would be sent through SMSs as usual to the mobile phone number provided by the user to the software "Mobile Q."
13. Even a user can get a token form the clinic and be in queue physically since the beginning as it was the case without "Mobile Q."
14. "Mobile Q" is having instant messaging feature.
15. "Mobile Q" provides a user-friendly GUI to the service provider having a number of features including File of SMS sent, Settings option in Tools, Basic for instant messaging, Mobile Queue having fields of Token Number, Time of reception of the SMS, Sender i.e., mobile number, START, Name, Add, Sorry, Skip and NEXT, etc. A snapshot of the GUI of "Mobile Q" is shown in Figure 1.

ALGORITHM

1. Suppose a doctor's "Mobile Q" with its mobile number as "0987654321" running on his system is having settings as follows: start of time as 10 am, average service time

as 3 minutes, waiting capacity i.e., physical queue of 3, max size of the queue as 25, registration keyword as *abc*. Further suppose a user can reach at the doctor's clinic within 9 minutes.

2. Suppose a group of twenty six users, say A, B, C, … … …, P, Q, R, … … …, X, Y, Z are willing to consult the doctor and P is the sample user. Each of them sends an SMS to "0987654321" with message < *abc space* * > where * is the name of the user.
3. Suppose "Mobile Q" receives all these SMSs in the given order. "Mobile Q" adds all the first twenty five users in the queue and the GUI will display that queue as follows:

Token No.	User mobile number	User name	Expected time for turn in minutes
0		Default	
1	Mob-A	A	0
2	Mob-B	B	3
3	Mob-C	C	6
… … …	… … …	… … …	… … …
16	Mob-P	P	45
17	Mob-Q	Q	48
18	Mob-R	R	51
… … …	… … …	… … …	… … …
23	Mob-W	W	66
24	Mob-X	X	69
25	Mob-Y	Y	72

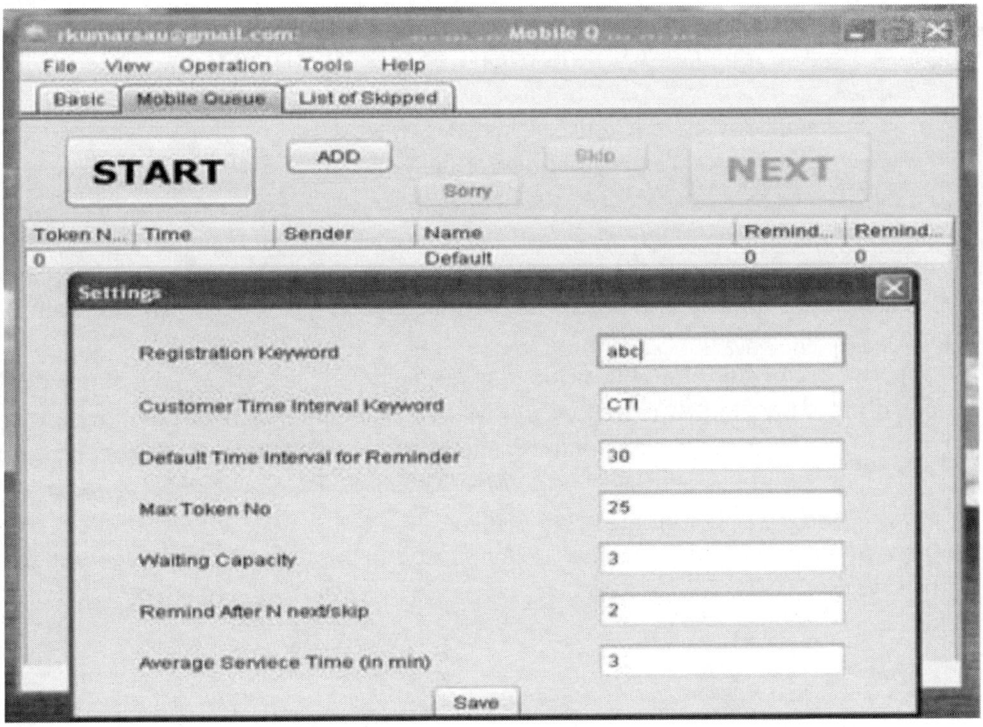

Figure 1. A snapshot of the GUI of "Mobile Q."

4. All the users, except the user Z who will be denied the service by receiving an SMS < *Mr./Miss Z! Sorry! The queue is full. Please try next session.* >, will receive an SMS < *Mr./Miss *! You have been registered. Your token no. is #. The service will start at 10 am. We will update you frequently* > where * is the user's name and # is the expected time for turn of *.
5. Suppose doctor enters in his clinic at 10 am and starts the service by clicking the "START" button of "Mobile Q." As the physical queue size is three, only first three users viz. A, B and C will be in the physical queue and A will receive SMS < *Mr./Miss A! Your token no is 1. The service has been started. Your turn may come any time. Please be present.* >, B will receive SMS < *Mr./Miss B! Your token no is 2. The service has been started. Your turn may come any time. Please be present.* >, C will receive SMS < *Mr./Miss C! Your token no is 3. The service has been started. Your turn may come any time. Please be present.* > As D is out of physical queue, he will receive SMS < *Mr./Miss D! Your token no is 4. The service has been started. Your turn may come after 9 min.* > D will move to the clinic to reach there within 9 minutes. The sample user P, out of physical queue, will receive SMS < *Mr./Miss P! Your token no is 16. The service has been started. Your turn may come after 45 min.* > and so on.
6. When doctor presses the button "NEXT." A will receive SMS <*Mr./Miss A! Your token no is 1. Please come in.* > As D has now entered into physical queue i.e., B, C and D are in physical queue, B will receive SMS < *Mr./Miss B! Your token no is 2. Token being served is 1. Your turn may come any time. Please be present.* >, C will receive SMS < *Mr./Miss C! Your token no is 3. Token being served is 1. Your turn may come any time. Please be present.* > and D will receive SMS < *Mr./Miss D! Your token no is 4. Token being served is 1. Your turn may come any time. Please be present.* >The sample user P will receive SMS < *Mr./Miss P! Your token no is 16. Token being served is 1. Your turn may come after 42 min.* >
7. In such a manner the sample user P will receive a series of SMSs regarding current token being served and expected time for his turn but he will not move to clinic until he receives SMS < *Mr./Miss P! Your token no is 16. Token being served is 13. Your turn may come after 9 min.* > P will move immediately to reach the clinic within 9 minutes. As P has to wait in queue for not more than 9 minutes as compared to minimum 45 minutes without facility of "Mobile Q", saving in waiting time is 36 minutes with "Mobile Q."
8. Suppose doctor finds it not possible to continue the service after token number 24, he could press the "SORRY" button of "Mobile Q" and enter token number 25 in the dialog box. Users with token number equal to or greater than 25 will get the sorry SMS i.e., X will receive SMS < *Mr./Miss X! Sorry! The service is discontinued. Try in next session.* > as well as Y will receive SMS < *Mr./Miss Y! Sorry! The service is discontinued. Try in next session.* > As a result both effort and time of X and Y will be saved.

ADVANTAGES OF "MOBILE Q"

"Mobile Q" is having a number of advantages in terms of affordability and suitability to a common man of India. Some of these are enlisted as follows:

1. "Mobile Q" can contribute in Gross Domestic Product (GDP) of the nation as "Mobile Q" reduces the waiting time in queue by an amount up to 70 to 80%. Reduced waiting time leads to higher productivity.
2. "Mobile Q" makes services more transparent and less frustrating to users.
3. "Mobile Q" saves time, consumption of fuel and amount of pollution avoiding travelling for just to get a token.
4. "Mobile Q" relaxes users as they remain updated about the status of the queue and can take decisions accordingly.
5. With "Mobile Q", there would be reduction in peak traffic as it would not be required for all the concerned users to reach the service place in the vicinity of the time of start of the issuance of token or start of the service.
6. With "Mobile Q", the service providers find it affordable to provide better facilities for the limited number of users waiting physically in queue.
7. "Mobile Q" is based on Mobile Communications Networks. To use "Mobile Q", users are required to have comparably cost effective and readily available SMS services only on their conventional mobile phones. As, the users do not require high cost Internet services and smart phones/tablets, it is possible to provide the facility of "Mobile Q" to a common man of India.

APPLICATIONS OF "MOBILE Q"

The concept of "Mobile Q" i.e., "Be in queue while on move using mobile phones" has applications in almost all walks of our life in urban as well as in rural areas facing problems of long queues as a matter of routine. "Mobile Q" may be used for Doctors and Patients; Health services, Hospitals; Form, Application, Bill, Ticket, Enquiry Counters; Public service related organizations e.g., Railways, Banks, Universities and Colleges, etc. Public Distribution Systems; Polling Booths; Courts, Advocates and Clients; Malls, Restaurants; etc. List would continue until long queues vanish.

Challenges in Implementation of "Mobile Q"

Few years back when the author conceived idea about "Mobile Q" like queue system, he was not having any know how or any inclination to develop it himself. Rather, he was just interested in sharing this idea with his friends in industry or with the then available free on line SMS service providers so that he could also be benefited by such type of service in case one of them found it viable to develop and implement it. The author communicated many of them but to no avail. Paying no heed at all to the idea fueled the curiosity of the author. Eventually curiosity got transformed into challenge and the author decided to make it a reality himself. In first phase, a skeleton to send SMSs and receive SMSs between a computer system equipped with a GSM modem and a GSM mobile phone got shape. The skeleton phase was followed by the phase of putting flesh of software on the skeleton to make it having feel and flexibility. At last, "Mobile Q" got its first public appearance three years back by demonstrating successfully formation of queues for users on move with mobile phones. Almost every common man including friends, colleagues, doctors, advocates, counter staffs, shopkeepers, etc. appreciated "Mobile Q" but no one showed interest in its implementation. The author initially could not understand reasons behind such response but one candid remark of a doctor helped him in getting it. The doctor told the author that though the "Mobile Q" was certainly of use in downsizing long physical queues in hospitals and clinics, no hospital or clinic would be really interested in its use as long queues were perceived by them as an indicator of their popularity. In spite of this mind set of society, the author continued his efforts relentlessly. Meantime, the author faced challenge of deciding mode of distribution of "Mobile Q" – should it be free or paid, should it be open source or proprietary as "Mobile Q" was developed using *freetts*-a free text to speech conversion software and *RxTx*- an open source LGPL licensed communication API. The author consulted a number of software and legal professionals in this regard but could not get an unambiguous opinion. Finally, the author realized that nothing could be more suitable than option of making it open source to avoid any sort of legalities. The effort was unabated and last year the author did have a communication with Department of Electronics and Information Technology (Deity), Government of India. Deity responded positively and asked the author to send details of "Mobile Q." The author sent it to Deity. Soon, Deity informed the author on the basis of remarks of CDAC- a technical wing of Deity that "Mobile Q" could not be considered for inclusion as Deity's "Mobile Seva" was supporting mobile apps only. The author argued that it was a deliberate decision not to develop "Mobile Q" as a mobile app and requested to Deity as well as CDAC to reconsider the case of "Mobile Q" taking into account the services being offered by "Mobile Q" and the set of objectives of "Mobile Seva." In response, CDAC asked the author to send an animated presentation of "Mobile Q." At present, the author is in the process of preparing an animated presentation of "Mobile Q" with hope that the day will come the citizens of India would have services of "Mobile Q" or "Mobile Q" like queue systems- a tiny step towards e-Governance in India.

ACKNOWLEDGMENT

The author is thankful to Mr. Pankaj Verma, Mr. Shailesh Dayal, Mr. Amit Kumar, Mr. Sandeep Srivastava, Mr. Praveen Dubey and Dr. Manish Khare for their help and suggestions.

REFERENCES

Garson XE "arson" , D. (2006). *Public Information Technology and E-Governance XE* "E-Governance" *: Managing the Virtual State.* Raleigh: Jones and Bartlett Publishers.

Mann, L. (1969). Queue Culture: The Waiting Line as a Social System. *American Journal of Sociology*, *75*(3), 340-354.

Mobile Governance. (2015). Retrieved 2015, from Vikaspedia: http://vikaspedia.in/e-governance XE "governance" /mobile-governance/mobile-governance.

Pierre, R. and Finger, M. (2007). Conceptualizing e-Governance XE "e-Governance" . *Proceedings of the 1st international conference XE* "conference" *on Theory and practice of electronic governance XE* "governance" , (pp. 399-407). New Yor: ACM.

Saugata, B. and Masud, R. R. (2007). Implementing E-Governance XE "E-Governance" Using OECD XE "OECD" Model(Modified) and Gartner Model (Modified) Upon Agriculture of Bangladesh XE "Bangladesh" . *IEEE*, *9*(1), 4244-1551.

In: e-Governance in India: Problems, Prototypes and Prospects ISBN: 978-1-63484-830-5
Editors: P. Kumar, R. Sharma and U. Kaushal

Chapter 13

LEGAL FRAMEWORK OF E-GOVERNANCE IN INDIA: PROBLEMS AND PROSPECTS

***Rupendra Singh**,1 *and Deeksha Sharma*2**
[1]Advocate Supreme Court of India and Visiting Faculty
Guru Gobind Singh Indra Prastha University, New Delhi, India
[2]Assistant Professor, College of Law and Governance,
Mody University, Laxmangarh, India

ABSTRACT

Governance in general and e-governance in particular are the methods of providing better means of life and standard at international, national and grassroots level. The Information Technology revolution has resulted in the employment of internet communication in the delivery of public services and to achieve good governance by supplying emphasis on e-governance. In the world of 3G and 4G, the governmental authorities in India are working to provide infrastructure and public services in digitized way via internet and accountability in governance has been attempted to be brought on the palm of the "common man." However, there is a lack of concrete legal framework to regulate the matters of e-governance. For instance, many privacy concerns are raised because of the collection, retention and management of personal data without adequate privacy protection legislation. This chapter is an attempt to critically appraise the historical growth and goals of e-governance and the current scenario of the legal framework which regulate e-governance in India.

Keywords: good governance, transparency, accountability, right to privacy

> E-Governance lies at the heart of two global shifts: the information revolution and the governance revolution.
> Both shifts are changing the way society works and the way that society is governed. (Richard Heeks, 1999)

---

* Rupendra Singh, Advocate Supreme Court of India and Visiting Faculty Guru Gobind Singh Indra Prastha University, New Delhi, email: r.singh@dme.ac.in.
[2] Deeksha Sharma, Assistant Professor, College of Law and Governance, Mody University, Laxmangarh, India

1. Introduction

The use of information technology and more specifically internet has increased many folds in recent years. The heavy duty computers and high priced internet services have given way to sleek devices, laptops, smart phones and an affordable internet service. (Gupta, 2010) The convergence of electronics and tele-communications has enunciated new vistas of transmission, storage and exchange of information among the masses. Irrespective of the fact whether an organization is a corporate or a government undertaking, it has chosen the information technology as a new mode of communication, resulting into rapid and prompt tool of decision making. Hence, terms like e-commerce and e-governance are the new buzz words.

The e-governance has played a prominent role in replacing the undesirable features like cramped spaces; shabby ambience; discourteous dealing personnel and their chronic absenteeism; demands of gratification; inefficiency in work; long queues; procrastinating officials; procedural complexities; etc. *(Monga, 2008)* e-governance, which has made the traditional approaches in public administration obsolete, has ushered in transparency in the governing process; saving of time due to provision of services through single window; simplification of procedures; better office and record management; reduction in corruption; and improved attitude, behavior and job handling capacity of the dealing personnel. Therefore, e- governance made the public administration more accountable, responsible and translucent.

Present paper titled as 'the Legal Framework of e-governance: Problems and Prospects' elucidates the divergent laws regulating the e-governance in India. Paper examines the inter-relationship between Right to Information Act, 2005; Right to know and transparency in government functioning as advocated in the Constitution of India. Moreover, a comparative study of legal framework of e- governance in India with United States of America has been drawn. Paper further examines some recent judicial pronouncements like Uniform Identification Number (Aadhar Card case), Reform in Civil Servants Service case where Supreme Court reiterates the importance of e-governance as a new mode of governance and reconciled the transparency with right to privacy.

2. Objectives and Research Methodology

2.1. Objectives

1) To study, understand and analyze the evolution of concept of e-commerce in India.
2) To appraise and analyze the existing legal framework of e-commerce in India.
3) To study and understand the problems of legal framework of e-commerce and to suggest methods of improvisation.

2.2. Database and Research Methodology

In this research doctrinal method has been employed, which relies upon secondary sources mainly text books, commentaries, All India Reporter and articles from internet.

3. E-GOVERNANCE: EVOLUTION AND GOALS

3.1. From Governance to e-Governance

The need for governance exists whenever a group of people come together to accomplish an end. Though the literature on governance proposes several definitions, most rest on three dimensions: authority, decision-making and accountability. (Governance, 2015) United Nations Development Program (UNDP) has very aptly defined the governance which covers all three dimensions: "The exercise of economic, political, and administrative authority to manage a country's affairs at all levels. It comprises mechanisms, processes, and institutions, through which citizens and groups articulate their interests, exercise their legal rights, meet their obligations, and mediate their differences." Therefore, governance is a process by which individuals and institutions, public and private, manage their common affairs. It refers to the interaction between the public sector and civil society for collective decision making. (ICT and Rural Development, 2012)

With the technological advancement and to make governance more transparent and accountable, a new way of governance was enunciated with the help of Information and Communication Technology (ICT). E-Governance is in essence, the application of ICT to government functioning in order to create 'Simple, Moral, Accountable, Responsive and Transparent' (India, 2001) (SMART) governance. E-governance ensures accountability in decisional processes by making the use of ICT for wider participation of citizens in public affairs. Citizens are participants in e-governance. E-governance is a generic term for web-based services from agencies of local, state and federal governments. In e-governance, the government uses information technology and particularly the internet to support government operations, engage citizens, and provide government services. (C., Jain, & Sharma, 2007) United Nations very aptly in a concise manner had defined the e-governance: "e-governance is defined as utilizing the internet and the world-wide-web for delivering government information and services to citizens." (Kumar, 2014) Therefore, governance as well as e-governance is premised on grundnorm theory of Immanual Kant who says, "So act as to treat humanity, whether in their own person or in that of any other, in every case as an end withal, never as means only." This observation is even more valid today. The citizens are ends in themselves, rather than as means to other ends. (Haq, 1995) The colonial view of the role of government as that of a 'controller' and 'ruler' has now become as that of a coordinator and provider. Government is responsible for providing certain services to the citizens, just like an organization is responsible for managing a value chain that leads to output. With the technological developments, government is obliged to provide those services at the doorstep of the individual.

3.2. Historical Growth of e-Governance in India

With the advent of the World Wide Web (WWW) in the nineties, global shifts towards increased deployment of Information Technology by governments emerged. The technology as well as e-governance initiatives have come a long way since then. Recognizing the increasing importance of electronics, the Government of India established the Department of Electronics in 1970. *(Yadav & B.Singh, 2012)* The subsequent establishment of the National Informatics Centre (NIC) in 1977 was the first major step towards e-governance in India as it brought 'information' and its communication in focus. However, the main thrust for e-governance was provided by the launching of National Informatics Center Network (NICNET) and national satellite-based computer network in 1987. This was followed by the launch of the District Information System of the National Informatics centre (DISNIc) program to computerize all district offices in the country. *(India, Saransh, 2011)* NICNET was extended via the state capitals to all district headquarters by 1990. In the ensuing years, with ongoing computerization, tele-connectivity and internet connectivity established a large number of e-governance initiatives, both at the union and state levels. The formulation of National e-Governance Plan (NeGP) by the Department of Electronics and Information Technology (DEITY) and Department of Administrative Reforms and Public Grievances (DAR&PG) in 2006 has boosted the e-governance process in India. *(India, Central Initiatives, 2015)*

3.3. Perspective and Goals of e-Governance

E-Governance aims to make the interaction between government and citizens (G2C), government and business enterprises (G2B), and inter-agency relationships (G2G) more friendly, convenient, transparent, and inexpensive. (Gupta S. B., 2012) Therefore aimed at to achieve (Technology, 2001):

a) Better service delivery to citizens
b) Ushering in transparency and accountability
c) Empower people through information
d) Improved efficiency within Governments
e) Improve interface with business and industry.

E-Governance is not about 'e' but about 'governance'; it is not about computers and websites, but about services to citizens and businesses. E-governance is also not about translating processes; it is about transforming them. The four pillars of e-government are (a) People (b) Process (c) Technology (d) Resources. *(Bhattacharya & Goswami, 2011)* The challenges in e-governance have been described as centered around for key areas viz people, process, technology and resources.

4. Legal Framework of Governing the e- Governance in India

There are various benefits provided by the technology whether it is at an individual level, or development of the country as a whole. It's a tool which makes a platform for the growth and development of the country. As observed by Albert Einstein, technological progress is like an axe in the hands of a pathological criminal. Therefore, to regulate this technological progress we need laws. Though India has no specific e- governance law but same has been regulated by various legislations and policies. The National e-Governance Plan (NeGP) has been formulated by the Department of Electronics and Information Technology (DEITY) and Department of Administrative Reforms and Public Grievances (DARPG). The NeGP aims to provide services to citizens and businesses with the vision of, "Make all Government services accessible to the common man in his locality, through common service delivery outlets and ensure efficiency, transparency and reliability of such services at affordable costs to realize the basic needs of the common man." *(India, Central Initiatives, 2015)* Diverse policies and laws governing the e-governance are as follows:

4.1. Policies Governing the e-Governance

The National e-Governance Plan (NeGP), takes a holistic view of e-governance initiatives across the country, integrating them into a collective vision, a shared cause. The end objective is to make available public services closer home to citizens, as articulated in the vision statement of NeGP as "Make all Government services accessible to the common man in his locality, through common service delivery outlets, and ensure efficiency, transparency, and reliability of such services at affordable costs to realize the basic needs of the common man" *(India, Central Initiatives, 2015)* Further, the scope of NeGP is very wide covering almost all aspects of governance – right from delivery of services and provision of information to business process re-engineering within the different levels of government and its institutions. It is essential that NeGP is implemented, monitored and regulated through a legal framework so that it can attain the desired goals.

4.2. Right to Information Act, 2005

Though the Constitution of India mandates right to information under Article 19 since the time it came into existence *(State of U.P. vs Narayan, 1975*), but legislature gave it an effective shape in 2005 in the form of Right to Information Act, 2005. This Act ensures the transparency in the functioning of the government by placing an obligation on the central and state governments to provide citizens the information about the policies, rules and regulations passed by the government; provided that the information so asked should not be an exempted information. Also, the penalties are provided in case of failure of the government to provide them the information. There is a nexus between e-governance and the RTI Act as former emphasizes on the use of technology by the government to provide information to the citizens. Moreover, Central Information Commission has also set a website, www.cic.gov.in to display the information related to it.

4.3. Information Technology Act, 2000

The Information Technology Act, 2000 was enacted to"…provide legal recognition for transactions carried out by means of electronic data interchange and other means of electronic communication, commonly referred to as "electronic commerce", which includes the use of alternatives methods of communication as emphasized by United Nations Commission on International Trade Law (UNCITRAL). In order to give true color to this legislation, the Indian Penal Code, the Indian Evidence Act, 1872, the Bankers' Books Evidence Act, 1891, the Reserve Bank of India Act, 1934 and various other laws have been amended. (Dalal, n.d.) (India, 2nd Administrative Reforms Commission, 2008)

The Act contains provisions on digital signatures and authentication of electronic records, attribution, acknowledgement and dispatch of electronic records, security of electronic records, regulation of certifying authorities, cyber appellate tribunal etc. This is the only legislation which provides for the data protection by incorporating penal provisions within the enactment. Section 43 of the Act provides protection against unauthorized access of the computer system by imposing heavy penalty up to rupees one crore. Section 69 says that the right to privacy can only be taken away by the provisions established by law. Section 72 of the Act provides protection against breach of confidentiality and privacy of the data. Person convicted shall be punished with imprisonment which may extend to two years or with fine which may extend to one lakh rupees or both. Though, the IT Act, 2000 makes penal provisions for the misuse of information or for unlawful use of information, yet these have been found to be inadequate.

4.4. Constitutional Framework

Constitution of India in its Preamble has talked about the justice: social, economic and political. Justice in its wider sense include, access to information and ascertainment of accountability of government functionary. This idea has further been manifested in other provisions of Constitution. Part III and Part IV of the Constitution impose a duty on government and make them accountable towards the citizen of India. E-Governance which advocates transparency, sharing of information and accessibility thereof frequently conflicts with right to privacy.

4.5. Judiciary on Good Governance to e- Governance

The concept of good governance is undoubtedly linked with the citizens' right of life, liberty and pursuit of happiness. This could be secured in a democracy only through the rule of law. As observed by Y. K. Sabarwal, Chief Justice of India that the concept of governance is as old as human civilization. What is "Governance"? It simply means the process of decision making and the process by which decisions are implemented. The quality of governance depends, in a large measure, upon the indulgence shown by subjects. Supreme Court of India recently in the case of *Shreya Singhal vs. UOI* W.P. (Criminal) No. 167 of 2012 observed that "an informed citizenry is a pre-condition for meaningful governance and advocated for e-literacy. In its judgment in UID case the Supreme Court raises its concern on the protection of privacy and hold that UID cannot be mandated except for few services like PDS, LPG and Kerosene subsidy until larger bench settle out the issue of inclusion of right to privacy in the Article 21 of Constitution of India. *(Justice K.S. Puttaswamy and Another Versus Union of India and Others, 2012).* The Apex Court accepted the contention of petitioner that in absence of any data protection laws the information so collected can adversely affect other rights like privacy, self-incrimination and others.

4.6. International Legal Frameworks

International law and various conventions have mandated on all the member countries to take measures for e-governance, in order to make the society transparent, corruption free and accountable. Article 5, 8, 9, 10 16 of United Nations Convention on Corruption talk about the transparency and also state the measures to be adopted for making government more accountable. In addition to this, the majority of members of Organisation for Economic Co-operation and Development and developing countries have formulated national e-government strategies. World Bank, United Nations Development Program, and WTO spend huge money to help the developing and under developed to promote e-governance. *(Holzapfel, 2014)*

Therefore, e-governance can be regulated by these variety of laws but above analysis depicts e-governance cannot be administered and implemented with this existing legal frame work.

5. Problems in the Existing Legal Framework and Its Way out

As discussed above there are diverse laws to regulate the e-governance in India but the implementation of these laws is not satisfactory. Laws like Right to Information Act, 2005 and Information Technology Act, 2000 and various judicial pronouncements have rather constrained the scope of e-governance in India. Some of them are discussed as under.

5.1. The Administration of e-Governance in India Is Subject to Policy Decision Presently Subject to NeGP

The initiatives of and the institutional aspects of NeGP are similar to those undertaken in the USA. But in USA e-governance is supplanted by legislative measure. The e-Government Act of 2002 is a United States statute enacted on December 17, 2002. The fundamental purpose is to improve the management and promotion of electronic government services and processes by establishing a Federal Chief Information Officer within the Office of Management and Budget, and by establishing a framework of measures that require using internet-based information technology to improve citizen access to government information and services, and for other purposes. The Act of 2002 defines clearly the "e- Government" which provides certainty and put a blanket on the scope of e-governance resulting into the crystallization of concept of e-governance. The Act then establishes an Office of Electronic Government, headed by an Administrator appointed by the President, in the Office of Management and Budget (OMB).

Indian e-governance mission though try to define the e-governance but has no legal sanctity, in absence of any statuary limitations to the definition of Indian e-governance is subject to wide interpretation which may subject to huge litigation. In addition to this, Indian e-governance mission is only confined to NeGP controlled and monitored by DeITY. Therefore, it is suggested that legislature should appreciate that since India is a developing nation, sensitive subject like e-governance should not merely be left on the discretion of policy makers. Hence, a statutory sanctity to the e-governance mission of India is necessitated.

5.2. Apart from the NeGP, Indian e-Governance Has Been Closely Associated with the Right to Information Because the Provisions of the Right to Information Act, 2005 Are Supplementary to the e-Governance

As e-governance accentuate on availing of government of services by internet and key service was to receive information from government. This purpose is much manifested by the fact that an online portal www.rtionline.gov.in has been created to apply online for information from government offices. Despite the legislative framework of RTI Act, 2005 the Act doesn't totally take up the responsibility of its proper implementation due to lack of enforceability procedures. For the Act to be more effective, there need to be better information flow among people at the village level who are unaware of their rights. Cause needs to be taken up by the States and NGO's to create awareness at the level where it's needed the most. Though RTI Act, 2005 is closely associated with the emission of the information and advocates the e-sharing of information but doesn't make any direct provision of e- governance. Therefore, it is suggested that either RTI Act, 2005 should be amended in light of e-governance or if any specific e-governance legislation so passed in the future, the legislation must be construed in the light of Right to Information Act, 2005.

5.3. Information Technology Act, 2000 Is the Legislation Which Regulates the e-Governance in India in Its True Sense

The Information Technology Act, 2000 was enacted to provide legal recognition for transactions carried out through electronic data interchange and other means of electronic communication which basically confined to the digital signature certificate and e-commerce. However, the scope of NeGP is very wide covering almost all aspects of governance - right from delivery of services and provision of information to business process re-engineering within the different levels of government and its institutions. Thus, its task is of colossal proportion. It would therefore be advisable if such a gigantic task is implemented, monitored and regulated through a legal framework so that its vision becomes a reality. It is also noteworthy that across the globe countries like New Zealand, Canada and USA have an exhaustive legal set up for regulating e-governance. Moreover sections 49, 69 and 73of IT Act, 2000 highlight its own limitations which is subject to vulnerability of its misuse. Wide discretionary power is given, in the case PUCL vs. UOI it was held that the procedure is inadequate as the Controller has been given discretionary power, and there is no mention of consultation with the accused before punishing him.

5.4. In Fact, While Implementing the NeGP, Various Structural and Institutional Issues Have Already Arisen Which Clearly Call for a Statutory Mandate for Their Resolution

The Eleventh Report on Second Administrative Reforms Commission in its report also made an reference about it (India, 2nd Administrative Reforms Commission, 2008) while examining the constraints experienced in the implementation of various Mission Mode Projects under the NeGP, the Standing Committee on Information Technology found out the Central Line Departments were facing difficulties on account of the fact that these projects were 'large, complex and technology driven.' Some of these issues were related to: (India, 58th Report Demand for Grants for 2008-09, 2008)

5.4.1. Lack of clarity on composition, role, responsibility and financial powers of the Empowered Committee.
5.4.2. Laying down policy changes for fast-track approval of MMPs and Special Scheme for State MMPs.
5.4.3. Issues regarding the role and responsibility of the States and the Union Line Ministries in project implementation. (Project specific interfaces between the State and Line Ministries also need to be provided urgently).
5.4.4. Policy for inter-ministerial governance structure for Integrated Services Projects.
5.4.5. Setting up an organization structure to deal with issues arising during post implementation period.

Underlying reasons of such issues are that numerous functions of NeGP are separately implemented by the Union and State Governments because of their specific functional jurisdictions. (Supreme Court Note No. 33)

5.5. Another Major Setback to the e-Governance in India Is the Privacy Law

The UID scheme of the Central Government has been stalled by the apex court of the country as it stands in conflict with the right to privacy. In addition to this, India though entered into the e-governance mission but not able to come up with any Data Protection Laws which raises serious concern of privacy and misuse of such information once collected by the authorities. Other countries like United Kingdom have Data Protection Act 1998, which put restrictions on collection of data. Personal data can be obtained only for one or more specified and lawful purposes, and shall not be further processed in any manner incompatible with that purpose or purposes. United States have chosen to adopt the sectoral approach that relies on mix of legislation, regulation, and self-regulation. In United States, data are grouped into several classes on the basis of their utility and importance. Thereafter, accordingly a different degree of protection is awarded to the different classes of data. They have Privacy Act 1974, Electronic Communications Privacy Act, and Children's Online Privacy Protection Act 1998 etc. Though India, upon the footprints of foreign laws, has proposed its Data Protection Bill but not yet passed by the legislature. Therefore, it is suggestible that government should pass Data Protection Laws and Privacy laws as soon as possible. The Privacy laws so passed must contain the different schedule specifying which information can be shared on what occasion, as is done in USA.

5.6. It Is Suggested That Legislature Should Act Promptly on the Recommendation of the Second Administrative Reforms Commission Report Submitted in December, 2008

The commission has recommended that components of the NeGP may be enshrined in a legal framework keeping the purpose would be to give statutory mandate to the institutional entities, setting up of a separate Fund, defining responsibilities of state and central government respectively and providing for time frames and oversight mechanisms. Thus, this legislation may, inter alia, contain provisions regarding the following (Supreme Court Note No. 33):

5.6.1. Definition of e-Governance in the Indian context, its objectives and role.
5.6.2. Coordination and oversight mechanisms, support structures at various levels, their functions and responsibilities.
5.6.3. Role, functions and responsibilities of government organizations at various levels.
5.6.4. Mechanism for financial arrangements including public-private partnership.
5.6.5. Specifying the requirements of a strategic control framework for e-Government projects dealing with statutory and sovereign functions of the government.
5.6.6. Responsibility for selection and adoption of standards and inter-operability framework.
5.6.7. Framework for digital security and data protection etc.

This legislation should have an overarching framework and be able to provide flexibility to organizations.

Conclusion

E-Governance is an initiative to respond to the demand for "maximum governance and minimum government." The decade of 1990's marked a shift in the manner of the functioning of government. The long cumbersome procedures and the indifference of the *babus (bureaucrats)* gave way to the computerized government departments and quick disposal of matters.

The recent governments have increasingly emphasized the importance of information and communication technologies in all areas of governance by digitizing the transactions and citizen-state communications and establishing integrated database of various government departments as well as citizens. Consequently, obtaining information from any government department, filling forms, register for government services, etc. has become less time consuming exercise for the citizens. This surely has marked a major achievement towards ensuring good governance. E-Governance is not only an attempt to reach the citizens and make the major public services available just a "click" away but also a major tool in making the governance transparent, accountable and inclusive.

However, e-governance in India is largely unregulated due to the lack of an exhaustive legislation in this regard. It mostly depends on the policy decisions and piecemeal legislations.

The National e-governance Plan as envisaged by the government was an initiative towards establishing various State Data Centers and Common Services Centers (CSC). CSC's are computer resource centers designed to provide an accessible facility for the delivery of services like health, education agriculture etc. in rural and remote areas. However, the NeGP can function effectively only when regulated by a law.

The piecemeal legislations in respect of e-governance such as Right to Information Act, 2005, Information Technology Act, 2000, The Indian Citizenship Act, 1955 and the Rules made there under give a glimpse of e-governance but no legislation in India has dealt with the matters related to e-governance in exhaustive manner. This has raised many privacy concerns. Recently, various e- governance projects has been stalled by the Apex court on the ground of privacy only. Globally, countries which have undertaken the e- governance projects recently have exhaustive legislation. Unites States of America has e-governance Act, 2002 likewise New Zealand, Australia and Canada has E- governance legislation. For e-governance to succeed in India, the need of the hour is that there should be a concrete legislation.

REFERENCES

Bhattacharya, S. and Goswami, J. (2011). Study of e-Governance: The Attractive Way to Reach the Citizens. *CCSN.* Rourkela.

C., S., Jain, P. and Sharma, S. S. (2007). *E-Government and e-Governance: Definitions.* Retrieved November 1, 2015, from ICEG: www.iceg.net.

Dalal, P. (n.d.). *The Expending Horizons of Right to Information.* Retrieved November 11, 2015, from Central Information Commission: http://www.cic.gov.in/.

Governance, I. o. (2015). *Defining Governance.* Retrieved November 7, 2015, from IOC: www.iog.ca.

Gupta, M. (2010). Tracking the Evolution of e-Governance in India. *International Journal of Electronic Government Research, 6*(1), 46-58.

Gupta, S. B. (2012, March). e-Governance in India and its Future. *International Journal of Management Science, 1*(1).

Haq, M. u. (1995, July 6). Special Advisor to the Administrator of the United Nations Devlopment Program. (O. U. Press, Interviewer) USA: Oxford University Press.

Holzapfel, S. (2014). *The role of indicators in development cooperation.* Bonn: The German Development Institute.

ICT and Rural Development. (2012, November). *ICT as Tools for Improving Local Governance.* (X. C. Kristina, Compiler).

India, G. o. (2001). *Report of the Working Group on Convergence and e-Governance for The Tenth Five Year Plan (2002-2007).* New Delhi: Planning Commission.

India, G. o. (2008). *58th Report Demand for Grants for 2008-09.* New Delhi: Government of India.

India, G. o. (2008). *Promoting e-Governance the Smart Way Forward.* New Delhi: Public Grievances and Pensions Department.

India, G. o. (2011). *Saransh.* New Delhi: Ministry of Communication and Information Technology.

India, G. o. (2015, November). *Central Initiatives.* Retrieved November 22, 2015, from India.gov.in (National Portal): www.india.gov.in.

Justice K.S. Puttaswamy and Another Versus Union of India and Others, 494 (Civil August 11, 2012).

Kristina, X. C. (2002, 11th May). *Overview on e-Governance Prepared in the Framework of the ICT Cross-Cutting Project.* Working Paper.

Kumar, T. V. (2014). *e-Governance for Smart Cities.* Springer Publishing House.

Monga, A. (2008). e-Governance in India: Opportunities and Challanges. *JOAAG, 3*(2), 52-61.

Singh, S. (2010, November). Promoting e-Governance Through Right to Information: A Case Study of India. *International Journal of Scientific and Engineering Research, 1*(2), 1-9.

State of U.P. vs Narayan, AIR 1975 (Supereme Court 1975).

Supreme Court Note No. 33.

Technology, M. o. (2001). *Electronic Governance- A Concept Paper.* Retrieved November 2015, from inistry of Information Technology: egov.mit.gov.in.

Yadav, N. and B.Singh. (2012, September). e-Governance: Past, Present and Future in India. *IJCA, 53*(7), 35-47.

In: e-Governance in India: Problems, Prototypes and Prospects ISBN: 978-1-63484-830-5
Editors: P. Kumar, R. Sharma and U. Kaushal

Chapter 14

AN E-GOVERNANCE STEP THROUGH KISAN SEVA KENDRA (KSK) TOWARDS INDIAN RURAL DEVELOPMENT: A STUDY OF NEED AND ROLE OF KSKS IN GHAZIABAD

Prateek Gupta[1,*] and Deepa[2]
[1]Associate Professor, Department of MBA, KIET Group of Institutions, Ghaziabad, Uttar Pradesh, India
[2]Assistant Professor, Department of MBA, KIET Group of Institutions, Ghaziabad, Uttar Pradesh, India

ABSTRACT

The Indian government has, since independence, subsidised many industries and products, from fuel to food. Loss-making state-owned enterprises are assisted by the government and farmers are given access to free electricity. An article published by International Herald Tribune (2005), stated that in India, subsidies amounted to 14% of GDP. As much as 39% of subsidised kerosene is stolen. An agricultural subsidy is a governmental financial support paid to farmers and agribusinesses to supplement their income, manage the supply of agricultural commodities, and influence the cost and supply of such commodities. The challenges before Indian Agriculture are immense. This sector needs to grow at a faster rate than in the past to allow for higher per capita income and consumption. It is an accepted fact that the sound agricultural development is essential for the overall economic progress. *Kisan Seva Kendra (KSK),* is a fast growing arena to transform Indian rural landscape. *KSK* has been formed with an exclusive mandate to design, develop, source and supply state of the art, economical and rural communications with value additions of content and services. This study is an attempt to highlight the need and role of Kisan Seva Kendra especially towards Indian rural development.

* Corresponding author: P. Gupta. Associate Professor, Department of MBA, KIET Group of Institutions, Ghaziabad. E-mail: dr.guptaprateek@gmail.com.

Keywords: economy, subsidy, agriculture, financial support, Kisan Seva Kendra

1. INTRODUCTION

Government of Indian is playing vital role in agriculture sector development. Some of the cited reasons for vital role are self-sufficiency, employment creation, support to small-scale producers for adopting modern technologies and inputs, reduction of price instability and improvement of the income of farm households. This vital role can take a number of forms such as import-export policies and domestic policies like price support programmes, direct payments, and input subsidies to influence the cost and availability of farm inputs like credit, fertilizers, seeds, irrigation water, etc. Among all of the domestic support instruments in agriculture, input subsidies and product price support are the most common. Various benefits are cited in justifying input subsidies: economic, environmental and social (World Bank 2008). Input subsidies can bring economic benefits to society. Inputs like fertilizers, irrigation water and electricity have a significant share in agricultural subsidies in India and fertilizer subsidy has attracted much attention of policymakers, and researchers in the recent past (Sharma and Kalla, 2001) (Sharma and Sharma, 2012).

An agricultural subsidy is a governmental financial support paid to farmers and agribusinesses to supplement their income, manage the supply of agricultural commodities, and influence the cost and supply of such commodities. A subsidy, often viewed as the converse of a tax, is an instrument of fiscal policy. Derived from the Latin word subsidium, a subsidy literally implies coming to assistance from behind. In India, as also elsewhere, subsidies now account for a significant part of government's expenditures, although, like that of an iceberg, only their tip may be visible (Khandelwal, Rathore, and Sharma, 2011). The objective of subsidies, by means of creating a wedge between consumer prices and producer costs, lead to changes in demand/supply decisions. The forms of subsidies are a cash payment to producers/consumers is an easily recognizable form of a subsidy. However, it also has many invisible forms. Thus, it may be hidden in reduced tax-liability, low interest government loans or government equity participation. If the government procures goods, such as food grains, at higher than market prices or if it sells as lower than market prices, subsidies are implied. The subsidy is very important for growth of farmers in India. Many persons have presented their views on agriculture subsidies at national and international level through research papers and articles (Sharma S. 1989) (Singh, 1999).

In case study of escalating costs of agricultural subsidies in India, published in Joint Learning Event: Promoting Pro-Poor Growth, Policy Instrument Note # 1, Farm Input Subsidies author focus on costs of agricultural subsidies in India. India originally introduced subsidies on fertilizer, irrigation water and rural electricity — that drove many of the irrigation pumps — in the 1960s to support the successful drive for the green revolution (Rathi, 2015). In India, agriculture production of two main cereals i.e., of rice and wheat, accelerated notably after 1967. While studies confirm that payment of subsidies on inputs contributed to rapid expansion of production of cereals in the early phases of the green revolution, once fertilizer use had spread, then it is less clear that the subsidies contribute to further increased production (Sharma S. 1989).

In research paper of "Agricultural Subsidies in India Boon or Curse" by – *Rajwinder Kaur and Dr. Manisha Sharma* has established a relation between subsidies (including fertilizers, electricity and irrigation) distributed in zone and productivity of zone in India.

The paper titled "The Effects of Agricultural Research and Farm Subsidy Policies on Human Nutrition and Obesity" by *Julian M. Alston, Daniel A. Sumner, Stephen A. Vosti* examined trends in agricultural policies, agricultural productivity, commodity prices and food prices in order to assess the nature and extent of effects of the main elements of US agricultural policies (commodity price and income supports, import barriers, and public agricultural R&D) on human nutrition and obesity (Singh, 1999).

2. Objectives and Research Methodology

2.1. Objectives of Study

The present research focused on the following objectives:

- To analyze the magnitude and incidence of subsidies, their burden on government finances being unbearable, and their cost being felt in terms of a decline of real public investment in agriculture.
- To study whether agricultural subsidies are biased against small and marginal farmers.
- To investigate the need of KSKs in India for subsidies distribution.
- To examine the role of KSK in appropriate distribution of subsidies.

2.2. Research Methodology

This research work has used both primary and secondary data. The main sources of secondary data were various journals, periodicals and newspapers. The study was completed under the following stages:

2.3. Collection of Secondary Data

In this phase, the data and information about the agriculture subsidy, distribution of subsidies, Kisan Seva Kendras, etc. were collected through various books, journals, magazines, newspapers and websites.

2.4. Collection of Primary Data through Field Survey

In this phase, as it reflects, the data, materials and information regarding KSKs were collected from the various offices, agencies of the Government and by making discussions and interviewing the officials. The primary information was collected through Direct Field

Survey. The mode of data collection method was survey, which was usually incorporated for collecting raw information. One questionnaire was prepared to gather the relevant information by conducting a sort of personal interviews with 100 farmers from the villages near Ghaziabad (Uttar Pradesh).

2.5. Desk Research

First and second phases were used time by time as per the demand of the research work. In the third phase, the data and material collected during the first and second phases were tabulated and analyzed in clear reference to the research objectives.

2.6. Research Study

Subsidy is a form of financial aid or support extended to an economic sector (or institution, business, or individual) generally with the aim of promoting economic and social policy. Although commonly extended from government, the term subsidy can relate to any type of support - for example from NGOs or implicit subsidies. Subsidies come in various forms including: direct (cash grants, interest-free loans) and indirect (tax breaks, insurance, low-interest loans, depreciation write-offs, rent rebates). Mathematically, the subsidy (S) in a service is obtained by:

$$S = RX + (d + i) K + i (Z + L) - (RR + I + D)$$

where: RX = revenue expenditure on the service L = sum of loans advanced for the service at the beginning of the period K = sum of capital expenditure on the service excluding equity investment at the beginning of the period. Z = sum of equity and loans advanced to public enterprises classified within the service category at the beginning of the period. RR = revenue receipts from the service I + D = interest, dividend and other revenue receipts from public enterprises falling within the service category. d = depreciation rate i = interest rate.

3. Subsidy Issues in India

Subsidies have proliferated in India for several reasons. In particular this proliferation can be traced to 1) the expanse of governmental activities 2) relatively weak determination of governments to recover costs from the respective users of the subsidies, even when this may be desirable on economic grounds, and 3) generally low efficiency levels of governmental activities. In the context of their economic effects, subsidies have been subjected to an intense debate in India in recent years.

4. Kisan Seva Kendra (KSK)

Kisan Seva Kendra, was first established in 1987, as the National Centre for Management of Agricultural Extension at Chandigarh, by the Ministry of Agriculture, Government of India as an autonomous Institute. In recognition of its importance and expansion of activities all over the country, its status was elevated to that of a National Institute in 1992 and re-christened to its present name i.e., National Institute of Agricultural Extension Management. Kisan Seva Kendra is the Indian response to challenges of agricultural extension in a rapidly growing and diverse agriculture sector. The policies of liberalization and globalization of the economy and the level of agricultural technology becoming more sophisticated and complex, called for major initiatives towards reorientation and modernization of the agricultural extension system. Effective ways of managing the extension system needed to be evolved and extension organizations enabled to transform the existing set up through professional guidance and training of critical manpower. **Kisan Seva Kendra** is the response to this imperative need. KSK has been formed with an exclusive mandate to design, develop, source and supply state of the art, economical and rural communications with value additions of content and services. The focus is to take the advantage of latest in technology to address several issues faced by the farmers for simple need for communication, access to input from experts and services of reliable quality. The objective is to empower people living in villages of the country in a sustainable and viable manner. Cooperative Societies form the core of the strategy which are enabled to be a catalyst for promoting these products and services in an economically viable manner.

4.1. Services Provided by KSK

Service for subscribers are available every day on areas of interest to rural subscribers.

- Dedicated helpline for query resolution by Experts
- To listen to voice messages once again
- Mobile quizzes, Phone in Programmes for expert advice
- Focused services for groups with common interest

Farmers can get a solution to their problems, queries by using this short code. Experienced professionals are accessible on this helpline, who provide solutions to farmers. Where required, subject matter specialists are taken on conference call to provide a satisfactory resolution to queries.

4.2. The Kisan Call Centre

To make information transfer more effective, greater use will need to be made of modern information technology and communication among researchers, extensionists and farmers. Public extension system requires a paradigm shift from top-down, blanket dissemination of technological packages, towards providing producers with the knowledge and understanding with which they solve their own location - specific problems. Continuous two-way interaction among the farmers and agricultural scientists is the most critical component of Agricultural Extension. At present, the issues have been addressed by the Extension Systems of State Departments of Agriculture, State Agricultural Universities (SAUs), KVKs, NGOs, Private Extension Services through various extension approaches in transfer of technology. A limitation in Transfer of Technology (TOT) model continues to remain a challenge for the public and private extension systems. With the availability of telephone and Internet, it is now possible to bridge this gap to quite a large extent by using an appropriate mix of technologies. The Department of Agriculture and Cooperation, Ministry of Agriculture, Government of India has launched Kisan Call Centres with a view to leverage the extensive.

5. Data Analysis and Result Discussion

1. Is agriculture farmer's main occupation?

a) Yes b) No

OPINION	NO.OFRESPONDENTS	PERCENTAGE
YES	98	98
NO	2	2
TOTAL	100	100

Result - From the above it is evident that 98% of the farmers feel that agriculture is their main occupation.

2. Are farmers aware of government plans and facilities?

a) Yes b) No

OPINION	NO. OF RESPONDENTS	PERCENTAGE
YES	84	84
NO	16	16
TOTAL	100	100

Result - From the above data it shows that 84% of farmers feel that government plans and policies facilitate productions, where as 16% of farmers feel that government plans and policies do not facilitate productions.

3. Do farmers know about the subsidy?

a) Yes b) No

OPINION	NO. OF RESPONDENT	PERCENTAGE
YES	92	92
NO	8	8
TOTAL	100	100

Result - From the above data it is evident that 92% of the farmers know about subsidy where as 8% farmers do not know about the subsidy.

4. Do farmers have any bank account?

a) Yes b) No

OPINION	NO. OF RESPONDENTS	PERCENTAGE
YES	80	80
NO	20	20
TOTAL	100	100

Result – From the above data it is evident that 80% of the farmers have their bank account, where as 20% of the farmers do not have their bank account.

5. Are farmer in the favour of online subsidy?

a) Yes b) No

OPINION	NO. OF RESPONDENTS	PERCENTAGE
YES	75	75
NO	25	25
TOTAL	100	100

Result - From the above data it is evident that 75% of the farmers 'agree' that online subsidy should be introduced, where as 25% of the farmers disagree for online subsidy.

6. Do farmers have any Agricultural Institute, Seva Kendra Office, etc. in farmer's area?

a) Yes b) No

OPINION	NO. OF RESPONDENTS	PERCENTAGE
YES	40	40
NO	60	60
TOTAL	100	100

Result - From the above it shows that 40% of the farmers agree that they have agriculture institute in their area, where as 60% of the farmers do not agree that they have any agriculture institute in their area.

7. How much government facilities helpful to farmers?

a) 0%-25% b) 25%-50% c) 50%-75% d) 75%-100%

OPINION	NO. OF RESPONDENTS	PERCENTAGE
A	35	35
B	55	55
C	10	10
D	0	0
TOTAL	100	100

Result - From the above data it shows that 10% of the farmers said that 0%-25% government is helpful in agriculture, 74% of the farmers said that 25%-50% government is helpful, 16% of the farmers said that 50%-75% government is helpful.

8. Are farmers a member of co-operative society?

a) Yes b) No

OPINION	NO. OF RESPONDENT	PERCENTAGE
YES	45	45
NO	55	55
TOTAL	100	100

Result – From the above data it shows that 45% of the farmers are members of cooperative society, where as 55% of the farmers are not members of cooperative society.

9. Do farmers have BPL Card?

a) Yes b) No

OPINION	NO. OF RESPONDENTS	PERCENTAGE
YES	65	65
NO	35	35
TOTAL	100	100

Result – From the above data it shows that 65% of the farmers have BPL card but 35% of the farmers do not have the BPL card.

10. Do farmers have any government warehouse facility in farmer's area?

a) Yes b) No

OPINION	NO. OF RESPONDENTS	PERCENTAGE
YES	35	35
NO	65	65
TOTAL	100	100

Result – From the above data it shows that 35% of the farmers said that they have government warehouse facility in their area, but 65% of the farmers said that they do not have government warehouse facility in their area.

11. How much agriculture land farmers have?

a) 0–10 b) 10–20 c) 20–30 d) 30–40 e) 40–50

OPINION	NO. OF RESPONDENTS	PERCENTAGE
A	10	10
B	40	40
C	30	30
D	15	15
E	5	5
TOTAL	100	100

Result - From the above data it shows that 10% of the farmers said that they have 0–10 bigga land, 40% of the farmers said that they have 10–20 bigga land, 15% of the farmers said that they have 20–30 bigga land, 15% of the farmers said that they have 30–40 bigga land, 5% of the farmers said that they have 40–50 bigga land.

12. How much crop farmers grow in a year?

a) Wheat b) Rice c) Sugarcane d) Mustard e) any other

OPINION	NO. OF RESPONDENTS	PERCENTAGE
A	30	30
B	25	25
C	22	22
D	18	18
E	5	5
TOTAL	100	100

Result - From the above data it shows that 30% of the farmers grow wheat, 25% of the farmers grow rice, 22% of the farmers grow sugarcane, 18% of the farmers grow mustard, and 5% of the farmers grow other crops.

13. How do farmers market their crops?

a) Private owners b) Government

OPINION	NO. OF RESPONDENTS	PERCENTAGE
A	60	60
B	40	40
TOTAL	100	100

Result - From the above data it shows that 60% of the farmers market their crops with private owners, and 40% of the famers market their crops with government.

14. How will farmers get subsidy?

a) Through Central government b) Through State government c) Through other Institutes

OPINION	NO. OF RESPONDENTS	PERCENTAGE
A	42	42
B	37	37
C	21	21
TOTAL	100	100

Result - From the above data it shows that 42% of the farmers get the subsidy through central government, 37% of the famers get the subsidy through state government, and 21% of the farmers get the subsidy through other institutes.

15. Method of doing agriculture?

a) Traditional method b) Modern method

OPINION	NO. OF RESPONDENTS	PERCENTAGE
A	67	67
B	33	33
TOTAL	100	100

Result - From the above data it shows that 67% of the farmers adopt traditional method, and 33% of the farmers adopt modern method.

Conclusion and Result Discussion

Agricultural extension is an important force in bringing agricultural change and development. Structural and functional change in agricultural extension service is unavoidable to meet the needs and challenges of 21st century. In the era of globalization and liberalization, it has made us to search the effective alternative approaches for public extension. To address the needs and challenges of farmers in this globalization and liberalization era, there is a need for change over from commercial agriculture to sustainable agriculture. Specifically competitiveness at the global level needs multiplying technological information inflow. In this climate, extension experts have suggested that, extension should be 'demand driven' and it should reduce the financial burden on government in the budget required for alternate extension that has come to vogue as Kisan Seva Kendra to meet the needs and challenges of future generation.

The Kissan Seva Kendras have been operating since more than 27 years in India but still farmers are not very much aware about this. Hence it is the high time to make them aware about this. Some important results are found in the present study such as:

1. In Ghaziabad region, farmers not have so much land for agriculture. Therefore, maximum farmers are not totally depended on agriculture, they have other source of income from jobs, business, etc.
2. Maximum farmers are aware with term subsidy and its benefits.
3. In majority, farmers are more prefer and favor of online subsidy.
4. Farmers are most prefer seeds and fertilizers subsidy then others such as agriculture machinery, animal husbandry, etc.
5. Farmers prefer different medium to get subsidy. In which, online subsidy is at the top and then cash and on the product subsidy.
6. The choice of farmers to get subsidy through central government.
7. The farmers of Ghaziabad region are not a part of any co-operative society.

SUGGESTIONS

The following suggestions are made:

- The farmers are to be aware about the various subsidies given by government.
- The farmers are to be aware about the online subsidy available for them.
- Despite the fact that majority of the farmers had very nominal level of knowledge regarding the KSK, therefore, there is a need to create awareness regarding the specific objectives of KSK among the members of Kisan Seva Kendras in specific and farming community in general.
- The Farmers who have knowledge about KSK feel that KSKs are ill equipped and carries poor market information. Hence the role of KSK towards providing the latest information communication technologies is to be aware.
- KSK facilities should be available for all types of farmers i.e., small, medium and large level with 24x7 support.
- There is a need to strengthen KSKs by providing additional staff hitherto agriculture supervisor is only person who takes care of KSK.

References

Khandelwal, S., Rathore, R. and Sharma, S. (2011). Variables associated with knowledge of farm women regarding home science technologies. *Proceedings of International Conference on Innovative Approaches for Agricultural Knowledge Management: Global Extension Experiences.* New Delhi: Indian Council of Agricultural Research (ICAR), New Delhi, India.

Rathi, N. (2015). Innovations in Adoption of Indigenous Knowledge of Livestock Management. *International Journal of Advanced Research in Computer Science and Software Engineering*, 5(1), 1009-1012.

Sharma, R. and Kalla, P. (2001). Factors affecting knowledge of dairy farmers about improved animal husbandry practices. *Rajasthan Journal of Extension Education*, 8(9), 118-120.

Sharma, R. and Sharma, S. S. (2012). Attitude of Farmers towards Kisan Mandals and Kisan Seva Kendra. *Indian Res. J. Ext. Edu*, 12(2), 38-42.

Sharma, S. (1989). A critical study on Training and Visit system of agriculture extension operating in Jaipur district.

Singh, G. (1999). Impact of extension wing on the farmers. *Rural India*, 63.

Editors' Contact Information

Dr. Puneet Kumar
Assistant Professor in Computer Science,
Department of Computer Application,
College of Engineering and Technology,
Mody University of Science and Technology,
Laxmangarh, Sikar, Rajasthan, India
E-Mail: professor.pkumar@gmail.com, puneetkumar.cet@modyuniversity.ac.in

Dr. Rajesh Sharma
Assistant Professor in Economics,
Department of Economics,
College of Business Management, Economics and Commerce,
Mody University of Science and Technology,
Laxmangarh, Sikar, Rajasthan, India
E-Mail: professor.rajeshsharma@gmail.com, rsharma.cobmec@modyuniversity.ac.in

Dr. Urmani Kaushal
Assistant Professor in Computer Science,
Department of Computer Application,
College of Engineering and Technology,
Mody University of Science and Technology,
Laxmangarh, Sikar, Rajasthan, India
E-Mail: urmani10kaushal@gmail.com, urmanikaushal.cet@modyuniversity.ac.in

INDEX

C

D

E

F

G

H

I

J

K

L

M

N

O

P

Q

R

S

T

U

V

W

Y